No Sanctuary

NO SANCTUARY

The True Story of a Rabbi's Deadly Affair

Michele Samit

A Birch Lane Press Book
Published by Carol Publishing Group

A Birch Lane Press Book
Published by Carol Publishing Group
Birch Lane Press is a registered trademark of Carol Communications, Inc.
Editorial Offices: 600 Madison Avenue, New York, N.Y. 10022
Sales and Distribution Offices: 120 Enterprise Avenue, Secaucus, N.J. 07094
In Canada: Canadian Manda Group, P.O. Box 920, Station U, Toronto, Ontario M8Z 5P9
Queries regarding rights and permissions should be addressed to Carol Publishing Group, 600 Madison Avenue, New York, N.Y. 10022

Carol Publishing Group books are available at special discounts for bulk purchases, for sales promotion, fund-raising, or educational purposes. Special editions can be created to specifications. For details, contact: Special Sales Department, Carol Publishing Group, 120 Enterprise Avenue, Secaucus, N.J. 07094

Manufactured in the United States of America
10 9 8 7 6 5 4 3 2 1

Library of Congress Cataloging-in-Publication Data

Samit, Michele.
  No sanctuary : the true story of a rabbi's deadly affair / by Michele Samit.
      p.   cm.
  "A Birch Lane Press book. "
  ISBN 1-55972-182-0
  1. Murder—California—San Fernando—Case studies. 2. Green, Anita I. Title.
HV6534.S29S26   1993
364.1'523'0979493—dc20   92-39498
                                                          CIP

This book is dedicated to the memory of Anita Green, who is missed more than words can say, but whose memory lives on in all the people whose lives she touched.

At first sin is like a spider's web; in the end it becomes as thick as a ship's cable. At first it is a visitor; in the end it becomes the master of the house.

—*The Midrash*

Contents

Contents

Acknowledgments

I wish to express my sincere appreciation to the scores of people whose cooperation, encouragement, and trust have made this book possible. With few exceptions, those involved candidly shared their information and insights with me, even when it was difficult for them to do so.

Given the book's tragic subject matter, I thank Melvin Green for trusting me enough to tell his story. Without his recollections, *No Sanctuary* would have been little more than a journalistic retelling of the court transcripts. Despite his conviction, Melvin continues to profess his innocence.

I would also like to thank Riva Rice for her absolute and unflinching commitment to the truth, no matter what it uncovered. I think Riva is perhaps the bravest person I have ever met. She has always encouraged me unconditionally, and she made me feel like she needed to have this book written. I feel fortunate to have met her.

Special thanks and appreciation are due to both the defense and prosecution teams who supported this project from its inception, giving freely of their time and information. It is rare to meet a group of lawyers so willing to take time from their busy schedules to help a writer. Their perceptions about Melvin Green proved invaluable, and it was a privilege to come to know all of them.

Unlike most defense lawyers, who often avoid talking about their high-profile cases, Gerry Chaleff and Arthur Alexander provided not only details, as long as they didn't compromise Mr. Green, but offered their insights into the legal system as well. I am grateful for their friendship and trust.

I'd like to single out Gerry Chaleff in particular, though he was often difficult to interview due to his absolute and unflinching belief in the attorney-client privilege; he tried valiantly to help me whenever I asked.

Without the assistance and encouragement of Deputy District Attorney Kent C. Cahill, this project might have been abandoned months ago. Kent's meticulous notes, documents, files, and sources saved me hours of research time. In addition to the interview time I needed with him, Kent spent countless hours explaining the trial to me, listening to my theories of who the gunman was, and explaining why certain things were inadmissible in court. I thank Kent for sharing his knowledge, his talent with words, and his often challenging friendship.

I also wish to thank Kent Cahill's colleagues from the San Fernando District Attorney's Office, who generously shared their time and office space with me, and helped me with my seemingly endless questions. The input, advice, and patience of Billy Webb, Steven Ipsen, and Darren Levine were very much appreciated. All four San Fernando deputy district attorneys are true believers; decent and caring men who really want to make the world a better place and will take risks to do so.

Judge George Trammel generously answered all my questions as soon as he was able to, and the insight his participation gave to this project was appreciated greatly.

In addition to the judge, I would like to thank everyone else in the Los Angeles Criminal Courts Division 104 for their concern: court reporters Anita Paul and Pat Cuneo, judicial assistant Steve Johnson, and deputy sheriff Steve Piel.

Thanks to Lieutenant Moorehead of the California Sheriff's Department for giving me access to Melvin Green while he was housed in the Los Angeles County Jail. In addition I'd like to thank all the helpful and supportive people at the Calipatria State Prison: Warden Bryan Gunn, Lt. Earl Upton, Lt. Armando Fabila, Lt. John Grant, Danny Paramo, and Melvin's counselor, Galyn Morgan.

I am grateful to Phyllis Baltin for providing me with tips and background information on many of the book's principal characters. Phyllis was brave enough to articulate what others only hinted at, and her courageous words helped shape my manuscript.

Completing this task would have been impossible without the help of the local police department. In particular, Detective Ray Hernandez, whose hard work and diligent commitment kept the fire in me burning.

I would like to thank Supervising Detective Michael Coffey for putting up with me, taking my calls, and just for listening. His honesty in describing his police department's weaknesses, as well as its strengths, was very courageous. He showed me how frustrating being a cop in a large city like Los Angeles can be.

Thank you to Detective Steven Hooks for working tirelessly to complete this case. A special thanks to private investigator James Sloman for caring enough to teach me how to stay safe and for helping me learn how to see just the facts.

There are so many others who helped out that it is impossible to thank everyone. But these kind individuals deserve mention: Scott and Clarissa Arnow, Roger Arnow, Michael and Cary Green, Bernyce Green, Shelly Hirsh, Hy Green, Susan Artoff, Lily Lopez, Irene Sherwyn, Miriam Jacobs, Nata Preis, Barbara Wolpow, Dr. Warren Line, Dr. Susan Selser, Robert Gerstein Esq., Aaron Sheldon Esq., Ann and Stanley Sludikoff, Michael Hirsh, Caren Gitlin, and all of the detectives at LAPD's North Hollywood Homicide Division, and the many present and former members of both Temple Judea and Shir Chadash who chose to remain anonymous. Thank you for generously helping me whenever I asked.

Thank you to my editor, Hillel Black, whose excellent, thoughtful, and merciless editing helped turned my often-rambling words into what I hope is a fast-paced and exciting story.

A heartfelt word of thanks to my literary agent, Russell Galen, for his emotional support, understanding, advice, and unwavering backing of not only this story, but of my ability to tell it as well. At the risk of sounding melodramatic, Russell's encouragement and friendship have changed the course of my life.

I would also like to thank my television agent and dear friend, Susi Weissman, for her continued support of my professional life. Working with her has been a treat that most writers can only hope for.

A heartfelt word of thanks to Melvin Wulf for keeping me legal.

There are no words to adequately acknowledge the inspiration and assistance of my loving husband, Jay. Often he made me work around the clock and was forced to take over my duties at home. His suggestions, comments, and influence are everywhere in this book and in my life.

I'd like to thank the lights of my life, our two sons, Benjamin and Danny. They are to be commended for their understanding and compassion. They learned very quickly to share their mommy with the computer and to wait patiently for my attentions, even when they missed me the most.

Thanks to my parents for always being there to love the kids, for having taught me to take a stand for what I believe in, even when they disagree, and for encouraging me, and then forcing me, to see sides of this story I never wanted to see. Thank you for your help and unconditional love.

Lastly, to all the wonderful friends and family members who forgave me for never having the time to call, for helping out with my children, for accepting the project I was working on, and for worrying about me at all hours of the day or night, thank you for your tolerance and devotion. This book is really for all of you.

Author to Reader

I first met Anita Green in an expensive clothing store, the Sherri Dee Boutique, located in Encino, California, on a smoggy Friday morning in September 1988. We were both looking for dresses to wear to the upcoming Jewish New Year services. We had to fight our way through the other shoppers, all looking for the perfect outfit. The Jewish New Year (Rosh Hashanah) and the Day of Atonement (Yom Kippur) are known as the High Holy Days. Temples are crowded, and this is the time of year many women choose to make a fashion statement. Encino women go all out. The stores were mobbed, and their selections limited.

I complained to a saleslady about the lack of feminine dresses to hit the racks that year, pointing out the store's abundance of tailored suits. A shopper in the next fitting room eagerly shouted over the partition, exclaiming she shared my sentiments. She explained she was the president of a large temple and would love to find a dress to wear to services.

I asked her, "What temple?"

She replied, "Shir Chadash–The New Reform Congregation."

I laughed and exclaimed that my husband and I had finally joined the congregation, just two weeks earlier, now that our five-year-old son was ready to begin his formal Jewish education. I told her how happy we were there and how much we looked forward to Rabbi Steven Jacobs's upcoming services. I had belonged to his former temple, Temple Judea, for many years. Services just weren't the same without his special magnetism.

As we exited our fitting rooms, Anita Green formally introduced herself. I reached out and grasped the hand of a blond woman in her early forties. She wore a blue denim jumpsuit that showed off her summer tan. Even in the hundred-degree heat, her makeup appeared fresh and perfect, as if it had just been applied. Her hands were perfectly manicured with bright red nail polish. They were covered with the most exquisite and unusual silver rings I had ever seen. The rings might have been designed by Indian artisans. They were like the jewelry that can be found in the offbeat galleries of Santa Fe and Phoenix.

She wore a Gucci watch. On her neck hung several gold chains. On one chain there was a gold charm of the number nineteen. On another there was the beautiful Jewish star, or Magen David.

During the year that I knew Anita, I never saw her go anywhere without her "19" charm. About a month before her death, I glanced at it during a swimming party at the rabbi's pool. "What does that symbolize?" I asked. Anita laughed, "My age." It wasn't until after her death that I discovered its true meaning. She had told girlfriends that it was the date she and Rabbi Jacobs began their affair.

I bought a sweater and Anita bought two pairs of earrings and a leather skirt. We exited the store together and decided to stop at the delicatessen next door for a quick lunch and to plot where to shop next for dresses, and, hopefully, get to know each other a little better.

Perhaps Anita wanted me to feel welcome at temple. Who knows? Maybe she was just hungry. But looking back on that moment, I am struck by the fact that Anita wanted to become friends quickly. Yet, when we were together, Anita always wanted to talk about my life, and not hers. From our first conversation, she was exceptionally warm and caring, with a genuine interest in everything I did. Many other friends and congregants described her that way too.

But with Anita, the appearance was always what mattered most. She clearly remained the temple president, and not just Anita Green, throughout our lunch and throughout our temple friendship, allowing her to avoid emotion or intimacy on her part.

It was as if Anita had a glass wall around her—you could see her but not really touch her. She never wanted you to know about the things in her life that were less than perfect. She was too embarrassed by them and wanted desperately to escape anyone's scrutiny.

We sat in a corner booth in the back of the smoking section. The waiter knew Anita. She was obviously a regular. I ordered a salad, and Anita asked for the heel of the rye bread, filled with soft-boiled eggs. I watched in amazement as she ate a dish I had never seen before, though my father-in-law had been in the deli business for years. She said it had always been her favorite as a child growing up in Long Beach, New York, where she adored her weekend trips to delicatessens with her father, a kosher hot dog and salami casings manufacturer.

When we dined at delicatessens, Anita always ordered the soft-boiled eggs or a liverwurst sandwich. She always drank a Diet Pepsi with a slice of lemon in it. If we met for breakfast she loved to eat garlic bagels.

From the start, I liked Anita. She was tough and aggressive, but loving and sensitive at the same time. She was an excellent listener and knew all about me in no time. She expressed her hope that I would become involved in the temple and quickly assessed my talents and weaknesses, telling me where I would be most needed and what I should watch. The temple, it seemed, was her life. I had never seen anyone so devoted to a cause.

After a lovely meal, filled with laughter, I knew I had found an ally. It usually takes me longer to trust women, especially strong ones like Anita. I often feel threatened by their power. Yet that day I was trusting, sensing a bond between us.

I later realized that I wasn't special. Anita was like that with everyone. Most of Anita's friends felt they shared special ties. One called me when she found out about this book and said, "Anita had the ability to make you think she was there for you alone. Her friends meant a lot to her." Anita knew instinctively how to be a friend and what people needed to hear.

Very quickly, Anita told me her parents were Holocaust survivors and how that experience had changed her life. We talked about so many things in just an hour, from child rearing to men, from vacation spots to how to find the best doctors in town. Anita seemed to have a source for everything.

Though Anita talked freely and openly about many things, she remained evasive about others. What I didn't learn, then or ever, was how dark her days at home had grown. Throughout most of our friendship she tried valiantly to hide the abuse she suffered from Mel, her husband. Only a few of her closest friends and her therapist knew about it, even when she filed for divorce in the summer of 1990. The very act of talking about Mel and her personal life seemed difficult for her to do.

When Anita finally broke down and confided in me about Mel, at a temple fund-raising dinner where he was making a fuss, it was only to say that his explosive temper scared her. Even then, Anita made light of the situation, jokingly referring to Mel's threats as attention seeking. What I sensed then, and throughout her divorce, was that Anita felt that if she ignored the situation and didn't give it all that much attention in her life, it would somehow fix itself.

Anita called Melvin a "blowhard," a man who liked to make threats. I was as shocked as everyone else when Anita was murdered just a year and a half after our first lunch together. The only thing that shocked me more was Mel's arrest six months later.

None of us really know how to make sense of Anita's death. The entire Jewish community in Los Angeles was horrified and outraged. Our congregation was devastated by the loss. Our rabbi, Steven B. Jacobs, was at a loss as to how to comfort us, and uncharacteristically, he seemed saddened beyond belief at her tragic death.

Anita was our community leader, our role model, the driving force behind the building of our future temple home. I do not think a single member of our synagogue had ever known someone who was murdered. It wasn't something we could easily comprehend in our sheltered community.

Our temple's offices were located in Encino, California. Encino was also the city where Anita Green had lived for many years. It is worlds away from the gang-infested areas in Los Angeles that capture national headlines. A wealthy suburb in the western part of the San Fernando Valley, Encino is part of the city of Los Angeles, but is, in reality, a world of its own. In Encino, at least on the surface, people seem to live idyllic, fairy-tale lives.

Encino is a town of contrived appearances where most people seem to have everything and want more. Many of the residents are caught up in a never-ending cycle of materialism. The more you own in Encino, the more affluent you appear to others. For many there, like Anita, appearances are important. Appearances make a statement to your neighbors about who you think you are and who you want to be. You are what you drive, what you wear, where you send your kids to school or camp, where and how often you vacation each year. In Encino there is another distinction, whether your house is on the south or north side of Ventura Boulevard, with the south side's hills being infinitely more prestigious.

Encino, California is one of the wealthiest communities in the Los Angeles metropolitan area. But the wealthy people of Encino, the Michael Milkens and the other nouveaux riches, are different from their financial equals in older parts of the city like Beverly Hills, Pasadena, or Pacific Palisades.

The San Fernando Valley is a residential community outside of Los Angeles made up of many small neighborhoods. Success in the Valley is defined by how much you seem to own, as if to prove that you could afford to live in the city proper if you wanted to. Many people here feel the constant need to explain why they do not have a 90210 zip code, or a Westside address, because the real estate in those communities remains even more costly than in the suburbs.

Los Angeles, as a city, grows more dangerous daily. The riots after the first Rodney King verdict touched most of us in this city in many ways. But we were all touched in profoundly different ways.

In the Valley, schools, parks, and restaurants were closed for almost four days, forcing many to stock up on groceries and then to visit the malls. Sitting at one mall, watching my young children play video games, I was shocked by how isolated we were. A few miles away, parents were throwing their children to the ground to shield them from flying bullets, or taking them out on their first looting expeditions. Our kids were carelessly throwing more quarters into the latest state-of-the-art video games, enjoying the extra time their parents had off from work.

The children from the affluent areas of the Valley wondered what all the fuss was about; their only knowledge of the riots came from television, school, and their frightened parents' whispers. For our privileged kids of the western San Fernando Valley, the war that had broken out in our city seemed as far away and remote as the war in Iraq.

Many of us felt guilty and decided to help, and hopefully, give our children a small dose of reality. We cleaned out closets and brought clothes to riot victims. We filled our Volvo and Mercedes station wagons with bags of groceries to carry downtown. Some of us brought our children along to help, so they would see how fortunate they were. But in the end, we went home to our safe little world, doubtful that we could make a difference.

Encino and neighboring Valley communities like Sherman Oaks, Tarzana, and Woodland Hills appear to be succeeding at providing parents with a security that the horrors of life on the streets won't touch their lives. Not only their malls are different, but many of the neighborhoods in these communities are gated in an attempt to keep outsiders at bay. Neighbors live on the same street for years and never talk to one another except when they meet at the tennis or health clubs or in the market. There is always a need for privacy.

The offices of Shir Chadash–The New Reform Congregation are located in the heart of Encino, directly across the street from Encino Park, where my children play. I feel comforted having my children play in this park, and though it isn't the best equipped park in the Valley, I believe they are safe here. Crimes just don't happen here, at least not violent ones. Anita Green's murder showed many of us in these communities just how thin the veneer of safety had grown.

Anita's murder seemed at first both isolated and incongruous. A masked motorcyclist coolly followed her as she drove to the office and then, just as she stepped out of her cherry-red Corvette convertible, professionally put a single bullet through the base of her skull. The gunman then rode off on his bike without taking so much as her purse. What motive could he possibly have had? Weren't we safe from random acts of violence here in suburbia?

The story that has surfaced during the past two and a half years goes beyond what any of us could have imagined. This wasn't a chance happening; Anita the indiscriminate victim of a stranger's anger. Illusions about people I had known for years were shattered the day Anita was shot. I wanted to give these people unquestioning love and trust, yet my instincts as a reporter told me this crime's circumstances were so sinister that many people in my life were somehow involved. The facts plunged me deeper into the story every day. As I uncovered new leads, delved deeper into my neighbors' pasts, and studied the evidence, I entered a world filled with obsessive individuals unable to control their passions until it was too late. All involved had an insatiable need for power and control over the other individuals in their lives.

The Green case unnerved me for many reasons, but none more powerful than the realization that many people in my life had so much to hide. As a reporter, I wanted to know who had killed my friend and why it had happened, but I was not supposed to be involved with or close to the people I interviewed. Invariably I would find out things that would cause me great pain. But I also knew I had many questions to which I wanted answers, and I was not content to listen to the rumors circulating around the city. Besides, how was I to ascertain what was malicious gossip and what was the truth?

Had Anita really had an affair with Rabbi Jacobs? Would she have been alive today if she had not? Had Mel hired someone to kill her? Did he deserve the life sentence? Why did so many of the witnesses hate Mel? Had Mel acted alone? Why hadn't Anita's friends who knew about his threats toward her, warned her? Would it have made a difference if they had? Why would so many good people try so hard to hide the truth? Why had others lied on the witness stand at Mel's trial? What was everyone so afraid of? How deep were the scars left on the temple, the families, and the friends by this crime? Who was left to pick up the pieces?

It seemed as if nothing was as it appeared to be. With all the rumors, the facts would certainly be hard to determine, let alone the whole truth. One thing was certain, so many people had broken the rules for so long that, to some, even death had seemed escapable.

I probably knew in my heart that I would write a book about Anita's murder the day it occurred. When I naively mentioned my intentions to my rabbi, asking him for his cooperation and insight, he was strongly opposed to the idea, telling me I would have no support or assistance from him. He warned me about the pain I would inflict on others and stressed that, in his opinion, Anita's memory would not be well served by any book about her death. At the time, I had no idea why he felt so strongly. It was my first indication that the rumors of their affair might be true, and that at least something was gravely wrong.

No matter how many times or ways I approached Rabbi Jacobs his response remained consistent. He "categorically and unequivocally" refused to participate and would not grant me any interviews.

As others in our small temple community began to hear about my project, more and more called daily begging me to stop writing. I was surprised because, at the time, I really didn't understand why everyone was so terrified. Call me naive, but I never expected to find out the things I found out about Rabbi Jacobs, Anita, or Mel Green.

As the facts surfaced, I came close to abandoning the project. I now understood everyone's concern. It would have been much easier on me emotionally to close my eyes. I found myself uncomfortable and unwelcome at a synagogue that I really did love being part of. I spent many nights crying myself to sleep. I knew if I did not write this book, someone else would. I wanted the right story told.

As ironic as it seemed, I still hungered for the rabbi's approval of my project and for what I had once received from him: wisdom, courage, spirituality, and the magic his presence created in my life. I also missed my temple friends because they had been my extended family, and we often shared holidays and special occasions together. Now they had abandoned me, and they didn't even know what I was really writing about. The rumors had hit the Shir Chadash Temple and everyone claimed to know exactly what was in this book.

How could I set them straight? How could I expect anyone else to understand my motives without sounding like I was spreading rumors myself?

No one at the Shir Chadash Temple had actually watched Melvin Green's complete trial, and only one or two members had even stopped by to support Anita's family and watch an hour or two of testimony. It was as if there was an unwritten code that said that they shouldn't be there. It just wouldn't look right. Nobody wanted to appear too curious.

I had agreed to watch Mel Green's trial as a reporter. Even I was worried about who would see me there. Rabbi Jacobs seemed distressed by my presence. Early on in the trial, Anita's mother, Riva Rice, leaned over to me in the hall outside the courtroom. "I want you to hear what your rabbi is going to say," she whispered. She literally led me to the courtroom's huge wooden doors and opened them for me.

Thinking back on this moment, I am certain she wanted me to hear his words and agree with her, that the story was indeed unbelievable. Riva was asking me to share her pain, trusting that I would then tell others the real circumstances surrounding the events that led up to her daughter's death. "How can things like this have been allowed to continue, Michele?" she asked.

I went into the courtroom and sat in a corner seat. Rabbi Jacobs appeared flushed and anxious, obviously a reluctant witness. Unlike Riva, he abhorred the fact that I was there. He had shunned all publicity and was trying desperately to keep a low profile. After court, he called an acquaintance of both of ours and asked why I had been in court. He made it clear that my presence there bothered him.

The next morning, when I returned and listened to my rabbi's testimony, I realized why he was so upset, why he could never have cooperated with me, and why I had to find the courage to write this book.

This was the stuff of tabloids and miniseries: a shooting, rumors of sex between two spiritual leaders in the temple setting, accusations, criminal charges, and people lying on the witness stand to save their reputations.

A titillating drama was unfolding before me; would my greatly loved and powerful, but not always respected, rabbi remain the focus of embarrassing allegations of impropriety that would ultimately destroy him? Or would the scandal and trial have little impact, the rabbi's followers covering up as the rabbi continued his leadership? The writing of this book was sure to be a personal odyssey of sorts.

Two years after Anita's death, the outcome is still uncertain. Rabbi Jacobs's power base remains strong; his phenomenal pulpit skills, his consistent eloquence at sermons and life-cycle events, and his ability to provide compassion to those in pain, are in great demand. He is one of those religious leaders with the wondrous ability to move and inspire people in dramatic ways, often bringing an entire congregation of people to tears with his inspirational sermons and moving stories.

Indeed, Rabbi Jacobs has the ability and talent to become one of the truly great rabbinical speakers of our time, but his personal past continues to stand in his way, a major obstacle he is not likely to overcome despite his impressive résumé. His temple, Shir Chadash, remains unbuilt, and the congregation continues to pray in a neighboring Christian church.

Some of his followers have grown frustrated and have chosen to leave the flock. There is a feeling among many who have stayed that if Anita were alive today, the temple would stand finished. In the minds and hearts of these followers, her tragic death and California's economy have delayed the process, and the rabbi has nothing to do with the situation. Others are not as certain that this is the case and say they left the temple because they were tired of having a religious leader with questionable morals.

"Rabbi Jacobs teaches us if we want our children to live ethical and moral lives, we need to set examples for them. We need to act as we want them to act. But what about our leaders? Shouldn't they lead the moral lives they ask their congregants to lead?" one former Shir Chadash member asked.

Whether it has anything to do with the rabbi or not, two years after Anita's death there is talk that the temple may never be built and the congregation may be forced to merge with another floundering Valley synagogue.

For a myriad of reasons, I resisted writing about a murder that involved so many people for whom I cared so deeply. I would have to invade innocent people's lives and possibly hurt them in the process to find my answers. I did not want the book I was writing to have a negative impact on the building of the temple. Yet, after just two days at Melvin Green's trial, I knew, as I knew the day of Anita's murder, that it was a story I could not ignore.

Even then, I sensed that writing this book would change my life. If I could endure the hatred I would inevitably face from the rabbi and my friends, then perhaps I would be able to make sure Anita's horrible death was not meaningless. If one abused woman could be saved, if the world could see that domestic abuse can and often does lead to violence and death, if we can learn that the struggle for power and control is so often a tragic struggle, and if people can be made aware that there are many times in life when those in power abuse their power to prey upon the innocent, then Anita's death would symbolically take on a new meaning.

And so, in a sense, Rabbi Jacobs's and the temple community's outrage are ultimately what kept me going and gave me courage. Throughout my life, I have clung tenaciously to my belief that the only stories worth writing are those nobody wants told. The fact that the rabbi was acting as he was only reinforced my belief that he had a great deal to hide. I knew as a journalist I had to expose what had really happened.

For years Los Angeles and the San Fernando Valley have had one of the largest and most influential Jewish populations in the world, exceeded only by New York. The Jewish population in Los Angeles has prided itself on its leaders remaining close to "scandal free."

Until the 1980s brought us Ivan Boesky and Michael Milken, the attitude here was: Jews don't steal, don't commit adultery, don't commit murder, and, heaven forbid, don't do anything scandalous, especially not our religious leaders. The Los Angeles Jewish community prides itself on its high values, moral superiority, and insularity. My temple leaders and members seemed to worry more about this reputation than about what had happened.

I felt guilty because I did not completely agree. Jewish leaders are like everyone else, and, given the complexities of life in America, Jews face the same temptations as members of other religious groups. Certainly the laws, commandments, and teachings of Judaism inherently help us live righteous lives. But the allure of money, sex, and power are as seductive to our leaders as to anyone else. Human beings make mistakes. Trying to deny our vulnerability to the world's evils seems absurd and intolerable to me. There is no way around it, what happened transpired in a Jewish setting. That does not make it any more shocking or any less horrendous.

The people in this book are real, and what follows is an accurate and faithful rendering of the series of events that led up to the death of Anita Green and to the conviction of her husband, Melvin Green, for arranging her murder for financial gain.

The story and dialogue have been compiled directly from court transcripts, police interviews, pretrial depositions, the victim's letters, the defendant's letters and audio recordings, newspaper accounts, medical records, and pertinent individuals' recollections, as well as from my extensive interviews. There are times when conversations have been reconstructed to make the book read more easily. When I have done this it was because I was relatively certain of what was said in the actual conversation.

Some scenes have been recreated as well, from combining information gathered and the recollections of others. In a few cases scenes have been created from what I believe must have transpired, as in the first chapter.

I have used many quotations from Melvin Green's letters, all of which are paraphrased, except for the ones that appeared as evidence or exhibits in the trial. The same applies for passages taken from Anita's letters, the rabbi's love letters, or other correspondence.

In Anita's case, the police provided me with other documents that were never used in the trial but were kept as part of the public record anyway. They had been listed on the police department's discovery index and then provided to the defense attorneys. Some of these are paraphrased, and others are printed verbatim.

While most of the book's main characters are referred to by their real names, many others who were interviewed chose not to be identified. By disguising their identities they feel it would perhaps be harder for someone to seek vengeance on them or their families if angered by this story. In other cases some just want their privacy protected. I have given these people new names and in some cases new professions as well.

Although Melvin Green has been convicted and the retrial motion denied, there is the uncertainty that the conviction might be appealed and a new trial granted. Some fear that

Melvin might seek revenge. Others believe they might be ostracized by the Shir Chadash community if it was discovered they had helped me tell this story. Still others are embarrassed by their knowledge of things. Finally, there is fear because the gunman has never been arrested and at this time still lives as a free man.

Part I

The Crime and the Community

October 1990

1

The Stranger

The stranger waited on Oxnard Street, studying the picture one last time. He glanced at the photo of a woman who was quite sexy for her age: pretty, blond, and alluring. He couldn't imagine why someone would want to kill a classy broad like her. It didn't matter who she was, this was just a job for him. All that mattered was the thirty thousand or so he would be paid. The more desperate they were to have it done, the more you could get.

Still, he was nervous and edgy; he would have preferred working under the cover of darkness. But he was told it had to be done now, today. Thursday morning, October 25, at 10:30 A.M. sharp. So here he was, on a busy street in the middle of North Hollywood. He would be glad when this job was finished. He stayed on his motorcycle, ready, waiting for the red Corvette to drive past.

He put on his gloves and checked his jacket pocket for his gun, his body welded to his bike—fast, agile, and great on corners, the perfect assassination vehicle.

The morning passed slowly. Since Oxnard was a busy street, there was no place for him to hide, no shrubbery to camouflage his presence. He didn't want to call attention to himself, but he didn't want to miss her. He remained parked a block away from Wilkinson, trying not to appear conspicuous. Whatever he was doing seemed to be working. Nobody appeared to notice him as he smoked a cigarette and drank a cup of stale coffee from Winchell's Donuts.

He had been through the plan several times already this

morning. He went over the approach one more time in his head. He had driven his escape route last night, timing it. He was ready.

Was he forgetting anything? Careful planning was essential. If you forgot a single detail, you increased your chance of being caught. He had avoided prison before because he was smart, paying great attention to detail. Still, others among his friends had run out of luck. His rap sheet was short. He was still the new guy on the block.

He went over his list mentally, remembering to cover his face. He grabbed his black motorcycle helmet and placed it over his head, carefully tucking his long blond hair into it. In seconds he felt the sun beating down on him and the sweat began to pour from his cheeks. It was unusually hot in North Hollywood for October and the air was oppressive.

He always sweated more when he was nervous or excited, and today he was a little of both. Hits were a difficult and dangerous way to make a living, but he fantasized about how easy a lifestyle it could bring. Certainly there was nothing like it to get the adrenaline flowing.

He owed a lot to the guy who had hired him. He wasn't about to let him down. Besides, they would never be able to tie him to this murder. Still, he didn't like that this guy had a big mouth. That's the one thing that continued to bug him.

In moments, he saw the red Corvette pull in front of him. He waited a full minute before pulling away from the curb. Then he grabbed the handlebars and was off, making sure not to arouse the driver's suspicion by following too closely. He noticed she glanced at him in the rearview mirror before turning onto Wilkinson. The motorcyclist stared straight ahead into the car one more time, making sure she was alone.

He zoomed around the corner right on her tail, almost running over some guy. Shit, a witness, he thought. Nobody was supposed to be out on the street at this time, and yet there seemed to be a lot of foot traffic. He would have to be more careful.

The lady made a left turn into a parking lot, pulled her car into a space and stopped. He was right behind her. Stay calm, the closer the better, he told himself. Getting off his bike, leaving it parked facing the wrong direction with the motor running, he walked right up to the blonde and grabbed her firmly by the arm, forcing her head away from the car.

Terrified, she didn't have time to struggle or scream. Without looking at her face, he fired a single bullet from a small caliber handgun into the base of her skull.

The man ran quickly back to his motorcycle, jumped on, and zoomed away, almost riding into a moving truck. To reach the freeway, he could make a U-turn and go back in the direction from which he had come, or he could speed down small residential streets, winding his way up to Oxnard. He decided to avoid the U-turn because he would have to pass the man who had just seen the shooting.

In a split second he decided to speed down Wilkinson and turn on Erwin. In the moment's confusion, and in his nervous condition, he momentarily lost his balance and fell off his bike.

Frightened for just a second, he slid the bike onto its tires, hopped back on, and kept on going, gunning it even harder now. Mistakes like that could destroy him.

On the way back to the freeway he realized he needed to change his appearance. Unfortunately, several people had seen him. His description would be broadcast on the police scanner within minutes. He pulled off his Army jacket and removed his black helmet, hanging it on his bike's handlebars. He decided not to dump the gun. It was the best he could do under the circumstances.

He pulled onto the freeway at the Oxnard on-ramp and sped away, realizing he'd just made the quickest money ever. Not a cop in sight. Christ, it was a good day for a killing.

2

Friends And Lovers

Despite the lateness of the hour, Anita Green could not sleep. As she lay in the darkness and looked at the sleeping rabbi, she could only think of how wonderful making love with him was. At forty-two she felt like a teenager again. The hot June night intensified their heat. The rest of the world, the rabbi's divorce, her loathsome marriage, her terror, melted away whenever they were together.

Though they had made love before, this was the night that Anita would describe to her closest friends as being particularly wonderful. This was the night, in the early summer of 1990, when Anita Green finally made the fateful decision to leave her husband, Melvin.

"There is something I have to tell you, I am finally going to leave him. You have changed my life and have taught me how to love again." Anita's words came from the heart. Later she told her mother, "I told Steven first. I am moving out in a few weeks. He is very proud of me."

Anita Green told friends that she did not want to spend one more miserable minute living in the same house with Melvin Green when life could indeed be so wonderful. Why torture herself any longer? She loved spending time with Steven. He made her so happy, and, as of this summer, he was a free man. His twenty-five-year marriage was finally over and his divorce almost final. But before she left Melvin, Anita had to be certain she and the rabbi would have a future life together.

Anita asked Steven how long she should rent an apartment

for, stressing that if they married after her temple presidency was over, she would only need to sign a thirteen-month lease.

Apparently Rabbi Jacobs agreed. Anita told several close friends that she was renting her new apartment until the following summer, when she planned on marrying Rabbi Jacobs.

During this time of waiting, Steven Jacobs's one request was that Anita continue to keep their relationship a secret. At times his request worried her. Was he sounding uncertain again? Didn't he really need her to get the temple built? After struggling for some time, Anita decided that his hesitancy was caused by his concern about appearances. Rabbi Jacobs always had to think about what was right for the congregation, as well as for his children. To some congregants it might not look right for them to be together yet. Even with this explanation Anita was worried. She needed his assurances and asked him again what his plans were.

The rabbi considered how to answer the woman who had worked so long and so hard for him over the years. Professionally, she was one of the strongest, most devoted temple presidents he had ever encountered. Personally, her life was a mess. Still, if the temple were to be built it would be because of her relentless dedication. He did not want to upset her. He appreciated all that she had done. Rabbi Jacobs promised her that they would be together openly one day soon.

Anita smiled. As she got up to leave, she reminded herself to tell Phyllis how sincere he sounded. Phyllis Baltin was one of Anita's oldest friends, and she had never liked the rabbi. Phyllis thought Steve Jacobs was a big phony and had never trusted his sincerity. Just last week over lunch, she had told Anita that the rabbi was transparent and that she should not believe a word he said.

"Look at his track record. He has done this too many times before, Anita. Nothing personal, but what makes you think he is going to be faithful to you?" Phyllis asked.

"I believe in our love, Phyllis. Besides, he needs me."

"Maybe he does, Anita, but for how long? And why aren't you allowed to tell anyone that you are seeing him? What's the big secret anyway?"

"He wants us to wait. It might not look right to some of the congregants if they see us together now."

For Phyllis, who knew of the rabbi's long past, this statement proved too much to take. He hadn't worried about appearances when he had cheated on his first wife. That wife had finally left him. Phyllis looked at Anita and answered, "I think I'm going to be sick. He has the gall to be worried about how something is going to look? At least he's divorced this time. One point for the rabbi. But you aren't, Anita. You still have a husband. Remember that and please be careful."

Anita could not get Phyllis's words out of her head. She stared at the rabbi. Was he merely bluffing? Why was he so concerned about secrecy? People already suspected that they were together. Anita believed him when he said that he did not want their involvement made public "officially" until she finished her term as temple president. Perhaps he had learned from his previous mistakes about how important appearances were to keep up. He kept telling her that he was in the public eye, with a certain moral standard to adhere to. People were not as eager to forgive you for your transgressions when others knew about them. Had he said all of this just to buy time?

So people suspected. The gossip traveled quickly. What the gossips did not know was that Anita was secretly planning on marrying the following June, as soon as she finished her presidency. That is why she only signed a thirteen-month lease on her new apartment. On the application she listed Rabbi Steven Jacobs as a reference, calling him a close personal friend. She wondered if Steven had shared their marriage plans with anyone else yet.

Anita had tried to prepare her mother, Riva, who basically felt the same way Phyllis did about the rabbi. Anita wondered why two of the people who had meant the most to her over the years thought Rabbi Jacobs was so bad for her. Did they want her to remain unhappy? Breaking the news as gently as possible, Anita said, "We are only good friends right now, Ma, but I don't know what will happen in a year or so. I care very deeply for him and I want you to know that."

Riva had not been happy. Hopefully, Anita's sister would convince her mother that Anita had never been happier. Anita's little sister, Linda, and her husband, Andy, both therapists, seemed to approve of Steven. Linda had even called her mother and said, "What is so bad, Ma? He seems good for her and she is happier than ever now."

Anita was even traveling with the rabbi now. They had just been to a rabbinic convention together, and Anita concluded that the rabbi was both serious and sincere about their relationship. He visited her family. He took her out openly with his colleagues. They had even chosen and bought some furniture together which would first fill her new apartment and later their home. Melvin paid all the bills. If he only knew.

Anita scolded herself for worrying. It was making her sick. She vowed to stop feeling so insecure about the rabbi and so upset about Melvin. Sure, Steven had had plenty of liaisons since marrying his first wife, Ginger, but as far as Anita knew he had never wanted to marry anyone else. She was special to him. And Melvin deserved to suffer a little. He had made her so miserable for all these years. Let him pay for it.

Anita had to admit to herself that both men were driving her a little crazy this summer, making tremendous demands on her time. They were both needy and controlling. She felt like a piece of steel caught between two powerful magnets.

When Anita was at the temple working, Melvin would constantly beep her on her pager or call her car phone whenever the temple secretaries wouldn't put him through. When she was at the accounting office, Rabbi Jacobs would call five to ten times a day. Neither man could stand to have her out of reach.

The only difference was that Anita despised Mel's calls and looked forward to the rabbi's. But still, each of them expected her to drop everything for him. Their constant demands were exhausting and draining.

After Anita had worked especially hard for the rabbi, he would often thank her with a special token of appreciation, a piece of silver jewelry or a poem. Her prize possession was a poem Steven had written for her recently, a poem that, in her eyes, proved his love for her. In the poem, among other things, the rabbi thanked her for her "love and companionship" as well as for her "body and passion."

Anita had put it away in her panty drawer, in a red velvet Valentine's box that was filled with tokens of both Steven's and

Mel's appreciation. Anita kept them so that whenever she got depressed she could remind herself that she was indeed loved. Nobody could tell her that this wasn't for real—not her friend Phyllis; not Steven's first wife, Ginger; not Mel, who had suspected the affair for over a year and kept telling her that the rabbi didn't really care about her. Rabbi Jacobs loved her. Soon the entire world would know. Their romance would no longer merely be temple gossip. Anita smiled. She had certainly come a long way.

Anita Molly Green, at forty-two, looked much older than her years. The stress of leading a double life had finally made her begin to put on weight again. She always looked tired since she seldom slept through the night.

Despite the strain, Anita remained attractive, with shoulder-length blond hair, soft blue eyes, long nails always polished bright red, and skin that was weathered from years of too much sun. Always perfectly made up, she applied her face even when she was wearing shorts and an old sweatshirt or lying in bed with a lover. She just never felt comfortable without her makeup. Anita always smelled wonderful, feminine and soft.

Anita was a woman who stood out in a crowd, not because she was exceptionally beautiful, but, rather, because she always assessed a situation and knew instinctively how to act and what to say. That quality, and the fact that he had always preferred women who were needy and in pain, had drawn Steven Jacobs to Anita years before.

Anita thought about her lover. He was exquisite, and she had boasted to her friends about how handsome he was. Rabbi Steven Jacobs looked much younger than his fifty years. He was a short man, a little over five feet three inches without his shoe lifts. Anita, at five feet five inches, was taller, but their bodies fit together perfectly. His naturally chubby body was well toned from years of jogging. He loved the sun and, like Anita, had a permanent tan. His ruddy complexion gave his round face an open, warm appearance. The rabbi was always smartly dressed and generous with compliments and hugs. When he spoke from the pulpit, his eyes, his best feature, seemed to look directly into a person's soul.

Anita was not the only one who found Steven Jacobs

attractive. He was, and had always been, immensely appealing to women. He was hard to resist, and Anita was delighted that she hadn't, once she found out how tender he was in the bedroom. She had never known lovemaking like this. She would sometimes write her feelings down after making love, and she realized that she actually wrote differently after she spent time with Steven. He inspired her.

Later, Anita tried to describe her feelings to Phyllis while they sat around the pool in the Greens' backyard. She had so much she wanted to share with her friend, and yet she was not really supposed to tell her anything at all.

"Phyllis, if only there were some way for me to let you know how special our love is," Anita said. "I want you to understand. The sex is incredible. I actually hurt whenever we are apart."

Phyllis stared at her friend. Anita seemed happier than she had ever been before. This was what she really wanted. She was going to leave her husband for her sanity, her safety, and, most of all, for her lover. Phyllis hoped she was not about to make another mistake.

"I want what's best for you, but give me a break. I don't want to hear about sex with the rabbi. You sound like you're back in high school. Mel is just so repulsive to you now that you're always horny."

The two women laughed.

"You're right, you know," Anita confessed. "Sex with Mel is pretty disgusting. We haven't been together since early February. I moved into Scott's old room back then."

Phyllis looked surprised that Anita was back in her son's old room. She lit a cigarette, exhaling slowly. As Phyllis watched the smoke billow into the air, she looked at Anita.

"You never told me that. Mel must be climbing the walls. Who is he sticking it to?"

"Damned if I know."

Phyllis had her own ideas, and she was sure that Melvin was bound to brag about his conquests. She would hear soon enough. The thought nauseated her. Who could possibly find Melvin attractive? She had wondered how he and Anita did it for years.

"Anita, since we're talking so openly, I have to ask you something. When he was at his highest weight, how did you two do it? Did he actually get on top?"

Phyllis had never been shy; and she had always wondered how Anita and Mel had made love. Since the first day, when Anita introduced her to Mel, when he was over 550 pounds, she had pictured all sorts of scenarios in her head. Now that they had separated she was pretty sure her question was fair game.

Anita laughed. It was just like Phyllis to be so bold.

"It was not very pleasant, and I can't even remember when I actually last enjoyed sex with him. There was a time, though, when Melvin was a generous lover. He was not experienced, but he tried to please me. Still, I never experienced what I have with Steven. Mel was always very hung up about sex," Anita explained.

"For years I just endured sex with Mel," Anita continued. "The fatter he got, the more difficult making love became. We got very creative. God, when he was close to six hundred pounds it was almost impossible! If we did it then, he pushed the issue."

"Did he force himself on you?" Phyllis asked. She could picture Mel doing something like that. He was so demanding.

"Yes, but not violently or anything like that. He would just surprise me and mount me from the rear. He knew that was about all my body could handle, and it wasn't as difficult for him to maneuver himself that way."

"Was it any better after he lost all the weight?" Phyllis persisted.

"No, even though he has lost almost three hundred pounds, our sex life hasn't gotten any better. The bedroom only makes me hate being with him more. He smells like that nauseating diet powder he lives on, and he obsesses about what the rabbi and I do in bed together. I don't let him touch me anymore. He is mad as hell about that. He claims I am not acting like a wife."

Anita had met Melvin Green fifteen years earlier, when she was in her late twenties. Bored and frustrated with her life as a mother and wife, she had searched for a job to help add meaning to her empty days. Melvin took a chance and hired her to work at his accounting firm. At the time, he was a wealthy, married businessman in his thirties who was unhappy at home and unstable in general. Anita didn't think it would be too hard to get his attention. She told her friends back east about her new boss, "I think he's interested in me, and even if he's not, he will be soon."

Anita's prediction quickly came to pass, and little did she know that her wish would all too soon become her greatest nightmare. Within months after their marriage, Melvin began to torment Anita, wanting to control her every move. She felt like she couldn't breathe. When Anita told Mel's first wife, Bernyce Herzberg, about his actions, Bernyce answered, "At least you got a house out of it all."

Anita had her beautiful home in Encino, but some wondered if she was ever really happy there. She always seemed to be running from her new husband. It was twice as bad because she worked and lived with him, so she could never escape his tyranny. She couldn't turn to her girlfriends. Over the years, Melvin had forced her to give up many of them because he was jealous of the time she spent with them. Men were out of the question. Melvin did not believe that a man and woman could be friends.

There were times when Melvin was tolerable. He was generous, kind, and great to talk to. Anita justified his bad behavior by saying he was nervous and insecure. She could not abandon him.

Anita did not want her family to know how unhappy she was most of the time, so she did not turn to them for comfort. Anita had no place to go for refuge, and she felt very much alone.

During this time, the one place where Anita felt good was the synagogue. In 1980, Anita's son, Scott Arnow, was studying for his bar mitzvah at Temple Judea in Tarzana, California. A large reform congregation located in the heart of the Valley, Temple Judea was a warm, loving, and *hamish*, or down-to-earth, congregation. Anita found a home there, and so much more.

The senior rabbi at Temple Judea, Steven B. Jacobs, then in his forties, was known around the country to be one of the greatest rabbinical talents of his generation. He had been chosen by the rabbinical movement to lead a peace delegation to Vietnam, and he spoke eloquently before Congress about what he witnessed there. Rabbi Jacobs believed in the Jewish imperative *tikun olam*, which translates as "fixing the world." The rabbi worked tirelessly to help make the world a better place. He worked to resettle the Cambodian boat people and was instrumental in getting countless Jewish congregations in the United States and Canada to participate in this effort.

For many of his followers, Rabbi Jacobs's presence was magical. He had a tender and personal approach to the rabbinate. His compassion and warmth allowed many to reconnect to their Judaism, often in dynamic ways.

Anita, in her early thirties, was instantly smitten, completely taken in by the wonderful rabbi's charm and charisma. Anita talked about him for days. She had never found temple enjoyable before. But now, the same prayers and songs she remembered from her childhood sounded different and more meaningful when Rabbi Jacobs delivered them. He made her feel spiritual and helped her communicate with God.

After services, he went out of his way to talk with all his congregants. At one Sabbath service Anita told the rabbi how special his services were to her, and he was immediately jubilant. He seemed to thrive on the attention.

His second ex-wife, Miriam Jacobs, later described the rabbi's reactions: "After services, he loves hearing how wonderful he was. He lives for that. He doesn't want to hear how his sermons inspired someone, but rather how he did. His ego gets all swollen, and he struts around the temple like a cocktail-lounge singer."

Anita was touched that the rabbi cared about what she thought of his service. He was very attentive to her, but, unbeknownst to Anita, the rabbi's attentions were part of his act. He often lavished attention on women congregants, and at times he appeared to get carried away. Women found him charming, and his attentiveness toward them did not go unnoticed. The vulnerable ones were like putty in his hands. They hungered for the rabbi's approval and went out of their way to secure his attentions.

Soon Anita began to volunteer at the temple. First, because she enjoyed the temple members; second, because she was very fond of the rabbi; and, finally, to escape Mel's tyranny and craziness.

Mel initially approved of the time Anita spent at the temple because he saw the members as potential clients for his accounting firm. It was not until much later that he grew jealous and tried to put an end to her work for their synagogue, which was the only time she looked forward to.

By the early eighties, Anita had already fallen completely in love with the rabbi. For years, her feelings had intensified, and she vowed to herself and her friends that one day they would be together.

In the beginning, Anita became a good friend to the rabbi and his first wife, Ginger Jacobs. She worked at being close to his children and involved herself intimately in their lives. She knew how important they were to him.

Anita's friends weren't sure exactly when Anita fell in love with Rabbi Jacobs. The gossip had started years earlier. Certainly there were occasions that didn't seem right to people. At Tammy Jacobs's graduation from high school, Anita joined Ginger and Steven at the ceremony and sat next to Steven. At the Jacobs's boys' baseball games, Anita and Steven would sit together and cuddle. People commented that Anita always had her hands on the rabbi.

It was unclear when the sexual aspect of their friendship blossomed, but their actions indicated that an affair had been going on for several years. After Anita's death, the rabbi told Anita's mother, Riva, that he had shared a "special" relationship with her daughter for six years. "We were sorry we could not tell you about it," he added. "We always wanted to." Some people said Anita seemed to throw herself at him. It was clear to many that she was more smitten with him than he was with her.

By 1983, Rabbi Jacobs had been the controversial rabbi of Temple Judea, for fourteen years. A popular rabbi, adored by the temple's youth, Jacobs was always eloquent on the pulpit and at life-cycle events. Still, his years of battles and power struggles with Temple Judea's board members had left many of the temple's leaders scarred.

Throughout the years, there were rumors that Rabbi Jacobs

was sleeping with congregants. Some members were upset and embarrassed. His marriage began to suffer and he changed dramatically. Later, some would refer to this period as the time of his first breakdown, claiming that he had never recovered.

In addition to Jacobs's personal problems, Temple Judea's leadership found it difficult to keep assistant rabbis and religious school directors on staff. It seemed that whenever another temple leader became popular, Rabbi Jacobs would grow jealous. A power struggle would begin, and Rabbi Jacobs fought his battles to win. He had a terrible temper, and his views on everything had to prevail.

Some said Rabbi Jacobs suffered from a Napoleon complex. Certainly he fit the picture, a short man who loved control and the power it brought him. Many who had worked for him shared harsh memories of battles lost. For a rabbi, Steven Jacobs had certainly made a lot of enemies.

In 1983, the tension at Temple Judea came to a head when Rabbi Jacobs made an unusual request. He wanted the board to fire the temple's other senior leader, Cantor Jerry Miller. Miller had a beautiful voice. He taught music at nearby Monroe High School and worked hard at training the temple's Bar and Bat Mitzvah candidates. People were outraged.

The rabbi said Jerry Miller was not an ordained cantor and wasn't willing to become one. In reality, the rabbi simply did not like the cantor. The rabbi pitted family members against one another as he explained to the congregation that Cantor Miller wasn't religious enough, citing his inability to read "real" Hebrew and his refusal to learn.

Apparently, when the cantor sang he read the words from the transliterated pages of the Hebrew songbook. Rabbi Jacobs claimed the cantor's failure to read the actual Hebrew set a bad example for the temple youth, who had to learn to read the language of the Torah and whom the cantor trained for their Bar and Bat Mitzvahs.

Self-absorbed with his mission, Rabbi Jacobs was oblivious to the pain he inflicted on the congregation. He demanded that the cantor leave, immediately.

The temple's leaders and board members didn't know what to do. It was true that their rabbi was dearly loved, but so was their cantor. Rabbi Jacobs had delivered an ultimatum: the cantor or the rabbi. A full congregational meeting was held to settle the dispute.

As the date for the meeting approached, lobbyists for each side worked on their friends and neighbors. As soon as a congregant hung up the phone, another call would come in arguing the opposite position. And all of this happened because Rabbi Steven Jacobs did not want to share his pulpit with Cantor Gerald Miller.

The board had already agreed to remove the cantor at the end of the year, but they asked Rabbi Jacobs to allow him to finish out his contract, hoping he would be able to find another job in the interim. Rabbi Jacobs refused. The board sought the congregation's approval of its decision to permit Gerald Miller, their cantor of seventeen years, to remain on the temple's staff for one more year.

The dreaded confrontation filled the temple to capacity. It lasted for hours. Emotions ran high, tempers flared, tears poured, and friends attacked one another's positions.

This temple meeting had already made headlines in the *Los Angeles Times*'s Valley section and in the Los Angeles *Daily News*. Some Valley residents were sickened. Why was the rabbi fighting his battles in the press?

The newspaper articles had seemingly forced the Reform Movement to step in. Its West Coast rabbinic leaders, Ted Broido and Lennard Thal, attended the meeting supposedly to help the congregants make a decision. In reality, Rabbi Jacobs did not trust his own temple members to accurately count the votes, and the movement leaders were there at his request to support his position.

One temple congregant, a professional journalist, chronicled the spectacle. On one side of the pulpit sat Rabbi Jacobs, flanked by his educational director, Judith Aronson, and his associate rabbi, Steven Reuben. On the other side sat Gerald Miller, with a member of the oldest *havurah*, the small groups of friends that made up the congregation.

As the meeting began, a confident Steven Jacobs walked toward the podium. He stared solemnly out at his disciples, but before he could speak some congregants began to cry out, "Jan is here. Jan is here."

No one could possibly miss the shouts ringing out announcing the arrival of Rabbi Jan Goldstein, the highly respected and much loved young assistant rabbi, who had left Temple Judea three years earlier, in 1980. Goldstein remained the only rabbi who had ever stood up publicly against Rabbi Jacobs's abuse of power. After sharing a pulpit with Rabbi Jacobs, he had retired from synagogue life and become the rabbi at a Jewish day school.

Rabbi Jacobs stared at Jan. He began to tremble and his face turned red with anger. He was visibly shaken and whispered something into Rabbi Thal's ear. The arrival of another rabbi to challenge him had stripped away his confidence. Quickly the Reform Movement's secretary, Rabbi Broido, walked down the center aisle to speak with Goldstein. All eyes turned to the back of the room. "If you speak against Steven Jacobs, you'll never work anywhere again," Broido whispered.

"I quit when I had no place to go and three young children to support. I'll take my chances. This man needs to be stopped."

Rabbi Goldstein then approached his colleague, Rabbi Thal, and said, "I want it on the record that I've been threatened by the Reform Movement."

"Threatened? Come on, Jan, who are you kidding?"

"I have a right to speak to this congregation. Are you forbidding me?"

Since it appeared that the balance of power in the room could easily swing toward the cantor if Jan Goldstein was allowed to speak, he had to be silenced.

"I have a solution. I don't think we will be needing to hear from *any other* rabbis tonight. But if Rabbi Reuben gets up to speak in Rabbi Jacobs's behalf, then you can speak on Gerry's behalf as well." Rabbi Thal and Rabbi Goldstein had struck a deal.

Rabbi Goldstein seemed elated. At the height of dramatic tension, when emotions were at their most feverish, Rabbi Reuben, known to be a compassionate man and an eloquent speaker, stepped in. He picked up the microphone, but before uttering a word he looked down at Rabbi Goldstein. Goldstein stood up and slowly approached the bimah.

Rabbi Thal stood up at the same moment. "End of discussion. We'll take a vote now," he exclaimed, preventing either rabbi from speaking. With Thal in control, there would be no dispute over the speeches.

The temple narrowly voted to allow the cantor to stay. It was a cheerless victory. Nobody wanted to lose either leader's talents.

Rabbi Jacobs, surprised and hurt by the congregation's decision, had lost both face and power. No longer in control of his followers, he felt betrayed.

"You have spoken. I will leave at the end of my contract."

The congregation could not believe what they were witnessing. Rabbi Jacobs's children sat in the front of the sanctuary crying.

His followers had never believed for a moment that he would lose. In fact, his office was filled with balloons and champagne in anticipation of the victory celebration his inner circle had been certain of. Some said the rabbi had planned the party to symbolically dance on the cantor's grave. Anita and Melvin Green had helped plan this celebration that never occurred.

Ironically, Rabbi Jacobs's final High Holy Day Service as Temple Judea's rabbi, in September of 1983, took place in a large circus tent at a fairground known as Devonshire Downs. In his sermon, Rabbi Jacobs called for healing. People were deeply moved.

But ironically less than five years later, Jacobs would put his new congregation through a similar battle when he demanded they oust Cantor Debbie Friedman from her position. The reason: too many congregants were bonding closely with her. It appeared that once again Jacobs felt threatened. This time, after a bitter board fight, his supporters prevailed.

After Temple Judea voted to not remove Miller, Rabbi Jacobs's supporters rallied behind him, laying the foundation for a new congregation. They planned to build him the biggest temple in the Valley. Their rabbi would lead it and emerge as one of the great rabbinic leaders of all time. Steven Jacobs had the talent, the power, and the charisma. They had the money. Together they would build their dream synagogue.

Shir Chadash–The New Reform Congregation was born. Its name translated into English means "a new song." Eight founding families shared a pioneering vision of what that song would grow to mean. In its first year alone, many of Temple Judea's most prominent members would follow Rabbi Jacobs.

The West Valley's Reform Jewish community was torn apart by the temple split. In some cases, generations were divided as grandparents and parents stayed at Temple Judea, while their children followed the dynamic rabbi to Shir Chadash.

Temple Judea rebounded quickly. Capitalizing on the baby boom, the temple concentrated on building a wonderful parenting center for infants and toddlers as well as a premier nursery school for preschoolers. In this way, new young families were drawn to the synagogue to replace those that had followed Rabbi Jacobs to Shir Chadash.

Anita and Melvin Green were among the original charter members of Shir Chadash. Anita remembered being excited by the intensity of the founders' commitment. Families were not allowed to question Rabbi Jacobs if they hoped to be accepted into the new congregation's inner circle. The rabbi was not as trusting as he had once been, and he needed to make sure that his followers supported him fully.

Anita loved being part of this group. Over the next six years they became like family to her. She treasured the time she spent with all of them, especially the time she shared with Steven.

As the years passed, their relationship had at last flourished, raising troubling questions for temple board members who chose to ignore it rather than embarrass their leaders. Several staff members warned Anita that their relationship was not proper, but her pat retort was always the same, "I don't care what people think. It's my life."

At least one brave temple staff member told the rabbi, who was technically her boss, her opinion of the rumored relationship. He seemed to care, but only momentarily. Apparently he could not help himself.

"I'm not married and she is going to leave Mel," the rabbi answered in an attempt to justify what was going on.

"She hasn't left him yet, and you are both leaders of the congregation. Besides, I worry about Melvin. I don't know what he might do."

The rabbi nodded. "I know. I wish there was some way to keep him away from here."

Perhaps in Rabbi Jacobs's mind the relationship was not out of bounds morally, but in Mel's mind it was. It tormented him. His wife was being coveted by another. His prized possession was being stolen away. Rabbi Jacobs had broken at least one commandment, and, in Mel's mind, several others as well.

The rabbi and Mel may have differed on the issue of morality, but the rabbi must have known his relationship with Anita was hardly innocent. At the very least, a clergyman who sleeps with his congregant could appear predatory and manipulative to many. That's probably why Steven Jacobs so desperately wanted to keep what was going on a secret.

3

Lunch Between Friends

Phyllis Baltin pushed away her coffee cup and lit another cigarette. This lunch seemed to be dragging on forever, and she was getting nowhere with Anita. Phyllis was only lingering because of her mother-in-law's last dying wish: "Straighten things out with Anita. I can't tell you why, but there isn't much time."

Phyllis wasn't superstitious, but she believed those words were a warning. She had to convince Anita that she faced a grave danger. As the minutes turned to hours, Phyllis became more and more frustrated.

Anita and Phyllis were sitting on the patio of the Silver Grille, a trendy Encino eatery. They were nervously chain-smoking cigarettes, discussing Anita's dilemma.

Phyllis was six months older than Anita and, in her forty-two years, had suffered through divorce, poverty, more illnesses than she could remember, severe problems with her kids, and enough family crises to feed her favorite soap opera writers for many months. Her youngest son (Anita's godson) hadn't spoken to her in almost a year. The last thing she needed this fall was one more thing to worry about. Her own problems were making her sick, and now Anita's life was on the line. Despite her efforts, Phyllis couldn't make Anita understand the seriousness of her predicament.

"Anita, just take what he's offering you. Is money worth dying over?" she had warned her. "You know how violent Mel can be," Phyllis added.

Phyllis knew Mel hated to part with money and would rather pay it all to attorneys than any to Anita. And what about his business buddies, cronies, and advisors? Phyllis knew they were all in bed together financially. Were they a danger to Anita too if she took half of Melvin's working capital in a divorce settlement?

Phyllis didn't want to frighten Anita by telling her about the terrible Thursday night two months ago. She would never forget the date, July 12, 1990. That was the night Melvin had called her boyfriend, Lance Shoemaker, and asked him, "How much would you charge to kill Anita?"

Lance and Phyllis had taken it all in jest. Over the years they had grown to expect this kind of talk from Melvin. He liked to shock people. But sitting at the restaurant today, Phyllis wondered if her silence was a betrayal. Did Anita need to hear about Mel's threats? How could she continue to warn her without scaring her? Phyllis was troubled enough by Anita's appearance today.

Anita wore a soft nylon jogging suit in a beautiful shade of pink. She had on a pair of tennis shoes and silver earrings that Phyllis had never seen before. She had put on weight, and Phyllis attributed the gain to nerves. Anita always ate more when she was upset. Anita looked haggard and exhausted, her face drained of color.

"What's going on?" Phyllis asked. "Isn't it any better now that you're out?"

Anita looked up from her plate and saw the concern in her friend's eyes.

"Mel can't handle my relationship with Steven. He's so angry. It makes him feel like he's less of a man or something. This divorce is gonna kill me. I feel badly that he's hurting so because I still care about him. I just wish he would leave me alone."

Anita's voice was filled with tension, tight and cracking, as she continued. "I've got something on him. Something more than just tax improprieties. Once I tell him, he'll back off. You know how much his reputation means to him. I think that's why he's so upset about this divorce. In his mind it makes him look bad, he thinks people are laughing at him. What he doesn't know is they were laughing at him long before I ever mentioned divorce. I kept telling friends Melvin was not as bad as he seemed. They tolerated him for me. But, finally, I think I've got him where I want. He'll have to give me the money I'm asking for."

Phyllis didn't have any idea what secrets Anita was referring to, other than knowing some of Mel's business improprieties. What more could she possibly have on her husband now? Anita seemed confused, alternating between fear and sadness, elation and contentment. She was almost like a manic-depressive. Sometimes she expressed confidence that she would win a hefty divorce settlement, and the next minute she would tell Phyllis that she wasn't going to get a thing. Sure, Mel feared she might turn him in to the Internal Revenue Service, but did Anita know something else?

Phyllis thought that when she wasn't frightened, Anita was more content and busier than ever. Her friend was trying to gain control of her life, and Phyllis was proud of her attempts. She just hoped Anita had finally gotten to the point where she was ready to save herself at all costs.

"Can you make it without his money for a while?" Phyllis asked.

"Yes, Phyllis, for a little while anyway," Anita answered. "I've borrowed some money from my mother and I want to go to work. I've learned a lot about working from Mel and the temple. I think I might be able to do well. What do you think?"

Anita didn't sound all too confident about the work part. She found herself entangled in a tragic dilemma. She had finally moved out, she was in a wonderful relationship, and she held a position that gave her power and prestige in the community. She had plenty of friends, and obviously a lot of choices, but she was terrified about trying to make it on her own. Part of Anita wanted to get a real job, but the other part was far too afraid to really try to find one, and even more afraid of how hard she would have to work if she did find one. Anita wasn't a stranger to hard work, but the only work she really enjoyed was for the temple.

"I'm glad you have some money. Don't let him pressure you." Phyllis wondered if now was the time to tell Anita about

Mel's ominous proposition to Lance, since she was obviously suffering with her own fears about Melvin. Anita's voice brought Phyllis back to reality.

"Phyllis, I feel like someone is following me. I think I've seen a blond guy a few times. I hope its only a private investigator. Maybe Mel hired one to see if I'm going to the IRS. He's so paranoid."

As she shared this information, Anita lit up another cigarette. Phyllis looked up. Her voice was low, almost a whisper. "Anita," she said, "I wouldn't put anything past Melvin. You've changed the rules. He can't control you, so he's afraid of you now. In his eyes you have all the power and the respect too." Phyllis knew her words were true. Melvin might do anything to Anita now.

Anita listened to Phyllis's words. She was worried sick about Melvin's angry reaction to her knowledge of his improper business practices. Yet she kept taunting him with it. It was her way of scaring him into giving her what she wanted. The taunts coupled with her obvious relationship with the rabbi were finally pushing him over the edge.

"When did he find out about us, Phyllis? I know he's suspected for awhile, but when did he find out for sure? He told me you told him. Were you the first? Steven's and my future well-being depends on when he found out."

Phyllis was startled. She had told Mel about Anita and the rabbi six months earlier at Mel's mother's funeral in January 1990. Mel had been hounding her a long time. Phyllis finally relented and told Mel what she suspected, partially to get him to leave her alone and partially because she felt sorry for him. After all, he was still Anita's husband. He might as well know that he was not the only one who had grown suspicious about the rabbi and Anita.

Phyllis was not harsh to tell Melvin at the funeral, of all places. She could not avoid answering his loud questions. He had come right out and asked her over and over when they were back at the house after the burial. "Who's she screwing, Phyllis? I need to hear it all. Don't leave anyone out. What about the rabbi? The guy with all my money? I keep writing checks to build the temple. Over one hundred thousand dollars this year alone. I have the records. Is he fucking her? You have to know. You're always on the phone with her. What has she told you?"

Mel had badgered Phyllis and kept on until she finally relented. "Anita, you know how he gets. It was embarrassing. I had to tell him. I tried to calm him down and tell him of the affairs before the two of you met anyway," Phyllis explained. "But he wouldn't listen. He got crazy. I told him who I was certain of, as well as who I suspected."

"When?" Anita asked.

"I said, in January. Back at your house. Right after the funeral." Phyllis added,"You were busy in the kitchen. He knew anyway, Anita. You were not very discreet about it."

Mel hadn't taken the news well. He'd grown more physically, verbally, and mentally abusive toward his wife since January 1990. He spent every waking minute thinking about her affairs, torturing himself as he tried to picture the details. He wanted to know if Anita's lovers were more skilled than he was in bed. Did they satisfy her sexually?

Mel's mind unraveled, bit by bit. The death of his beloved mother, June Green, and the betrayal of his wife proved more than he could take. Perhaps June Green knew her only child was bordering on madness. She had begged her daughter-in-law not to abandon Melvin.

From January through July, life in Anita and Mel Green's Encino house had been hell on Earth. Anita thanked God that Scott was out of the house, living with his fiancée, Clarissa. Some days Mel would raze the house and office, looking through all of Anita's belongings for incriminating evidence to mail off to his divorce attorney. He'd rifle through and then throw out her temple files and rosters, explaining everything in the house was his, so he could do whatever he pleased.

He held meetings at his office that first stripped away Anita's powers at their accounting company, then her standing in the company, and finally whatever was left of her self-esteem. Mel took away Anita's access to bank accounts and changed the safe at the office. "She's a villain out to destroy me," he shouted to one confidant when the man questioned Mel's actions.

Every morning, Mel read Anita's appointment book to find out where she was going so he could torment her with his phone calls. He would empty her purse, searching for cigarettes, letters, anything he didn't approve of. He took away her checkbook and her credit cards. If Anita made telephone calls from either the house or the office, he would listen in on the extension. He would work late, call her when he knew she was already asleep, and then hang up the receiver.

Perhaps the worst times were at night. Mel had always had a sleep disorder. He just didn't get much sleep at all and survived on a couple of hours of rest each night. Now even a couple of hours was unheard of. Most of the night Mel would stomp around the house, the walls and foundation shaking, while he prowled through Anita's belongings. For Anita, the nights were the longest. She would bury her head in her pillow and hope the drugs the doctors gave her would calm her enough to allow sleep to take her away from her misery. When she finally fell asleep, there were many times when Mel would come in and wake her up, always screaming at her about something. After months of this nighttime abuse, Anita had finally left him.

Despite Anita's attempts at bravery in dealing with Mel's actions, Phyllis had noticed she had gone to great lengths to avoid contact with Melvin, and now that she was out of the house she tried even harder to stay away from him.

It seemed that whenever Anita would see Mel he would spend virtually every minute shouting insults at her, harassing her, and trying to embarrass her. In front of temple friends, family members, and business associates, he would call her a cunt, a lesbian, a whore, and whatever other obscenity he could think of at the moment.

Melvin drove around the Valley in a state of frenzied jealousy and anger, frantically dictating crazy letters into his "bitch box," the small tape recorder he carried everywhere. He would then force his secretary, Lily Lopez, to type them up. His divorce file was growing in size, locked in his safe. The letters were addressed to Anita, to Rabbi Jacobs, to his business associates, to himself, and to his attorney.

By the middle of August 1990, the number of letters had

increased dramatically. On some days Mel would write long letters a few minutes apart, as the stream-of-consciousness thoughts continued to torment him. Obviously, Mel Green despised living alone and could not stand the thought of his wife with someone else. Why was Anita telling him that Steven and she spent practically all their time together, especially now that Mel was so lonely? Anita knew it was not a very smart way of acting, but she couldn't help it. It was her way of abusing Mel and getting back at him for all the torture and abuse he had put her through.

Phyllis tried again to warn her friend. She had been trying to protect Anita all along, yet Anita, as usual, only heard what she wanted to hear.

"Do not let him know the things you do with Steven. Don't tell him how hard you are working on the temple. Leave him out of it."

Phyllis was sure Anita had not listened. She was staring into space as if Phyllis's opinion did not mean a thing. Anita was hotheaded and stubborn, with selective hearing. Phyllis knew Anita was working on this problem with her therapist. But if she was gaining anything from the sessions, it was not making things noticeably better. Phyllis hoped for her friend's sake that she would start to listen soon.

On the street, a car slowed down. The driver looked at the two women and then sped off. Phyllis realized that they could both be targets. They were like two sitting ducks, all alone, leaning against the wall and talking. Was someone looking for Anita? Or had Phyllis merely watched too many cop shows on television?

The car approached again. Phyllis saw the driver had long blondish hair. He looked like the guy they had both seen earlier in the summer in Anita's underground garage. Now Anita said she thought a blond guy was following her. Phyllis fought the urge to bolt from the table. After all, they were in a public place.

"Is that the guy, Anita?" she asked. Anita shook her head no. Finally, the driver disappeared.

Phyllis thought of the bizarre phone calls and letters she had received over the years from Mel Green. She remembered that for one Hanukkah dinner he had arrived at her house brandishing a gun. When she reacted negatively, he said it was only to protect her. Phyllis had made Mel put the gun away in a drawer in her bedroom.

Anita was embarrassed whenever Mel waved a gun around, but she had usually done her best to ignore the situation, trying instead to change the guests' focus of attention. "He's just odd. Thinks he's Kojak," she explained at one party. Friends laughed nervously. Mel seemed to like the attention his firearm brought him.

Phyllis knew the Greens' marriage had never been a normal partnership; it was more like an ownership. Melvin felt he had the absolute right to own and control Anita. That was his view of what came with a marriage certificate. Phyllis had read part of what he had forced Anita to sign before they married. She would never forget the line, "I am the absolute and supreme boss of Anita Molly Green. If she ever argues with me, my position automatically wins. I wear the pants in the house."

Phyllis was privy to hundreds of letters and documents that said things even more outrageous, and she reminded Anita of their existence.

"I know, and they're getting worse. You should see the letters he's writing nowadays." Anita tried to laugh. Her friend had been honest and tough with her today. She had made sure Anita knew just how dangerous she thought Mel had grown.

Phyllis pleaded again, "Anita, don't flaunt Steven to Mel. Don't pressure his lawyers for more money. Please listen to me. Get on with your life."

With the mention of Steven, their lunch was over. Apologizing, Anita said she had to leave. Perhaps she was overreacting, but she couldn't stand to hear anything negative about Steven.

As Phyllis sat alone smoking cigarette after cigarette, everything became clear. Anita's new friends and colleagues were richer and more powerful than Phyllis, but they certainly were caught up in the game their temple leadership was playing. They had to know that their rabbi was sleeping with Anita. It had to sicken many of them. After all, Mel Green was still donating a lot of money to build that temple. Couldn't the rabbi wait until Mel and Anita were divorced? Phyllis was also shocked that the temple had told Melvin he was no longer a member because of the way he made his pledges to the synagogue. Yet Anita, who paid her dues with Melvin's money, was the temple's leader. How could the board allow a decision like that? You can't throw someone out of a congregation. Mel never accepted the decision and wrote letter after letter explaining that he was still a member in good standing.

My God, Phyllis thought, the board and the whole community had condoned this behavior by their silence. This temple board, made up of pious good people, was accepting the breaking of a commandment by both of their spiritual leaders. If anything happened to Anita, Phyllis would hold them all responsible. The continuing affair would no doubt send Melvin Green even further over the edge, and put Anita Green in grave danger.

Grabbing her purse, Phyllis began to get up from the table. Glancing down, she saw the check. Phyllis took this as another sign. It was the first time ever that Anita had left her sitting with the bill.

4

A Fatal Appointment

October 25, 1990

A few weeks after her lunch with Phyllis, Anita Green woke up at Rabbi Jacobs's house and got ready to leave for her husband's office to pick up a check. Their divorce lawyers had spent months working out a compromise: Anita would continue to work for Mel at home, and Mel would pay her for the work when she brought it back to him. It was a little after nine on Thursday morning, October 25, and she was acutely aware of the danger in which she would be putting herself. Separated now for almost three months, Anita was terrified of keeping this appointment with Mel.

Anita had grown frightened of spending any time with her husband; during their separation his temper had rocketed out of control. Their last meeting together, in early October, with both of their attorneys present, had ended in disaster. In fact, Anita had agreed to today's meeting only because Mel promised to give her a much-needed check.

He had been withholding funds from her since their separation, and now she was in dire financial straits. On August 24, 1990, she'd written her divorce attorney, Janis McDonald, about the financial peril in which she found herself. "Would you please consider, since his attorney is going out of the country for a few weeks, calling her and trying to get some temporary support for me? I'm out of funds. If you do decide to call, please ask her to try to get him to stop with these letters. I do not want him to bother me, either by mail or on the phone."

Cunningly, Mel had waited until Anita was at her lowest

31

point ever, virtually penniless. He then offered her a proposition, one he knew she would take, because, in reality, she didn't have any alternative. She couldn't keep begging forever.

He had found her at the hairdresser on the morning before their appointment.

"Anita," Melvin said over the phone, "I have a check ready for you. You can pick it up at the office, at 10:30 tomorrow morning. I don't have time to drop it in the mail."

Anita begged him to mail it. "No, come in or you won't get it at all," Mel shouted. After hanging up the phone, Anita had confided tearfully to her hairdresser, Gina, about how her husband terrified her.

Gina wasn't the only one Anita confided in. Normally private, that summer Anita had told many people about her fears. In fact, over lunch just a few days before, she had told Phyllis Baltin that she suspected Mel had hired a private eye to see what she was up to at all hours, or perhaps to check if she was visiting the IRS.

Anita knew Mel was scared because she really could destroy him. She knew where the skeletons in his business were buried. But she was smart enough to know Mel would not tolerate the destruction of his business. Was he spying on her to set her up? Anita doubted it, but she couldn't be sure. So she grew even more frightened.

Anita had finally broken down and confided to close temple friends, fellow board members, and people on the building committee. "If something ever happens to me, it's because of Melvin. He'd be responsible. He's a dangerous man."

At one temple function she had begged her close friend Marcia Cayne to follow her into the bathroom so she wouldn't have to face Mel alone. He'd followed her into the ladies' room waving a gun one too many times. He was less likely to shoot her if she was with someone.

Mel had told Anita on numerous occasions that if she left him she wouldn't live to spend his money. In fact, only the day before, Mel had met with his ex-wife Bernyce. At their lunch, he told her he'd fight for his money until the end. He definitely had talked for years of killing her, but presumably she didn't really believe she was in danger. She kept denying to herself that he was capable of hurting her. The death threats continued, but Anita hoped he was full of hot air. Not thinking clearly, Anita was sure she could handle the situation. Mel's office was filled with people; surely he wouldn't hurt her there. His staff was obligated to remain loyal to Mel, but they thought the world of Anita as well. Mel would never risk losing their loyalty by having them witness a harmful act against her.

Anita knew in her heart that Mel still loved her. He was so appreciative of the way she'd cared for his mother, June, in her final days. She tried to convince herself that her past actions would protect her, but she wasn't very successful at her attempts.

In retrospect, it is surprising that Anita had put up with Melvin for ten years. During the first year of their marriage, while Scott, her son by her first husband, was still in school, Melvin began his tirades. At first it was just mental abuse, but it grew increasingly more physical over the years.

As she got ready to go to her meeting with Mel, Anita realized she was very depressed. She was feeling guilty about having left him and anxious he might really hurt her. At the same time, she was insecure in her relationship with Steven and always unsure what their future together would bring, especially if she and Melvin were prosecuted for tax improprieties.

Fearfully, Anita grabbed her purse and headed for the tax-consulting business she and Melvin ran in North Hollywood. It was already after ten, and she didn't want to be late, since Melvin had been quite specific about the time. If she was late, he might change his mind about the money.

Anita was concerned about her future. She knew the divorce would be difficult, and she really was beginning to fear that Mel might hurt her more than just economically. She expected him to continue cutting off financial support, and she knew that, whatever she would get, she would have to fight tooth and nail for it.

Anita had been able to get an apartment and fill it with new furniture because Melvin had reluctantly given her ten thousand dollars to cover her moving expenses. Now that the money was gone, she was only able to put food on the table because her mother had lent her twenty-five thousand dollars. She intended to pay back every penny from the money she expected to get in her divorce settlement.

Anita liked her new apartment in Encino. It was pretty, clean, and peaceful. But still she preferred staying at the rabbi's. She had spent another wonderful night with him last night, at his house in Northridge. She felt so much safer when they were together.

It was hot in Northridge, California, this morning. It had been hot all week long, and the mercury in the thermometers continued to rise. The Santa Ana winds had begun to blow, which promised to bring some relief to suffering Valley residents, but it was still sweltering.

Rabbi Jacobs lived in a quiet residential neighborhood in Northridge, California, one of the hottest parts of the Valley. His house was located on Mayall Street, directly off Balboa Boulevard. Anita would have rather spent the day cooling off in the rabbi's pool then venturing out in the early morning heat to her husband's office in North Hollywood. Still, she forced herself to set off on the short drive.

She left Steven sleeping soundly as she pulled out of the garage. She checked the street and drove away quickly as the garage door closed behind her.

Anita opted for the freeway and began the trip across the Valley. She encountered little traffic during the journey because the morning rush hour had long finished. She exited the Hollywood Freeway at the Oxnard ramp, which lets out onto Laurel Canyon, and traveled a half block to Oxnard Street, where she turned right.

Sometimes Anita felt funny about driving her fancy sports car in North Hollywood. The area was far less exclusive than Encino or Northridge, and she thought the shiny red car appeared conspicuous. She glanced into her rearview mirror to check her lipstick and noticed a motorcyclist following her closely. That was the last thing she saw before changing lanes and turning right onto Wilkinson Street.

Melvin had been busy all morning getting things ready for Anita. He nervously piled up work for her to take home to finish. It had been quite a while since she had done any real work. He had to lure her here with the promise of a check. Mel told Anita that he would calculate how much money he owed her after he figured out how much work she had completed.

As time passed, he grew restless. Adrenaline raced through him. Mel just couldn't settle down to do any work. He brought Anita's work into the library conference room where she liked to complete it. He spread the sheets out on the table. Maybe she'd do some work today. Mel doubted it.

The minutes seemed like hours. They dragged on as Mel paced and paced some more. It was important that Anita honor today's meeting time, more important than anyone realized. It would prove her loyalty still belonged to him.

Mel wanted his life to get back to normal. Anita couldn't expect to get away with the way she was treating him forever. He remembered a temple service just last month where she refused to sit next to him because she had already moved out. Hell, he was still paying the temple dues. She could at least sit with him.

Mel glanced up at the clock on the wall and noticed it was only 10:15. He walked to the front of his office and checked with Lily, to see if his wife had arrived yet. When Lily said no, he whipped himself into a frenzy, convinced that she was standing him up, though the appointed time of their meeting had not yet arrived.

He stomped down the hall toward his office, opened the back door, and looked down the street, craning his neck to catch a glimpse of his wife's approach. She was coming after all. All at once, inexplicably, he came quickly back in and stood calmly with Lily in the waiting room. Anita pulled her red Corvette into the parking lot, but she wasn't alone.

5

Shocking Statements

Just after 10:20, an unusual event occurred in North Holly-wood. The doorbell to Melvin Green's accounting office rang. Everyone who ever came there knew you didn't ring the bell; you just walked in.

Lily Lopez, the office receptionist, was busy typing in the front reception area. She had noticed a tenseness in her boss's expressions and actions. He was pacing back and forth in the front of the building where she worked. By the time the bell rang, he was quite agitated, which was the usual these days, given all he was going through.

Melvin Green had grown even more irritable and obsessed than ever, now that his wife Anita and he were finally in divorce proceedings. Lily attributed his strange behavior to his wife's momentary arrival. In fact, the whole office was tense. She noticed that Mel's uneasiness intensified after the bell rang.

Lily thought it odd that Melvin was up front in the reception area with her. Most days he worked alone in his office. Today he was trying to engage her in a conversation while she was trying to type. Perhaps he was lonely and craving con-versation. Melvin always liked to talk. The bell continued to ring.

"Who's there?" Melvin asked.

A hysterical woman barged into the waiting room, scream-ing loudly about a shooting in the parking lot.

"A lady's been hurt. Come quickly," the woman pleaded to a seemingly shocked Melvin Green.

At first, the desperate woman didn't seem to make much sense as she delivered her unbelievable message. But in seconds, both Melvin and Lily were following her out the door.

Melvin Green ran into the parking lot, not knowing that his actions there, and the way people would perceive them, would forever change the course of his life.

A sweaty-palmed, heart-racing, head-pounding Melvin Green raced to the injured woman, with Lily following at his heels. Both rushed over to the familiar car, gasping as they spotted the driver.

The blood-drenched body of his wife, Anita Molly Green, lay over the steering wheel of their red Corvette convertible. She had been shot in the head. Her beige dress and her blond hair were covered with blood.

"Oh my God, Oh my God," Melvin screamed. "That's my wife."

He stood there frozen for a moment.

Then he forced himself to look at his wife again. He knew immediately that the bullet had shattered her skull. He noticed a slight movement. Could she still be alive?

Then someone shouted, "Has anyone called an ambulance?"

"Yes, they're on the way. The police are too," was the answer.

At the mention of the police, Melvin walked even closer to the car and continued to stare at his wife's body. Wide-eyed, Melvin shook his head in disbelief. Despite the size and location of the wound, and massive blood loss, Anita wasn't dead yet.

From outside the vehicle, at a distance it looked as if Anita had merely collapsed onto the car's dashboard and was simply resting her head there. It was only when Mel came close to her and noticed the size of the huge hole in the back of her head, with her brains exposed and blood pouring out, that he appeared to lose control. He turned to Lily for support. She thought he was going to go into shock.

The dedicated secretary was momentarily immobilized by the sight before her. Before covering her face with her hands, Lily watched in disbelief as Anita's blood flowed out of her.

Mel glared at Lily. He quickly regained his composure and took control of the situation.

"I'm a medic. I need to stop the blood flow. I want to help Anita," he bellowed.

A bald-headed neighbor came running over with a towel. He handed it to Melvin.

Mel placed a finger gently over the gaping hole in Anita's neck. He then positioned himself carefully in the doorway of the car, preventing others from approaching her.

Melvin sat there at the foot of Anita's seat. He removed his sweater so it wouldn't get bloody. He looked at the people staring at them, seemed to think for a moment, and then grabbed Anita's hand and began stroking it. He continued to hold it and talk softly to Anita until the police and rescue personnel arrived and removed him from her side.

The emergency call had come in at 10:25 A.M. The police dispatcher listened to the voice of a man frantically notifying them of a shooting.

"This is an emergency! A lady's been shot!" he shouted into the phone. "She needs an ambulance. Please send the police," he added.

"Well, hold on. Where are you?"

"12431 Oxnard Street, North Hollywood. The parking lot is on Wilkinson Street. That's where she is. I saw it all."

"Is someone with the victim?"

"Yes, the lady I'm working for went over there and told them. They ran out and are with her now. They know her."

"We're on our way."

The emergency call to the North Hollywood division of the Los Angeles Police Department came in at a little before 10:30 A.M., on Thursday, October 25, 1990. It was already hot as hell and smoggy too, while the officers sat listening to the police scanner. It wasn't often the police received a report of a shooting in the morning. Usually the watch commander gave the nighttime shooting reports to the detectives when they arrived at 9:00 A.M. Perhaps it was the heat.

The dispatcher's message was odd enough to jar the homicide coordinator, Detective Michael Coffey, away from his mountain of paperwork. Running, the blond, muscular detective with the deep tan and well-toned body grabbed his car keys.

"This sounds like a good one, John. I'm on my way," Coffey shouted to the watch commander, John Stillo. The commander was right behind him.

The two police cars left the station in a matter of seconds, Coffey in a detective's car and Stillo following in a black-and-white police car. As he sped the few blocks to the crime scene, Coffey wondered who would shoot someone so early in the morning. It was so unusual in this area. Was it a robbery that the victim had interrupted?

Coffey arrived at the crime scene within five minutes of the emergency call. He found himself at a business located on the corner of a small residential street. The shooting had occurred in the parking lot, directly north of a small office building. A few people had already begun to gather around the victim's car.

Coffey, smartly dressed, exited his car and strode up to the victim's vehicle. A uniformed officer was already present.

"We've checked her purse. There's no sign of robbery. Her credit cards and cash haven't been touched." The uniformed officer told Coffey all that he had learned about the victim.

As Coffey moved closer, he saw a large bullet hole in her head. The door to the car was open, and rescue workers were trying to save her.

Coffey watched as paramedics carried the injured woman to a waiting stretcher. Lily Lopez covered her eyes and began to cry.

The noise of the shooting and the sirens of the police cars had brought people out of their houses. They started to mill about the parking lot, all trying to get a look at the victim. Coffey ordered a uniformed officer to mark the crime scene with yellow tape, hoping to keep the curious away.

Exactly five minutes after their arrival, at 10:32 A.M., the paramedics started CPR. They began full resuscitation four minutes later and worked frantically for another ten minutes to stabilize Anita.

Detective Coffey noticed a large male pacing nervously across the driveway, his eyes wild. Coffey made a mental note to ask someone about this man.

As paramedics struggled to stabilize the victim, Coffey

glanced back at the strange man. The guy was staring at him and walking back and forth across the lot. Approaching an officer, Coffey asked, "Who is that guy?"

"That's her husband. We had to pull him off her when we arrived. Claims he was administering first aid to her. I don't see how he could have though. There isn't a drop of blood on him."

The paramedics pushed the gurney into the ambulance. Before the ambulance doors closed, Coffey ordered a uniformed police officer to accompany the victim to the hospital.

Before the ambulance pulled away, Coffey took a closer look at Anita. She was still wearing several pieces of jewelry—a necklace, a watch, two bracelets, and quite a few rings. Her purse was still in her car, the money and credit cards lay undisturbed.

As Coffey touched the fabric on Anita's dress, he observed the fabric had not been ripped or torn. No fibers or threads hung from it. Anita had not had time to struggle.

The shooting looked like a hit. Indeed, the shooter even pulled his victim clear of the car, so the bullet would go straight through her head. Coffey did not think the police would recover the slug.

Michael Coffey, a Los Angeles police detective since 1978, had worked homicide for more than ten years. Just by looking at Anita, he knew immediately the shooter was a pro. Random shootings were seldom this accurate.

Coffey's experience and his ability to remain cool under pressure explained why he was in charge of the station's homicide cases. His instincts were usually right. He couldn't really explain it, but he always knew who to approach first for questioning. He glanced at Melvin Green. The detective sensed something sinister and strange about the guy.

A few minutes after the ambulance pulled away, Coffey strode up to Mel and directed him to the corner of the driveway. He began his questioning. "I'm Detective Michael Coffey, LAPD. Do you have any idea what this is about?"

Coffey's years of detective work, on hundreds of murders, hadn't prepared him for Mr. Green's surprising answer.

"I'm her husband. Why don't you check on the guys who

were screwing her? Um, Rabbi Steven B. Jacobs, Alan Lebowitz, and Hal Mitchell, to name a few."

Coffey thought to himself, why is he telling me this? The detective stared at Melvin Green. Mel did not appear to be upset and was very precise in what he told the detective.

To Coffey, the remarks were highly unusual, but he had no idea at the time how many lives would be altered forever by his having heard the strange words at the crime scene.

Melvin Green saw Coffey looking at him. He buried his head in his hands. Coffey noticed he seemed uncomfortable but not upset.

Coffey turned to an officer. "I don't want this guy going anywhere. Take Mr. Green back to the station so he can make a more detailed statement. I'll call for a detective to interview him."

Later, he would recall his reaction to Mel's statement. "His remarks really touched something in me. It was one of the coldest initial statements from a husband or loved one that you could ever imagine. He didn't appear to have any emotion. I'll never forget it. At that moment I knew this would be an unusual and highly complex case."

The detective had seen people react in all sorts of ways to violent crimes, but he had never seen someone, still in the grip of shock, trying to point the police in a different direction before they had even been asked who might be involved.

After thinking a moment, the detective decided that Melvin Green was trying to choreograph the murder investigation away from himself. He was providing the police with leads before they even asked for them. Was Green trying to keep them away from him? Coffey knew Melvin Green was hiding something.

The detective's thoughts were cut off by the arrival of his lieutenant, Ron LaRue. "What have you got on her?"

Detective Coffey replied, "We've learned that she's Anita Molly Green. She's forty-two years old and a community leader, the president of a large temple. She's supposed to be a well-loved lady. That's her husband. They're in the process of getting a divorce. I've talked to him. He's very strange. We're taking him to the station, lieutenant."

"I want you to do crime scene, Coffey," the lieutenant said.

"Think carefully about who you'll put on the case." Before leaving he added, "Keep me informed."

Picking up the radio, Coffey requested additional police units for crowd control.

Coffey's mind raced ahead. Although murders in Los Angeles were frequent, they usually occurred in the gang-infested ghettos of the inner city. And most of those occurred at night. There were plenty of murders in the Valley too, but not one that looked like this.

Michael Coffey noticed another man approach his uniformed officers. The detective listened to the man who was obviously distressed.

"Officer, I heard a pop, and when I looked up from my work I saw a person wearing a black, full-faced, dark-glass motorcycle helmet and green army-type field jacket with tan pants turn away from this red Corvette. The door of the Corvette was open, and the man was right next to the lady, standing between her and the inside of the open door of the Corvette. The guy then turned and sprinted very fast away from the car, toward the street. He jumped on a motorcycle and sped away. I'm the one who called the police and rescue." The man spoke quickly, the adrenaline making his heart pound in his chest.

The witness's name was Nicholas Foss. He was a roofer who had been working across the street from Melvin Green, Incorporated, at the time of the shooting.

"What did the guy look like?" Coffey asked.

Foss described a man with long blond hair, of medium build and height. It all had happened so quickly.

Mike Coffey thought Foss had provided a pretty good description of the shooter. He picked up his radio and told the dispatcher to send as many units as possible to search for the guy. They were looking for a young man wearing a black motorcycle helmet and a green army jacket. He had scruffy, long blond hair and appeared to be of medium height, with a muscular build.

Foss said the shooter jumped on his bike and sped away, traveling north on Wilkinson. Because of the close proximity of the freeway, Coffey guessed the assailant simply raced out of the area. He could have changed freeways in minutes, and given the immensity of Los Angeles's freeway system, he would disappear.

Detective Coffey checked Anita's car for evidence. Lying on top of the car were a pair of designer sunglasses. He wondered how they got on top of the car. Inside, he found a pair of shoes, a purse, and a cloth satchel. Opening the satchel, Coffey found a makeup case, an address book, a spiral notebook, another pair of shoes, some underwear, pantyhose, and a hairbrush. There was also a zippered case containing all sorts of prescription and over-the-counter medications. He left everything in place for the evidence and fingerprint units to examine and photograph.

Michael Coffey walked through the offices of Melvin Green, Incorporated. He entered the brick building from the Wilkinson entrance, but noted another entrance on Oxnard Street. He found television monitors in Melvin's private office and in the reception area up front, but upon examination saw they had not recorded the crime.

The accounting office was small and old-fashioned. The furnishings were done in brown and beige office tones and were not elaborate. Only the back office, Melvin's private retreat, was furnished more comfortably. The detective found a large overstuffed chair, a leather sofa, and a beautiful mahogany desk with an elaborate black-and-gray-marble top. The walls were paneled in mahogany, with shelves and drawers filling every corner. Pictures of Mel's children and family members stood on the shelves in beautiful frames. His diplomas and tax certificates hung on the walls.

Coffey walked back to his car and called Joe Shenk, North Hollywood division's watch commander. "Joe, find Boom Boom, wherever he is. Tell him to roll. We need him on this one. Get as many other detectives as you can find out here. Hurry."

Boom Boom was the name affectionately given to Ray Hernandez, a seventeen-year police-force veteran, with almost as many years as a homicide detective. He had earned his name his first day as a detective when he had shot at and apprehended a bank robber. Ray was a dedicated detective with a heart of gold and a passion for police work.

They found Hernandez and the other homicide detectives on the golf course finishing the third hole. Cursing themselves for having taken a long-overdue morning off, the guys hurried to the showers, with Ray leading the way. In just minutes, they were headed back to the station.

Coffey awaited his detectives' arrivals by making notes of everything that needed to be done. Some detectives would have to make lists of who to interview. Others would study the crime scene. Still others, his most curious men, would be sent to search the area for witnesses and clues. Crime photographs would be taken; prints would be completed. Coffey would send a detective to the hospital to observe the actions of family and friends. They would not leave anything to chance.

Coffey assigned another detective to go examine Anita's car with great care, in the hope of finding a bullet. Before Coffey had walked away from the vehicle, he had personally removed her pocketbook. Opening her wallet now, he saw that her license confirmed her to be Anita Molly Green, forty-two.

When Coffey's detectives removed the driver's seat, they observed a large amount of blood underneath it. Coffey doubted someone who had lost that much blood could survive. On the right side of the steering wheel the detectives noticed a small dent, just below the steering column.

There were a total of thirteen vehicles at the scene of the shooting, parked in the office's parking lot or in front of the building on Oxnard Street. Coffey made sure their license-plate numbers were entered into the crime-scene log for further investigation.

When Coffey's men from homicide began to arrive, his instructions for them to question everyone. He did not want to wait for people to come to them. He was looking for that special nugget of information that would provide a reason for this brutal and seemingly senseless attack. He was sure that was how they would find their killer.

Michael Coffey walked over to Melvin Green. "Let's take a ride, Mr. Green," the detective said as he led Melvin to a police car and opened the door for him.

Melvin saw his secretary, Lily Lopez, and Nicholas Foss were already seated in the car.

"Am I a suspect?" Melvin asked Coffey.

"Just as much as anyone else who knew her. This is just standard procedure in a homicide case," Coffey answered, slamming the door shut.

An agitated Melvin rolled down the window, no longer calm. He was almost frantic. "I want to see my wife at the hospital. You'll have to bring me right back here," he shouted.

Detective Michael Coffey watched as the police vehicle pulled away. Melvin Green's ominous words, "Ask the men she's screwing," still rang in his ears.

II

Melvin Morton Green

1935–1990

6

Fitting In

Little Melvin played on the outside patio, trying to block out his father's screams and his mother's sobs. Mommy and Daddy were at it again. Daddy always yelled at Mommy for everything. Melvin stood quietly, straining to hear what they were fighting about this time.

"You know what I'm gonna do to you?" his father shouted. "I'm going to teach you how to be a real wife. What's the matter with you? Can't you do anything right?"

"I'm sorry, Hy. I'll try harder." June Green would say anything to quiet her husband.

Mel's father kept shouting about anything and everything that came to his mind. It seemed that nothing was good enough for Hyman Green, and no matter how hard Melvin and his mother worked for Hy's approval, they never received it.

"When will you ever learn? I hate when you pay more attention to his needs than mine," his father bellowed. Hy Green had no intention of sharing June with his young son.

June looked to the floor and ignored him. It was a trait she had perfected over the years, one she would teach her future daughter-in-law, Anita. It was the only logical way to respond to someone who was out of control. Somewhere she heard footsteps.

Melvin ran into the house. Dressed in his Superman costume, he would save his mom. June Green was the bright light of her young son's life. He adored her and would do anything to end her misery. Melvin hated when his father acted this way.

49

"Daddy, Daddy, please stop," the little boy pleaded.

"Shut up, Melvin. This doesn't concern you. You'll get yours later if you don't leave us alone."

"Why are you angry, Daddy? What did Mommy do? Please stop fighting." Melvin's four-year-old eyes filled with terror.

"He's just trying to make peace, Hyman. Please leave him alone," June Green said.

At the moment, June decided the best course of action was to avoid her son's gaze. Hy was far more likely to overreact and hurt Melvin if she acknowledged his presence with a loving glance. Besides, eye contact while she was in her humiliated condition was more than she could bear.

His father gave Mel a look that told him he better get out or he'd get a spanking that would be closer to a beating, and hear enough yelling to last a lifetime.

"I mean it, Daddy. You better leave my mommy alone," Mel cried, sounding as tough as Hy did. Whatever he was doing seemed to be working. Mel could tell his father was backing down. The four-year-old bullied his father into submission. Defeated, Hy Green stalked away.

The little boy and the man constantly vied for June's attentions. As always, this fight was fueled by jealousy and the need to control. June had been reading to Melvin, and Hy didn't like her to read to their son when he was at home. Melvin felt responsible for the wars that continued to break out in his living room. If he had never been born, his parents wouldn't fight like this.

Melvin dealt with the outside world by trying to control it. He developed a tough-guy, bullying veneer to deal with his parents, playmates, and people in general. He would use the same facade throughout his life, especially during business meetings and with women.

Young Melvin was adept at hiding behind other masks as well. Like most preschoolers, he loved fantasy play and dressing up. The difference between Melvin and other children was that Melvin couldn't always differentiate between fantasy and reality, and all too often his make-believe world took over his life.

Melvin ran up and down the cement sidewalk in front of his

small house on Sampson Place, located in the East Los Angeles community known as City Terrace, playing Superman. This was Mel's favorite thing to do. Superman was Mel's hero—always in control, always powerful, and always well loved and respected. Nobody ever crossed Superman and lived to tell about it.

Of one thing Melvin was certain: he and his childhood hero, Superman, had the same burden to bear. They both faced great obstacles in getting the love and affection they needed.

According to the comic book, Superman's parents abandoned him when they sent him down to Earth. He couldn't turn to others for love because he would lose all his powers if he ever really fell in love. Superman was destined to live a life filled with loneliness, and even when he met Lois Lane, their life together ended in tragedy.

Melvin understood his idol's plan. His own parents were unable to show love and affection to him, seldom hugging or kissing him. His mother, June, wanted to, but couldn't be counted on to be consistent with the affection Mel needed because she was frequently too drained emotionally from the abuses his father rained down upon her. Even when she wasn't depleted, Hy wouldn't allow June to get close to Melvin. He was simply too jealous a man to allow it.

Mel's father didn't know how to love him or anyone else. He was insanely jealous of the time his pretty wife spent on their son, and resentful when others commented on how bright a child Mel was. Mel spent the majority of his childhood and most of his adulthood seeking his father's love and approval, which sadly was something he never attained. His father picked on Mel constantly. At every family function until the day she died, June Green would place herself between the two men to stop their warring.

Melvin continued playing. "I'm faster than a flying bullet, quicker than the speed of light...I'm Superman...Da, da, da, da." Melvin ran frantically back and forth across the cement, finally leaping off a precipice to fly away.

"I'm flying...oww," he screamed, falling to the ground. For a minute, Melvin wasn't certain what had happened. "Mommy, Daddy, I'm hurt," the child wailed loudly.

His parents ran out to him. His mother took him into the house to clean his head, checking his wound to see if he needed stitches.

His father screamed the entire time. "Stupid kid, what the hell did you think you could fly for?"

Melvin recalled his fall from the cement as both the best and worst moment of his life. "I mean, I was really flying. I was Superman, and I liked that. I enjoyed the power. But then I fell, and I realized in just one instant that I wasn't really Superman.

Melvin Morton Green was born on June 6, 1935, to Hyman and June Green. His mother was a housewife and his father a traveling salesman. The Los Angeles neighborhoods of City Terrace and Boyle Heights were filled with Jewish newcomers working hard to provide a good life for their families. The hub of both Boyle Heights and City Terrace was Brooklyn Avenue, a large street that looked and smelled like the New York borough it was named after. On Brooklyn Avenue, one could find merchants selling everything from pickles to Talmuds.

Melvin was raised with traditional Jewish religious values. Mel claimed his family kept a traditional home and celebrated all the holidays. The Greens worshipped in the large traditional shul on Wabash Avenue, where Mel loved to attend both services and Hebrew school.

From an early age, Melvin felt more at home in the synagogue than anywhere else. He loved the books, the prayers, and, most of all, the ancient melodies.

Every Saturday morning the Greens walked to services together, seldom greeting the other congregants as they marched by them, heads held high. The Greens weren't snobby, but rather, they just weren't social people by nature. They didn't consider themselves superior to other people; they just weren't comfortable around them. June worried Hy would get angry in front of other people, so she avoided them altogether. Family and friends claim June always tried to hide Mel and Hy's tempers from the world.

Friends say June Green wanted everyone to like her, and though most did, few felt the same way about her family. June saw this attitude as a reflection on her. Some said she never recovered from the shame.

Neighbors described the male Greens as bright but odd; which is a nice way of putting it. Father and son acted like they despised one another, yet their relationship was almost incestuous. Though they were always fighting about the strangest things, they spent all their free time together. They sometimes seemed to control one another's movements.

The temple provided the Greens with most of their social life. They expected the other temple members to function as their extended family; a family that would share their joys and comfort them in their sorrows; a family that would always accept their differences and would unquestionably forgive them for their sins. Melvin learned at an early age that this was what a synagogue was all about.

Melvin inherited his love of Judaism from his father's mother, whom he called Bubby. In the Jewish tradition, he was named after her deceased husband, Morris Mordechai Greenspan.

Melvin's paternal grandparents came from a religious part of Russia known for its close-knit and observant Jewish community. Bubby didn't like Los Angeles and often dreamed of going home to Russia. She remained in California for her family and was always particularly fond of her young grandson, Melvin.

Bubby would sit for hours telling Melvin stories from the Bible. The boy had a real aptitude for their meanings. Bubby told her daughter-in-law wistfully, "Perhaps he'll be a rabbi, he has the mind for it. Let's hope he develops the heart."

Melvin never seemed to develop the heart. He fell into the habit of putting people down, trying to make them feel as badly about themselves as he did about himself. "You'll never amount to anything...You're a horrible person...You're so ugly." These were the only words he knew because they were the words that he heard each day from his father.

Melvin liked to lie, often to see if people believed what he would say, and just as often because he believed lying let him control what others thought of him. He was quite good at it, and others sometimes swore he was telling the truth even when they caught him in obvious contradictions. "He was just so sincere with his stories, wanting you to accept them more than anything else. Always saying things like, 'My word is my bond. Is yours?'" Melvin Green preached honesty for others while practicing his own forms of deception.

His grandmother was upset. As she watched her precious *eineckle* grow up, it became apparent that he wasn't made of the right stuff to be a rabbi. Bubby washed her hands of him. She might as well let her son decide what was to become of him.

Mel's father, Hyman Green, was too wrapped up in his own life to think about anyone else's. He went through the motions of being a parent, but never really thought his son would amount to much.

Hy Green made a living doing the one thing he was really good at—selling. He was a modern peddler, successfully hawking women's sportswear for many different firms throughout his career. He spent a great deal of time on the road, often leaving Melvin and his mother alone for weeks at a time.

These were the best times of Mel's childhood. Though Mel fought with his mother too, their fights weren't as vicious as those with his father. He and his mother always found something wonderful to do together. They would read, bake bread, play cards, and talk for hours. Melvin loved to talk, and his kitchen conversations ranked among his happiest moments.

Both Melvin and June loved poetry, and they would spend many wonderful hours writing poems together. The poems were loving and sweet. They were the beginning of Melvin's love of writing.

Melvin Green attended City Terrace Grammar School, a public elementary school near his Sampson Street house. It was a large, decaying facility that has educated some of Los Angeles's finest minds.

Young Melvin was an excellent student who got along well with his teachers. "I was always the prime student. My head was an open pitcher and my teachers poured the knowledge in."

Melvin showed exceptional talent for reading and writing, and his teachers encouraged him with his stories and poetry. His earliest letters, stories, poems, and cards poignantly expressed his innermost feelings, secrets, and dreams.

When a teacher told him perhaps his writings would be published one day, Melvin took the compliment to heart. From that day forward he acted like his writings would someday change the world. Little did he know that the words he committed to paper would come back to haunt him. The only world they ever changed was his own.

Melvin's habit of writing long letters to others can be traced to the third grade, when he wrote a young classmate a letter scolding him for making fun of his jacket. The letter's tone was so harsh and intense that it was hard to believe it was written by an eight-year-old. Melvin wrote many letters berating others for not accepting him socially. This practice continued throughout his life.

At first glance, Melvin looked like a boy who had it made. He was a handsome young lad who always dressed well, his clothes immaculate. He performed well academically. But, somehow, he always remained an outsider, never fitting in at school or even at home. His good looks were ruined by the perpetual scowl on his face and the bossy attitude he displayed toward everyone who crossed his path. His teachers may have liked him, but his classmates didn't. They remember him as a bully who thought he was better than everyone else.

"He liked to yell at all the kids, boss us around and stuff," recalled one. "He had a holier-than-thou attitude and definitely thought he was better than anyone else."

When Mel was young, Hy yelled at him to discipline and to control him. He yelled at him for doing things, for not doing things, for making the wrong choices. It seemed whatever Melvin did, Hy wasn't pleased. Hy often said, "Everything with Melvin is a battle."

Melvin, in turn, acted like Hy on the schoolyard. The kids played the wrong games, wore the wrong clothes, and most certainly read the wrong books. Melvin kept his nose in the air to protect himself from his peers' rejection. If he considered everyone inferior to him, then they couldn't hurt him by keeping him out of things.

Because he alienated all the kids in the neighborhood, Melvin found himself in a position he hated the most, being alone. It was during these frequent periods of isolation that his obsessive behavior began to surface. Even as a child, he saw the world differently than most, and little things bothered him immensely.

Melvin tormented himself about how many questions the other kids answered in class, who was going to be elected team captain, or who would he have to sit next to at lunch.

He dreaded the notion that his teacher might like another student more than he and would worry about school or scouting events scheduled more than six months ahead. Would the kids tease him there? Melvin would obsess about these life-threatening issues for hours, and his teachers sensed that something was not right.

"It's hard to put into words," recalled one teacher, now long since retired, "But if my memory is correct, Melvin was a worrier. He was always very concerned that other people were talking about him. He was paranoid, putting an inordinate amount of focus on himself. Often there was simply nothing a teacher could do to convince Melvin that others weren't plotting against him or making fun of him."

There were brief periods of time when Melvin could stand to be by himself. He would read, draw, and sing to himself. But then his mind would start working overtime and his mouth would react. Often, he would insult someone because he imagined that person was out to get him. It was no wonder the kids kept away from him. His big mouth kept running all the time, getting him into trouble.

One day Melvin came home from school and announced to his parents that he was going to be very rich when he grew up. His father just grunted. His mother said, "Sure you will, Melvin. You can do anything you want to do."

June Green wasn't just saying that. She wouldn't be surprised if Melvin brought home the world. Somebody with his superior intellect was bound to become a big financial success.

Later in life, Melvin Green hated when others compared him with his father. He would say, "I'm not like him. I've made 'real money.'" It appeared Melvin thought he would finally get his father's approval by becoming wealthy. He is still seeking that approval today.

Melvin's lifelong love of singing and music started in

childhood. At school and religious school he was always in the chorus, singing the loudest of anyone in the room.

Melvin's singing embarrassed his father, who thought singing was for girls. Once again, Hy was successful in destroying what little self-esteem Melvin had left.

Melvin had an exceptional memory. He could remember every time someone embarrassed him. He got through his father's embarrassment by convincing himself that he was intellectually superior to him. This wasn't difficult to do, because Melvin abhorred the fact that his father was a salesman and wished he was something more respectable, like a doctor, lawyer, or even a teacher.

Melvin began high school in Los Angeles at Woodrow Wilson High. He remained there for two and half years, which were some of the happiest years of his childhood. When Melvin was a young teen, Woodrow Wilson was both a junior and senior high school and though he was one of the youngest in the school, he was also one of the brightest. That fact alone did wonders for his confidence, but he still had problems making friends.

When Melvin was in his early teens and halfway through the ninth grade, his family moved to North Hollywood in the more affluent San Fernando Valley. Boyle Heights and City Terrace were growing less and less appealing as more and more blacks and Hispanics moved into the rapidly decaying neighborhoods. Most of the Jews moved out. North Hollywood was a step up for the Greens, but it certainly wasn't as prestigious a community as Encino or others in the West Valley.

In the Valley, Melvin attended Walter Reed Junior High School and later, North Hollywood High School. Academically, he peaked at around ninth grade.

"At the age of fifteen or sixteen I thought I knew everything. At seventeen I had lingering doubts." Melvin explained that he was bored with school, and his good marks no longer had a positive effect on his parents. They expected them. Still, Melvin kept his grades high enough to make him a California Gold Seal Bearer at his high school graduation, an honor only held by students attaining a 3.5 grade-point average or above.

In middle school, high school, and college, Melvin's favorite subject was English. He enjoyed reading the classics and loved quoting from famous works of literature. Melvin assumed that using these quotes made others recognize him as the bright teen he was. "I want the world to know from whence I come."

Socially, Melvin didn't fare any better in the Valley than he had in the city. He spent a lot of time alone in his room. He didn't date much in junior high or high school because he was terrified of rejection.

Melvin knew he was odd and wasn't comfortable sharing that awareness with women. "I wasn't that interested in women yet anyway. I was a late bloomer sexually. I took a long time to get up the nerve to ask a girl out. It wasn't worth the potential rejection. They had to practically throw themselves at me or ask me out first. The same thing with my wives and my current fiancée; they made the moves first. But once I was with a woman, she never wanted to leave me. I could have dated a lot, but I didn't. I was too involved in sports to care."

Melvin's first date was with Sylvia Cohan. "I was so nervous I don't remember where we went or what we did. I think I took her to a school function first and another time to the movies or something. I really can't be certain. She wasn't a serious girlfriend or anything like that."

Hy Green didn't encourage his son to ask more girls out. Hy never encouraged his son to do much of anything.

In high school, Melvin grew interested in competitive sports, and for a while they provided the recognition he craved. At fourteen, Mel was over six feet tall and weighed 177 pounds, which made him one of the biggest kids in the school.

Sports gave him something he had never found before, an arena in which it was acceptable to be aggressive and dominating. On the playing fields or in the gym, his insatiable need to win was seen as a positive attribute. Whether playing basketball, running track, or wrestling, Melvin proved to be an exceptional athlete: aggressive, focused, and strong.

Melvin's high school athletic-awards dinner was a real letdown. His parents arrived late, and Hy glowered. Melvin accepted two trophies, a first place for wrestling and another for running. Hy's only comment was how come the school bought such chintzy trophies.

Traditionally, one of the benefits of being a jock is increased popularity among your peers. Melvin didn't reap this reward. Given his size and his fondness for bullying, no one even tried to befriend him. Kids warned one another to stay away from him. This attitude made Melvin even more difficult. He really believed he was untouchable. As his loneliness intensified, his bullying grew.

It is said, perhaps too easily, that we repeat our parents' behavior. In the Green family there were already many chilling signs that Hy's violent, abusive behavior toward June would be reenacted by Melvin. Like his father, Melvin saw women as objects. They were both frightened by women, so they always tried to control them, but they also saw them as "prizes."

By the time of his high school graduation, Melvin was a forlorn teenager with a huge chip on his shoulder. Angry that he wasn't his graduating-class valedictorian, Melvin claimed he should have been but nobody wanted him. Nobody had ever wanted Melvin Green. He was determined to prove them wrong.

7

In Charge of His Own Destiny

After his graduation from high school, Melvin spent many months trying to figure out what he wanted to do with the rest of his life. Up until the day he started the University of California in Los Angeles, he was not sure what he wanted.

Of course, his opinionated parents knew exactly what was best for him. Their son was to be a doctor, and medicine was the only acceptable career path for him to follow.

"It will be so wonderful to have a doctor in the family. I know you can do it." June Green called everyone she knew to tell them that her Mel was going into the world of medicine.

On the way to the campus for registration and his first day of courses, Mel took a deep breath to calm himself. He reported to his counselor, filled out the paperwork, and enrolled in mostly biology and premedical classes. He signed up for one English class that was required of all incoming freshmen. Thank God, Melvin thought, it would be a good diversion. Melvin felt like he was in for a long semester.

Melvin liked science, but the thought of four years of undergraduate school made up mainly of science classes did not seem at all exciting to him. He had fantasized that college would be stimulating, his course work inspiring. Now his parents' demands were crushing his fantasies.

One of the things Melvin Green never understood about his parents was their need to control him. Throughout his childhood, June and Hy Green tried to tell Mel exactly what he had to do with his life in order to become someone other than who he already was.

Now he was at UCLA, the first of the Greens to go to college, and they were dictating his courses and telling him exactly what he was to study. And he was listening. He wondered how his parents had managed to intimidate him again. Melvin knew it must be because of Hy. His mother may have wanted him to be a doctor, but only Hy had the power to try and force the issue. That made him angry. He considered himself far superior to both his parents intellectually, but especially to Hy.

Mel had always loathed the fact that his father was in the rag business and frequently unemployed. He would have preferred that his father was a professional. In fact, as a child Melvin had always been quite gifted at making up stories about his parents to make them appear more glamorous and successful than they really were. It was a habit that continued throughout his life, but as he grew older, the stories focused on himself as opposed to his parents.

A few months into his first semester at UCLA, at a time when Melvin was feeling particularly less than excited about his courses, he joined his parents for breakfast.

"Well, son, tell us, how do you find college?" Hy asked as he put down the paper.

Mel was shocked that Hy was taking an interest. However, something about his tone was sarcastic, as if he was mocking Mel about something. Mel had deep loving feelings for his father, but he didn't trust him. He was immediately on the defensive.

"It's no problem. I can easily handle all the work," Melvin boasted. "I can hold my own with my professors too."

Since childhood, Mel had had an overwhelming need for his teachers' approval. Perhaps he sought from them what he was so sorely lacking at home. Mel continued to brag about how easy his classes were and about how many sports he was playing. After he felt certain that he had reported his progress in glowing enough terms, he ever so hesitantly began to broach the topic of his specific courses.

"I'm not crazy about all this biology and physics. After a few hours of it my head aches and aches," Mel complained. "I think I'm going to study business, perhaps marketing or accounting. I've always had a real flair for numbers and I like making money."

His father was puzzled. "Accounting? Why would anyone want to count other people's money all day long?" Hy Green sat up in his chair as if anticipating a fight. Mel was ready.

"No! That's not what accounting is all about, Dad. It's like a puzzle. You use your brain to help people with their investments."

"Well, I still don't see why you would want to study it. Besides, it seems to me that figures would be far more boring than formulas."

Mel could feel his heart begin to beat fast in his chest. The sweat began to pour from his forehead. He was getting very upset.

"What's the big deal? Why do you care what I study? You have never really cared what I have done in the past. I'll live my life the way I want." Mel sounded both exasperated and angry, resigned to the fact that his father never listened to him, never heard what might really make his son happy.

Hy jumped up and began to storm around the kitchen. He said that Mel was an ingrate who didn't love his parents. He called him every name he could think of. Mel was selfish, inconsiderate, thought he was better than his parents, a real prima donna and a "no good" who would never amount to much of anything.

Mel let his father rant for a few minutes. He was tired of arguing, but his future was worth fighting for. He was to be in control of his destiny. Melvin had always hated being told what to do, what to wear, how to sing, how to act. It wasn't as if being a doctor would make his father love him any more. It was just a matter of control. The time had come to show his father who was boss. He was no longer going to be the angry child that Hy could push around and bully.

Mel looked his father straight in the eyes and raised his voice. "I hate to upset you, but there is no way I'm going to let you decide what I'm going to study."

"I'll decide as long as I'm paying the bills," Hy bellowed. "You'll never amount to anything anyway."

"What have you done that's so great, Dad?" Mel retorted. "How are ladies' separates selling these days?"

His mother had had enough. June Green had spent eighteen years watching these fights. She had recently spent time in the hospital for a nervous breakdown, and she was not about to let her husband and son send her back. June looked at the two men and her deep sad eyes said it all.

"Have you thought this all through, Mel?" she asked. "What if you studied both subjects, taking courses in each?" June had learned over the years to become the master of compromise.

Mel rolled his eyes and began to bang on the table. He stormed around the kitchen. Then he kicked the refrigerator and looked at his mother. "You don't get it, do you? This isn't about classes. This is about me. I decide what I do from now on. I dictate my comings and goings. You need to follow my plan, because I'm finally going to."

June took a deep breath, but now she too was getting angry. It was the same old issue, control. It made both Mel and Hy see things with a distorted perspective.

"Your father doesn't mean to upset you. He just wants what's best for all of us. Since the day you were born we knew you were destined to be something special."

"There's not a damn thing about him that is special," Hy hollered.

Mel charged out the door. Hy was putting him down again. In his father's eyes he didn't do anything right and he never had and never would.

Melvin obsessed about his father's remark for months. He grew angrier and angrier. He kept asking himself over and over why Hy cared what he studied.

By New Year's Melvin had worked himself into such a frenzy that, after just a semester at UCLA, he dropped out of school to join the army. The afternoon that he enlisted he spent worrying. How would he break the news to his parents? He wondered if he had made the right choice.

Melvin sat under a tree in the UCLA quad and, like so many college students before him, pondered his existence. He was reminded of his favorite philosophers, Bertrand Russell and René Descartes. He wrote a poem that he realized was partially his own and partially plagiarized, but that he knew would become part of his life.

There was a young man who said,
"God, must find it exceedingly odd
to think that this tree
could continue to be
when there is no one about in the quad"

Reply:

"Dear sir, I find your astonishment odd,
I am always about on the quad
And that is why this tree
will continue to be
since observed by yours faithfully, God"

This poem gave Mel the courage to move forward throughout his life and he referred to it often. He knew whatever direction he chose he had enough inside of him to make it on his own. He was bright, articulate, imaginative, and sensitive. God was by his side to guide him.

Of course, his parents initially went crazy, and the fighting continued for days. "Jewish boys don't make good soldiers," his mother protested, crying the entire time. "We don't believe in killing."

"There isn't a war going on right now, Mom," Mel replied.

Once again, in their eyes, he had failed and was making a mistake. Mel hoped one day they would approve of his choices. "I'll be the best soldier they've got," Mel bragged. "The army will even pay for school afterwards too. I've got it all figured out."

Melvin always liked to figure things out. Ever the logical one, he calculated that if the army paid for his education then perhaps his father wouldn't find fault with what he chose to study.

"What if a war starts and you have to kill someone? How would you feel about doing that? Could you ever kill a man?"

"I don't believe in killing, but there are times it's okay to kill, even in the Bible. We'll just see what happens."

Once Mel was in the army, things settled down at home. Army life was just what Melvin Green needed, and he thrived on the regimentation. In a letter to one of his few friends he wrote, "It is boring here. I work hard and am in great shape. I like the system, the army is a very just system."

The years Mel spent in the army were uneventful. He proved to be an undistinguished soldier, and his parents eventually forgave him, but things were never quite the same between them. They never gave up the hope that he would one day become a doctor. In the army, Mel studied first aid. His parents hoped his interest would mean medical school in the future. But it wasn't likely. Hy grew more disgusted with Melvin. He told his friends that his son didn't have what it took to be a doctor.

8

The Start of Something Big

When Melvin Green got out of the army in September of 1958, he reenrolled at UCLA and began to study accounting. He couldn't remember ever being happier. School was a breeze after the service and he excelled in all his classes. Mel was quick with numbers and had a real knack for economics. He loved figuring out ways to beat the system. For Mel, life was always a game. Mel loved the world of numbers because the rules were very clear. There was less room for error. He knew exactly what was expected of him.

His success at his class work bolstered his confidence. Since he was in such good shape from the army and as strong as he had ever been, Melvin began to wrestle in college. He was good, but his teammates did not like him. He was boastful and mean.

Mel, desperate for real friendship, began the practice of buying his friends by loaning them vast amounts of money that he earned on the side by doing accounting work. He made these loans to cement his fragile friendships, hoping that, in the future, his friends would remember how good he had been to them.

Mel saw that accounting could be very lucrative, and that perhaps great wealth would be the way to win his parents' approval and get back into their hearts. It would certainly give him the power over people that he craved so desperately.

As with everything else Mel ever attempted, he soon claimed to be an expert at taxes. He fancied himself the future Melvin Belli of the tax world. He took courses, bought books, and began making small investments with his own capital and that of his friends. One college acquaintance said, "Mel always had a way for us to make a buck without doing anything."

These tastes of financial success did little to get rid of Melvin's inferiority complex. He still claimed that he was studying premed, and to this day brags that he finished both the premed and accounting programs at UCLA, and both with honors.

The University of California's computer records indicate that Melvin Morton Green was indeed enrolled at their Los Angeles campus. In fact, he was enrolled for almost ten years, but he never graduated and was not awarded a degree in anything. This single fact made him paranoid for many years and set him on an insecure path of always needing to boast of his accomplishments whether they were true or not. It also helped the district attorney to assess his credibility when he found out that Mel never had a degree in accounting and that the diplomas that hung on his walls were fakes.

While studying accounting at UCLA, Melvin met his first love, a pretty would-be actress named Bernyce Herzberg. Melvin was supposed to take out Bernyce's roommate, Joyce. His friend Saul planned to join them on a double date as Bernyce's escort. When Melvin called to discuss the night's details, Bernyce answered. Bernyce found Mel Green bright, articulate, and interesting to talk to. The first of many things he talked her into was switching dates. Melvin Green was always a smooth talker.

Melvin and Bernyce became close friends. He had perpetually felt like an outsider with women before, even when they pursued him, but Bernyce made him feel comfortable and good about himself. His parents even approved of her. What wasn't there to like?

Bernyce was a stunning woman. She was full figured and all curves. She wore her thick brown hair in a stylish page-boy haircut, was always perfectly madeup, and dressed in classy clothes. Her family's traditional religious teachings and values were similar to the ones that the Greens thought they had given Melvin. In addition, the Herzbergs were worldly and sophisticated, which meant a lot to the Greens. The Greens were ecstatic.

Bernyce and Melvin's relationship blossomed slowly. She was impressed by his rugged good looks, his muscular body, and his devotion to her. But this adoration also worried her. Was he too obsessive? Bernyce never knew what to expect from him. Perhaps true love would come later.

The Herzbergs were somewhat less than charmed. To them, their daughter Bernyce was a shimmering diamond who shone upon the world. What could their daughter possibly see in Melvin Green?

What Bernyce, and later the two other important females in his life, saw in Melvin was whatever he wanted them to see. Melvin was a gifted actor who was able to attract them all by playing roles with them. When Mel courted a woman, he would find out exactly what kind of man she was looking for, then he became that man.

For Bernyce, Mel acted like he was a fantasy catch, the would-be perfect husband. He told her, "I really want a family and a home, and that's my number-one priority." He spent years making her believe him. Once they were married, however, he dedicated himself to his career and not his family.

To Anita and his intended third wife, Alexandra Leeds, Mel would play the rescuer. "I'll rescue you from your boredom and your struggles. I'll give you everything, and in exchange you give me your love and your soul."

Bernyce, Anita, and Alexandra were very different looking women, but, on the inside, they all suffered from low self-esteem and deep-rooted insecurities. As these women began to mature and grow, Melvin became an albatross around their necks. They still valued the friendship and companionship that he offered, but they despised his dark side, and they didn't trust him.

During their courtship, the more Bernyce put Melvin off, the more his love turned to total obsession. He wrote her poems rhapsodizing about the depths of his love. He sent her flowers, candy, and cards. While most men hid their feelings, Melvin showered Bernyce with outward displays to show the intensity of his passion.

Even in love, Bernyce and Mel fought constantly. He just couldn't interact with her in a normal way. Mel was always suspicious and controlling. Bernyce hoped once he grew more secure in their relationship things would change.

When she saw how good Mel was at his little investments, Bernyce urged him to try professional accounting, even if he was still in school. If Mel prepared people's taxes, he could make great money. Bernyce convinced him that he didn't need to be a CPA and that he could earn a good income while he was still in college. Melvin liked the idea. With Bernyce's encouragement, he started his own company.

Melvin became even more smitten. Bernyce was one of the first people ever to encourage him. It wasn't often that someone went out of their way for Melvin Green, and it seemed to have a calming effect on him.

Once he was making money, Melvin grew more desirable to Bernyce. He offered the unemployed actress security and stability. It would be great to start out with a husband who was already making a living. Bernyce had seen what happened to marriages when the husband was not able to provide. Melvin was a good choice since she was certain that he would be financially successful.

But still, Bernyce told friends she was worried. Mel's moods were erratic. He smothered her with love and he was obsessive about everything. "Why didn't you call me the minute you got home? Did you have to wait half an hour?" he would complain. Melvin's compulsions were hard to take.

This was about the time that Mel began to gain weight, claiming that he needed to bulk up for UCLA athletics. He began his practice of getting drunk on food. Mel would gorge himself for hours at a time, packing away more meals at one sitting than Bernyce had ever seen. Sometimes he was obsessed with her, and at other times he was obsessed with food. Bernyce felt sorry for him. She hoped her love would help him heal.

After a courtship that had lasted for five years, Bernyce agreed to give marriage a try. She would continue to love and be a friend to Melvin Green, but now she would do these things as his wife.

Mel was elated. Ever since she had flirted with him on the phone five years earlier, he had realized what a good catch she was. He promised her that their marriage would be the start of something big.

Mel had always felt like he owed Bernyce something because she had helped him get started in business. At the same time, he believed she was beholden to him. He allowed her the luxury of being a kept woman. It was always tit for tat. That was the way Mel viewed the world. People usually had something on one another, and that's what kept the world in line.

Mel decided that he and Bernyce would have a traditional marriage; he would be the breadwinner, and she would raise the kids. Initially, Bernyce protested. She wanted to be an actress, and he had no right to try to dictate how she was going to live. But a few years later, she realized that someone needed to be home for her young sons. That person would not be Mel.

By the time their first son, Michael, was born, communicating with Melvin had become nearly impossible. Though Mel appeared delighted with his son, carrying him around as if he were a trophy, he was having more and more difficulty interacting with people.

Being intimate was far too difficult for Melvin unless he needed to be. Otherwise, he locked himself in his office. It was just easier that way.

Bernyce was lonely, sorry, and sad. This was not what she had hoped her marriage would be like. She remembered the sensitive Mel who had recently courted her; the candles, the letters, the all-night soul-searching conversations. She supposed the honeymoon never lasted forever. Bernyce never forgave Mel for changing after they got married or for taking away her career.

Soon the Greens had two sons, and Mel would remain at the office for longer stretches of time. Perhaps he had lost interest in her. Perhaps he was having an affair. Bernyce began to ask questions.

She attempted to show an interest in Mel's business. She asked him questions and was shocked by his answers. She found Mel secretive and evasive.

"Why are you being so nosy?" Mel hollered.

"What do you have to hide?" she countered.

This wasn't a very good way to communicate. As her marriage both progressed and regressed, Bernyce realized that Melvin was always in one of two moods: ecstatic or mean. There was simply no in-between.

Once in a while he would exclaim his love for her and the boys. He would talk to her, share what had happened at the office, play with the kids, and, above all, talk about how wonderful life would become for all of them. When Melvin was in a good mood, he was a delight to be around.

More often than not, however, Mel would be his regular, terrible, bossy self. In his dark moods he would holler at Bernyce and the children about the most insignificant things. He would lock himself in his office, slam the door, and sulk for hours. During those times, his dark days, Mel could not stand it if anyone else in the family was having a good time.

As they grew, his two sons, Michael and Cary, hungered for their father's attention just as Mel had hungered for Hy's. Mel was an absentee father, a workaholic who was absolutely never there for his kids. He went to his office seven days a week and literally buried himself in his work.

Mel gave a little more attention to his younger son, Cary, than he did to his firstborn, Michael. In front of his wife, his parents, his associates, and his friends he would often compare his offspring. He made it clear that his fair-headed son was his favorite. Cary was handsome, bright, and a real go-getter. He always followed Mel's rules. Michael, who resembled Mel, was, in his father's mind, lazy, insubordinate, and obstinate. In Mel's eyes they really were like Cain and Abel.

On the few occasions Mel did parent, he played his sons against one another as a way to control them. They learned at an early age to vie for his infrequent attentions. Cary was usually the winner.

Mel never let up on his sons. Nothing they did was good enough. He would stomp around the living room and rage about their report cards, their rooms, and their dozens of other inadequacies too numerous to specify or holler about.

Now and then Mel would give Bernyce a list of all the things that bothered him about her and the kids. Usually it would come at three in the morning when he would wake her up and run through all his particulars. Mel was an insomniac and spent many nights obsessing about his life. He could not stand it if others slept through his misery. "Why aren't you more supportive of me?" Mel hissed through clenched teeth. "Why do you buy them so many damn toys?"

Once Bernyce asked Mel to spend more time at home with the boys. "They need you to be around more, to show an interest in what they are doing."

"What they need is someone to continue paying the bills. Do you think money grows on trees?" Mel bellowed.

By now the Greens had moved into the wealthy Los Angeles community of Bel Air. It took a lot of money to live in Bel Air and maintain the lifestyle to which the Greens had grown accustomed.

Money wasn't the problem and hadn't been for years, though Mel certainly fought with Bernyce about it. Melvin Green was a self-made man, and he continued to take in more and more money each day. He had a real aptitude for taxes and a creative way of finding loopholes.

Word spread quickly. "This guy can save you big money on your taxes."

Mel Green had it all: a beautiful wife, two sons to carry on his name, an exquisite home right outside of Beverly Hills, and a successful business that he had built up on his own. Still, his unhappiness ate at him, and his fits continued to rage on unabated. In the middle of this, Anita Arnow blew into his life.

Part III

Anita Molly Green

1948–1990

Anita Rice. The one who started a curious chain of events.

Anita Green's trade school yearbook, 1966

9

See How Different Girls Are

On a cold day in the midst of a bitter winter, a beautiful baby girl was born to Rebecca and Joseph Rice, immediately filling their lives with warmth and love. Anita, their firstborn and very much planned for child, was special from the beginning. Her bright smile gave Rebecca and Joseph, both survivors of Hitler's death camps, reason to live again.

Anita was light complected with bright blue eyes. Her father, Joseph, adored her. Her smiling face, beautiful blond hair, and plump rosy cheeks helped put the past behind him. Joseph would never forget the horrors he had lived through at the hands of his Nazi oppressors, but his new daughter gave him hope for the future.

Anita's parents had been through much in their young lives, and parenthood seemed easy after their struggles. Little did they know that raising Anita would prove to be another challenge.

Joseph and Rebecca Rice came from a small village in Lithuania, a world away from the New York that would later be their home. Their village produced rye, oats, barley, and potatoes. It supported a large dairy industry that exported food into the other Soviet republics.

Joseph and Rebecca married on March 11, 1942. Joseph was a professional soccer player. He was tanned, blond, athletic, and muscular. Rebecca came from strong peasant stock with features that could be considered pure German. She, too, was fair skinned and blond.

Joseph worked in his family's baloney factory with two of his five brothers, Charlie and Henry. The factory supplied the processed meat for most of the region.

Rebecca (affectionately known as Riva) cooked for her husband, kept house, and hoped that nobody would cause trouble because they were Jewish. When two of her Jewish girlfriends were killed in the road by anti-Semites for no reason other than their religion, Rebecca grew frightened. She hoped for a better life for her children, and promised not to have any until she could guarantee them that life.

Briefly, during their courtship and for a few months after their marriage, Joseph and Rebecca had hoped to raise a family in the tranquility of the beautiful Lithuanian countryside.

Miles of rolling green pastures were irrigated easily with water from the dozens of lakes and streams nearby. Eerie mists rose from moonlit lakes, the moon shining through the cloudy skies to light up the village. It was a wondrous setting in which to fall in love.

That fairy tale's spell was broken by the Nazis. Life in Lithuania grew hard for the Jews in the months preceding the war. Anti-Semitism was on the rise, fueled by the German propaganda, which rapidly spread to Lithuania's peasants.

World War II marched into Rebecca and Joseph's village in early June, just three short months after they were married. Once war broke out, the Germans were very interested in taking control of Lithuania as quickly as possible, not only because doing so would give them access to Russia, but because they wanted the bountiful farmlands and excellent, well-managed food-processing plants.

When the Germans came to their village, Rebecca and Joseph tried to escape into Russia. They sped out of Lithuania in the direction of Moscow on Joseph's racing motorcycle. Just before crossing the border, they ran into a Russian general covered with medals. Appearing confused, the general asked them the way to Moscow.

Joseph took the general's confusion as a sign. He explained to his young wife that if the Russians could no longer find their way to Moscow, then they were in trouble. The couple returned home to await their fate.

A week later, the Germans arrived and arrested all the Jewish men, killing some, putting others in jails, and still others into concentration camps.

Rebecca and Joseph were sitting in their apartment with a few other family members when the Germans knocked on their door. Rebecca spoke fluent German and with her Aryan features was able to persuade the Nazis that there weren't any Jews in the apartment. They were fortunate because all the Jews arrested in the first round were killed within a week, even those who had been taken to camps.

In the beginning of Lithuania's occupation, the Germans were disorganized. As more troops arrived, the Germans created a Jewish ghetto. That was where Joseph and his brothers were sent along with their wives. The young Jews were allowed to continue to work outside of the ghetto, but they had to return each evening before sundown. Everyone had to wear a yellow star at all times.

Rebecca tried her best to make life bearable for her husband. She always kept the small quarters they shared with many others as clean as possible. Their marriage was happy and loving, despite the terror under which they lived.

As the war progressed, Joseph was arrested and placed in Dachau, a German concentration and labor camp. Rebecca, who had tried so hard to remain strong for her man, suddenly found herself alone. Eventually, she too was arrested and placed in the Schufo internment camp near the Polish border.

The war passed slowly, and the two lovers almost gave up hope of surviving and seeing one another again. Though they lost most of their respective families, Rebecca and Joseph Rice found one another after the war through a chance of fate.

After her liberation by the Russians, Rebecca intended to return home to Lithuania. Her brother-in-law, Charlie, found her and his other sister-in-law and begged them not to go back. Dragging his reluctant sisters-in-laws along, Charlie orchestrated their escape into Germany.

In the middle of the night, traveling with forged documents and jumping from train to train like hobos, or hitch-hiking, the three traveled to Munich. In Germany, the women were reunited with their husbands, who had recently been liberated

by the Americans. They all became part of a group of Lithua-
nians living in an American refugee camp on the outskirts of
Munich.

After a few months in the camp, the young couples traveled
to Belgium, once again under cover of darkness. In Belgium
they applied at the American consulate for visas and began
their long wait. Six months later the visas arrived, and they
were finally off to join Joseph's two brothers, Henry and
Benjamin, already in America. Benjamin, the eldest of the five
Rice boys, was the first to arrive in America. He sent for all his
brothers, and eventually everyone arrived except Harry.

By 1946, after a perilous thirteen-day boat crossing from
Holland to Portland, Maine, they arrived in New York eager to
begin their new lives. The family settled in Long Beach, New
York. During the forties, Long Beach was mainly a resort
where the well-to-do residents of Manhattan came each summer to escape the city's sweltering heat.

This was the New York pictured in old Neil Simon plays,
where the sky is clean and families stroll happily together.
Long Beach back then was a first-name kind of community
filled with thoughtful, neighborly, amiable people. The locals
took pride in helping the "seasonals," or tourists, find their
way around. The community wasn't officially a town, but it felt
like one. It was big enough to have its own urban conveniences
and close enough to New York if you wanted the real thing, but
it was small enough to sustain a high degree of neighborliness
and pride.

Long Beach was filled with Jewish immigrants. The wives
cleaned house, shopped, took care of the children, and still
had time to prepare all the dishes from the old country. The
husbands took 6:00 A.M. trains into Manhattan, where they
worked all day, came home weary, and went to synagogue for
evening prayers, afterwards returning home to play with their
children. Life was lived close to the bone, and familiar customs
were preserved.

The Jewish immigrants mixed well with the other immigrants settling in Long Beach, and everyone mingled with the
local population. Long Beach was a true melting pot. Neighbors respected one another's traditions and customs.

Rebecca and Joseph Rice moved into an apartment with Charlie, his wife, and their young son, Anita's cousin Martin. Joseph, Charlie, and Henry took the train each day into Manhattan.

The Rice brothers worked in a factory that made casings for salamis and sausages. They toiled long hours each day, earning a meager living. Bright and aggressive, they watched everything, soon learning every aspect of how the business operated.

This was the life into which Anita was born, a world away from the small village in Lithuania where her parents had met and married just months before they were separated by the war.

In a few years, the three Rice brothers opened their own plant, United Casings. Given the large numbers of observant Jews who had moved into the United States both before and after the war, there was a real need for another factory that provided kosher casings. United Casings had two divisions; one made regular casings, the other made strictly kosher ones.

Given the Rices' combined experience in their father's baloney factory in Lithuania, and the need for a kosher product, United Casings rapidly grew and was able to support the entire family comfortably for many years.

Anita Rice lived in the small two-bedroom apartment in Long Beach with her extended family until she was two and a half years old, sharing the tight play space with her cousin, Martin, who was a few months older.

Living with another family proved difficult for Rebecca. Though she would work hard to keep the apartment immaculate, maintaining six people's belongings, including two busy toddlers' toys and diapers, wasn't easy. Invariably, dishes would stack up or clothes would be strewn about. Though she tried to be comfortable there, Rebecca always felt as if the apartment wasn't her own. Though it was filled with love and laughter, she hadn't had a home of her own since before the war.

One morning Rebecca and two-year-old Anita went out to look for a larger apartment. They were shown the bottom floor of a lovely, but old, three-family home.

"Why don't you buy the house?" asked the owner.

"We could never afford the payments," Riva answered.

"It will give you an income right away. That's how you can manage."

Later in the day when Joseph returned from work, Rebecca excitedly told him about what the man had proposed to her. Joseph went the next morning and listened to the owner explain what being a landlord was all about.

A few minutes later, with only a handshake as down payment, Joseph purchased the Rice's Chester Street house, where the family would live for over a dozen years. Rebecca quickly and lovingly turned it into a beautiful home.

The large white stucco house with green trim and green shutters was divided into three apartments. The Rices lived on the main floor and rented the two other apartments. All the tenants shared the basement, where the children played while their mothers used the washing machine and dryer.

Anita's grammar school, Chester Street Elementary, was directly across the street from her house. The family's orthodox synagogue was located a few blocks away.

Anita's childhood street was a safe, old-fashioned world, not very different from that depicted in the movie *Avalon*. Anita's family kept strong ties with their family in Eastern Europe and would often meet to discuss whether to bring a relative to America or to send money to another.

Anita always felt very strongly about her parents having been in concentration camps, and those feelings remained with her and affected the way she viewed the world for the rest of her life. It was what had attracted her to temple in the first place. Often she would try to understand and transcend her parents' pain through prayer.

Anita considered her parents strict and, at times, backward. That wasn't really the case, but her neighborhood, synagogue, and family were ethnic mirrors that reflected the hardworking old-fashioned values of her Russian, Polish, Lithuanian, and German Jewish ancestors who had recently fled from the Nazis. Naturally, survivors of the Holocaust tried to recapture their lost childhoods, ambitions, and dreams through their children.

As a young child, Anita loved to accompany her father to

work on weekends or after she finished both public and Hebrew school. She would bring giant dried salamis home from the factory to hang in the kitchen, filling the entire house with their pungent aroma. Many years later, Anita would bring those same kind of salamis home to California. Their smell reminded her of home.

From a very early age Anita Rice wanted the all-American dream: a handsome husband, a glamorous house, and a beautiful child. When asked what she wanted to be when she grew up, Anita often answered jokingly, "rich and famous."

Anita went to school but seldom paid much attention to her lessons. The teachers were frustrated; here was this bright and happy little girl who didn't want to settle down to work.

Anita never understood the correlation between work and success. She always thought someone else would do the work for her; that was just the way it was supposed to be.

One classmate recalled, "Anita didn't want to stay after school to participate in music or drama. She wanted to play. When we finished our lessons or tutoring after school, she'd be waiting by the fence for us to come out and play. She was always so much fun."

As young as six, Anita loved sitting in the den with her father while he told her stories of the old country. She would stare up at him for hours, listening to his soothing voice describe faraway places. This was the one time Anita was calm, often curling up next to Joseph and falling asleep by his chair.

Rebellious at home and bored in school, never finding the niche where she belonged, Anita got through grammar school. When she was in school, Anita preferred people to books and was more interested in having fun than in studying. This attitude bothered Anita's parents, especially her mother.

Later, Anita's friends attributed Anita's lack of interest in school to her need to defy authority; her mother insisted that school was important, and Anita always liked to do the opposite of what her mother wanted. Although Anita loved her mother very much, she told her school counselor that her mother was far too strict and that she didn't understand her daughter.

Anita's only sibling, her sister, Linda, wasn't born until

Anita was seven years old and entering the second grade. For many years Anita grew up surrounded with all the love, nurturing, and attention that the two adults could shower upon her.

Her sister, Linda, grew to be the apotheosis of academics and well-roundedness. She was quiet and studious and adored by all her teachers. After school Linda joined every club and activity available. Her scholastic records embodied the ideal her parents stressed: work hard and you will achieve your dreams.

Rebecca and Joseph tried hard not to compare their daughters, but it wasn't always easy. It wasn't just school that bothered them; it was attitude. Anita was rebellious, usually hard to control, and Linda was always so easy.

Still, Joseph admired his elder daughter's spunk, calling her zest for life remarkable. The sun rose and set on his Anita, and no perfect student could have been more adored.

Joseph Rice was a quiet man whose values made an impact on his daughters' lives. Though Rebecca was the real decision-maker in the Rice family, Joseph's values helped lead the family to the decisions they made. Anita always wanted his approval and usually got it.

As time passed, Anita would shield her father from her more serious pranks, often keeping secrets from him. When she was in trouble, instead of turning to her beloved father, she'd look to her mother and beg her to keep the news from Daddy.

Later in life, when Anita left her first husband, Roger Arnow, her mother found out before Anita confided in her father. Again, when Melvin Green bought Anita a large home in Encino, Anita wrote her mother a letter about it, stressing "please don't tell Daddy." Anita knew, since her father had never liked Melvin, that he would not approve of her marrying him.

While her children were at home, Rebecca was a traditional homemaker, but she aspired to more for her daughters. She tried to teach them that it was okay to take risks, and that they could do whatever they wanted.

Riva, a bright woman who spoke five languages fluently when she arrived in New York, struggled to learn to speak

English without an accent as quickly as possible so her young daughters wouldn't be embarrassed. She encouraged the girls to go to school and study hard so they could grow up to be ballerinas, teachers, lawyers, doctors, or businesswomen. Although she worked at home and their father earned the money, Riva explained how a woman needed to become self-sufficient. Riva prayed her girls would never be dependent on their husbands for survival.

Linda followed her mother's advice. Anita never understood what her mother meant until, in her mind, it was too late to change.

Anita found herself identifying with the wealthy American Jews who summered in Long Beach and with the even wealthier ones who went to Florida, where the Rice family spent its summers. She admired their carefree, free-spirited lifestyles; they always appeared to be having so much fun.

All Anita saw was the endless party of pretty people who didn't speak with an accent. She didn't see how hard these people had worked to give their kids a week or two at the beach, a place where she was fortunate enough to live all year round. The visitors' lives seemed far more glamorous than being the daughter of a greenhorn who made hot dog casings.

One evening when Anita was fourteen years old, her parents went into Manhattan with another couple for dinner and a play. A few nights a month the Rices had Anita help out by baby-sitting her little sister, who at the time was almost seven.

When the other couple arrived at their house, Joseph Rice thought nothing of leaving his jacket with the keys to his new Oldsmobile on the coatrack.

After her sister was tucked into bed, Anita's boyfriend, Steven Cohen, came over. Anita spotted her father's jacket, nabbed the car keys, and dared Steven to take a ride with her.

Several hours later, the police found Anita and Steven miles away in Leda, New York, the Oldsmobile completely smashed. Anita was in the front seat crying about the car, her parents, and her baby sister, who was home alone.

Like many small-town police departments, the Long Beach police knew the people they served. The Rices were hard working and upstanding people. The officers warned Anita to get her act together; her parents did not deserve to be hurt by her actions. Then, thoughtfully, the police tried to hide the car from the Rices until Anita could speak with them.

When her parents came home, Anita was waiting for them. Riva's friend had two sons, and Riva remembered her saying, "See how different girls are? She's waiting up for you."

The Oldsmobile accident was only the beginning. The Rices found raising their older daughter was always a challenge. Throughout her school years, Anita was more daring than her friends, consistently flirting with whatever was dangerous and forbidden, including cigarettes, liquor, and boys.

In the early sixties, in Long Beach, being daring also meant cutting classes, wearing lots of makeup, dressing glamorously with gobs of jewelry and furs, and hanging out with an older crowd. These were Anita's trademarks.

After graduating from high school, it was clear that, despite her parents' encouragement, Anita was not college material. The Rices sent their elder daughter to a trade school where she learned how to be a physician's assistant.

Immediately upon finishing the year-long program, Anita went to work in a doctor's office. Bored stiff, unhappy in a small, confined office with few people to talk to, Anita set herself up for failure by deciding that the working world wasn't for her. She complained constantly to her parents and friends about her job. It was boring, it was hard, the people were mean.

Anita's freedom came when she was nineteen years old. Lacking the incentive needed for a career, she began looking seriously for a mate. She quickly met the man who would become her first husband, Roger Arnow.

Roger was a loving man who adored Anita. Captivated and charmed by her friendly ways, it wasn't long before they were dating seriously.

"Anita was great then," recalled Roger. "She was a very special person and had a great way of looking at the world. I could listen to her talk for hours, with her humor and spontaneity. I loved her family. She was never boring and she seemed to care about me so much. We were both so young."

Roger, at twenty-one, was only two years older than Anita. He worked for Warner Bros. as a publicist and lived in a small co-op in Queens. Roger and Anita had little in common, but both loved to party and have a good time. They would frequent bars and nightclubs, convincing themselves that they were perfect for one another.

Although Roger didn't come from a family with money, Anita figured that in time he would advance at Warner Bros. and soon make a comfortable living. "Besides," she told her mother, "there are no men now. They're all at war in Vietnam. I love him and I want to get married." Anita made it perfectly clear that getting married was what she had to do.

Even after the marriage, Anita's parents continued to pamper her. Riva and Joseph would buy Anita and Roger expensive presents. In fact, they even bought Roger and Anita their first home, just half a block away from their own. Nothing was ever too good for their daughter. She would always be their little princess, and they would give her the world.

Anita and Roger's marriage was a traditional one. Roger went to work each day, and Anita kept house. She loved her home and took pride in keeping it beautiful for her husband. Roger would return home each evening and find Anita looking contented. Soon she announced that she was pregnant.

The Rices were thrilled with Anita's news, hoping parenthood would be what she needed. Anita had always been fond of children, her warmth and fun-loving spirit attracting them. With the baby due shortly, perhaps Anita wouldn't be bored. There was so much to do.

Within weeks, Anita's pregnancy turned difficult. First, she suffered from terrible morning sickness. Then, just as the morning sickness began to lessen, she started to bleed. Four months into the pregnancy the doctor put her to bed. Anita had to lie down with her feet up. She soon grew bored and depressed. She felt like her fun-loving carefree days of youth were now permanently behind her. She would lie in the bedroom at her mother's house while Riva took care of her.

Riva had not realized how lonely and empty Anita's life was until this period. Without a job, her husband at work, Anita lay in bed, the twinkle gone from her eyes. Visitors were few and far between. Anita's school friends were either away at college or busy with new jobs.

Riva tried to hide her sadness about Anita's predicament.

She did the best she could to make Anita's pregnancy brighter, talking about how much fun a baby in the house would be.

Riva remained devoted to her pregnant, bed-ridden charge; cooking Anita tempting meals, bringing her books to read, encouraging her other daughter, Linda, to keep Anita company. Riva would stand in the doorway of the room shaking her head as she watched Anita smoke cigarette after cigarette while her unborn grandchild fought to survive.

Anita's appearance deteriorated rapidly. This was partially due to her condition, but perhaps just as much to her personal agony. For the first time in her young life Anita seemed not to give a damn about how she looked.

Riva was grateful that her new son-in-law was tender and attentive toward his wife despite her appearance. Roger's tenderness touched Riva deeply, and she would never forget it. Roger had found his way into her heart.

Not quite seven months into her pregnancy, Anita's contractions began. The doctor watched her writhe in pain for several days. After a long and difficult labor, Scott Arnow entered the world weighing less than two pounds. Anita didn't know at the time that she would never go through such hell again. She was never able to carry another child to term.

Riva recalled, "Scott looked like a chicken. He was so tiny. But his features were still adorable." Scott remained in the hospital for many months, fighting to survive, and making it against all odds.

Giving birth to a premature child gave Anita new responsibilities. The baby's bills were mounting, and because her parents paid for everything, Anita felt guilty. She wished Roger earned more money. It wasn't up to her to make up the difference; her job was simply to take care of Scott.

As her baby grew bigger and stronger, he became the favorite in the hospital's nursery. He was delightful, and the nurses were happy when it was finally time for him to go home, but they felt a tinge of sadness as well. Scott Arnow was their baby too. Everyone had worked so hard to save him. The nurses prayed his life would be filled with joy, and that his mother and father would love him and treat him well.

His grandparents loved and cherished Scott, doting on his

every achievement. Roger proved to be a particularly devoted father, ecstatic about his new son's smallest accomplishments.

"Look, he moved his hand, he's waving," the proud father would exclaim to anyone who would listen. "He's smiling now. See how bright he is."

Anita loved her infant, but he was so little and she was terrified she would hurt him. Changing, burping, rocking, and hugging him frightened her. She never seemed to grow comfortable in her new role.

Anita didn't take to parenting the way Roger had. She had planned on long, loving days with her baby, but found caring for Scott boring and stifling. Her pregnancy had kept her confined. She had no intention of letting her child encroach on her young life the same way. Anita couldn't wait to have fun again.

Shocked, her parents decided Anita wasn't ready for the demands of parenthood, especially since Scott was premature. Rebecca, Joseph, and Roger argued over Anita's indifference toward Scott, and wound up showering him with more attention than ever. The baby thrived.

Riva told herself that in many ways, as old as she always tried to act, Anita was still a child herself. Like a child, whatever she wanted came first. Riva hoped motherhood would eventually make her grow up.

Anita's parenting, or lack of it, didn't make Riva or Joseph love her any less. They knew that she had difficulty with responsibility. Ignoring her baby or being impatient with him didn't mean she didn't love him. There were many different kinds of love. Perhaps one day Anita would learn how to express her love to her young son.

About a year later, as Scott entered toddlerhood, Anita grew slightly more smitten with him and began to seem interested in his development. Perhaps Anita was one of those people who just couldn't relate well to infants. Watching her new baby grow stronger as he turned into a real person seemed to fill Anita with wonder and love.

On the surface, life appeared to be turning around for Anita; she was enjoying being a mother and at long last had her parents' approval. She saw it every time they looked at their grandson. She paraded Scott around town in his carriage, telling old friends that she had finally done something right. Inside though, she felt emptier and emptier.

Life passed slowly for the Arnows, a perpetual vacation of sorts for Anita, though she didn't know it at the time. Anita took care of the house, cooked the meals, and played with Scott, often walking him to the seaside or park. There were zmany leisurely days spent with her toddler on the beach, where Scott ran and laughed with all her friends' young children. At night Grandma and Grandpa were always eager to help out and baby-sit, so Roger and Anita could take in a movie or go to dinner.

Life might have gone on forever this way for the Arnows were it not for one fateful night early in the fall of Scott's third year. Roger returned home from work with important news that would alter the course of their lives, although no one could foresee at the time that it would be the beginning of a move that would ultimately destroy their marriage. In hindsight, had she known, Riva says she would have fought harder to keep her daughter in the East.

Roger had been transferred to Los Angeles, and the young family was on its way to the land of dreams. Anyone who had ever known Anita would have predicted she would be ecstatic. She had always wanted excitement.

However, when Roger broke the news to her, Anita just stared at him, wondering what it would mean to them. Why us and why now? Somehow, moving away didn't seem as glamorous as it once had. Her family was comfortable here and life was easy. Who knew what would be waiting for them in California?

Anita was scared. For all her bravado and big talk, she was very naive and unsophisticated, and Los Angeles was a different world, miles away from her support system. But, on the other hand, after four years of marriage in New York, life was becoming boring and Anita felt older than her twenty-three years. She hoped Los Angeles would bring the sparkle she was looking for, and she dutifully followed her husband to California with her young son.

"Don't worry," Anita said to Roger. "We'll be just fine, and we'll all be together. It's going to be so exciting to get away from here."

Anita appeared to be the perfect wife, anxiously trying to make the best of a situation that she wasn't all too sure about. Roger recalled, "She was as supportive as possible, and very loyal. She seemed really excited about the move."

Loyalty was a trait Anita would always value highly. She chose a life of devotion and stood by her man despite the personal sacrifices she had to make when he decided to move. This trait would later prove to be a dangerous one indeed.

On the eve of their departure, nothing seemed real. It was as if this were just a big adventure and Anita would soon be returning to her family. "I think that's how she got through it," Roger added. "She just didn't think the transfer was forever. She couldn't. She'd have some fun, see some new places, and then she'd come home. She worried about all the normal things mothers worry about. What would she do alone with her three-year-old in a strange city? How would she make friends? These things were always very important to Anita."

"We'll visit often," Anita told her sad parents, who clung to Scott until the last possible moment, only reluctantly handing their grandson over to her. "You'll love coming to see us in California," she added, trying to sound cheerful.

Anita didn't cry; she was too proud for that. Besides, how could she admit to her family that moving away bothered her when she had talked about doing it all her life?

"I felt like we lost her then, like things would never be the same," Riva said. For a family as close as the Rices, and for one that had endured forced separation during the war, a voluntary separation was almost too much to bear.

For most people, there are times in their lives when a single moment can be the turning point; from happiness to despair, from wealth to poverty, from childhood to adulthood. Saying good-bye to her mother and father and feeling their pain was Anita's moment. She knew her world would never be the same. Standing in front of her childhood home, Anita appeared to realize for the first time ever just how much she meant to her family. It didn't matter that her life hadn't turned out the way anyone expected. These were her people, her beginning, her shared heritage. Would she ever find a connection in Los Angeles—a place to go for affection, support, and unconditional love and approval?

Uncertain about what the future would hold, Anita left Long Beach for someplace called Encino, in California's grand San Fernando Valley.

Her husband Roger later explained, "We were both very lonesome at the time, and it took quite a while for us to adjust. I had my work and other outside interests like sports. She really didn't have anything other than Scott. She met Mel in this condition, and he took advantage of her. She was like putty in his hands. Mel thought he could mold her into his fantasy wife, so he smooth-talked her and promised her the world. California was rough for us, right from the beginning. The move set the stage, made her more vulnerable to everything else that happened to her."

Roger described Anita's mental state accurately. She was lonely, insecure, and vulnerable at the time of her move, hoping something nice would happen to her in Los Angeles. It was quite a shock when her life became even more boring.

10

The California Lifestyle

"What's happening? I want to go home," Anita screamed hysterically to Roger. Anita and Roger grabbed Scott and ran from their small apartment as the earth shook and rumbled under their feet. It felt like they were going to be smashed by a giant bulldozer.

Unless you've been through an earthquake before, or have stood at the edge of an erupting volcano or on a train track with a locomotive speeding toward you, a quake's few seconds of shaking are a never-ending nightmare in which seconds seem like minutes. Anita and Roger clung to one another, practically squashing Scott between them.

Los Angeles was crowded, smoggy, and expensive. Now it was also shaking. Anita and Roger Arnow of New York would gladly have endured many winters of snow and ice to avoid having to go through such terror again. They had moved to California only two weeks ago and now were experiencing the Valley's biggest earthquake in decades. It was the last thing they expected.

"Mommy, Daddy, why is everything moving?" Four-year-old Scott asked incredulously. He didn't seem at all frightened by the shaking.

The Arnows took their inquisitive son outside and remained standing on their apartment patio, petrified with fear, until a kind stranger rescued them. Later, Anita told their rescuer she had been sent from God.

"It's over; stop crying. You'll scare the kid. Shit, it looks like you two need a drink. Come on, follow me." A pregnant

Phyllis Baltin pushed them into her apartment, chattering the entire time.

"Where are you from? I saw you move in a little while back. Earthquake virgins, huh? I'll never get used to it." Phyllis talked a mile a minute.

Opening the door to her apartment she shouted, "Rick, we've got company. Get the drinks."

Anita protested and Phyllis insisted. In just seconds, the Arnows were nursing scotches in Phyllis and Rick Baltin's comfortable living room. Anita glanced up from her drink in time to see Scott run off with the Baltin's son, looking like he had found his long-lost best friend. Anita smiled. She felt the same way about Phyllis.

After talking for many hours, Roger finally got up to leave. Anita was disinclined to follow. She was especially thankful for the companionship and was reluctant to return to her lonely apartment.

Phyllis Baltin had a sixth sense about loneliness. "Don't worry, we'll talk more in the morning." Anita seemed grateful. "The moment she entered my home, I knew how lonely she was," Phyllis said. "She missed her family and friends back east so much. I could feel her anguish. I wanted to be there for her."

Even then, in 1971, Phyllis had the distinct impression that something more than loneliness was bothering Anita. She actually seemed in pain. The depression that would surface on and off for the remainder of Anita's life, and for which she would later be treated, had begun to surface. But even at the end, when Riva handed Phyllis all of Anita's prescription drugs that the police had given her, Phyllis was surprised at the extent of Anita's misery. "Come back whenever you want. I've enjoyed the visit, and the boys played so nicely with one another." Phyllis Baltin liked Anita, and she looked forward to a long, special friendship.

Touched, Anita told her, "I won't forget today. I'll always remember your kindness, especially during earthquakes." Both women broke into giggles.

Anita was true to her word. Three weeks later, when Phyllis Baltin suffered a miscarriage, it was Anita who brought her to the hospital and stayed with her throughout her ordeal. Phyllis recovered, and when she delivered a healthy son the following year, Anita became his godmother.

On the day of the earthquake, after her visit with the Baltins, Anita called her mother. "We're okay, Ma. We made our first California friends today. They rescued us from the shaking!"

Anita and Phyllis celebrated "earthquake day" on February 9 every year until Anita died. Even if they were busy, they would always meet for lunch. Both women thought it particularly poignant that a life-long friendship marred by shaky times began during an earthquake.

"That's how life in California began for Anita and Roger," Phyllis recalled. "They didn't plan it. Their move, her boredom, it just happened to her, as is often the case with many of us. She needed to marry Roger. He got her out of the house. But her grand life plan didn't surface until after she moved out to California and realized how unhappy she was."

A few days after Phyllis's miscarriage, Anita and Scott knocked on the door. "Come in," Phyllis shouted.

Anita entered, arms laden with food. "I've brought us lunch. Where are all the good delis out here?" she asked.

"There aren't any," Phyllis moaned. "I'm so mad at Rick leaving me and going back to work. Roger seems so devoted," she added wistfully. "He's great with your son and mine has already adopted him. You're so lucky."

"I don't feel lucky," Anita replied anxiously, not wanting to reveal too much too soon. "I'm a little bored with my life right now; he's part of it."

Phyllis figured Anita just needed to get laid.

"Isn't he good in bed?" No one could ever say Phyllis Baltin beat around the bush.

"That's not it at all," Anita laughed. "He's a great lover." Anita wasn't sure what she was trying to say. "Roger helped me break away. We got married and sort of grew up together. But I keep thinking there's something more out there." Anita added, "He's a wonderful father though."

Phyllis sighed. "That's what matters. Don't lose sight of what's most important in life. You can always play around. Good men are hard to find."

Phyllis already knew her friend was romantic, materialistic, fun-loving, and bored. So Roger and marriage had been Anita's ticket to freedom, and now they were suffocating her. Phyllis wondered what Anita would do about it.

At the time, Phyllis supposed Anita had viewed getting married as the only thing to do. Her groom's social standing or financial prospects weren't as important then as the fact that she wouldn't have to make a decision about how to spend the rest of her life. To justify her decision, Anita convinced herself that Roger was indeed her knight in shining armor, and that he'd work hard to provide her with her version of the American dream. Now it wasn't enough for her. Phyllis felt sorry for her, but she felt Anita certainly had a lot of growing up to do.

Anita's first marriage began a practice that would plague her for the rest of her life. Where men were concerned, Anita had tunnel vision. She saw them only as vehicles to provide her with whatever she could not obtain for herself. Anita, like many lonely women, deluded herself into believing that a relationship would bring her whatever she lacked: self-confidence, money, happiness, fulfillment and power. She should have followed her mother's advice, "Love yourself and you'll find what you're looking for." Riva Rice was a smart lady.

One hot day in August 1974, Anita hit rock bottom. Emptiness tore at her heart. Alone most of the day in a small apartment, she longed for Roger's company and didn't know what to do to fill her days. Often Roger played baseball or boxed after work, or took Scott on an outing. Anita felt abandoned. She got up the nerve to call several therapists, left messages, and, when they returned her calls, told them she had changed her mind.

This was the summer that Anita had one of her earliest extramarital affairs. It started innocently enough, a few quiet lunches with a good friend from her apartment building. But the attention he paid her was great for her ego, which at this point seriously needed boosting.

The affair didn't solve anything and over time didn't make her feel any better. If possible, things were worse. She felt guilty. Anita loved her family, her son, her parents, and Roger. She didn't want to hurt them and prayed they wouldn't find out.

Anita's life continued its downward cycle. She took Scott to school, to Little League and soccer, and to his friends' houses, but her heart wasn't really in it.

Scott, at just six years old, was already aware that something had changed between his parents. His mother appeared to be growing more hostile toward his father. She was impatient, testy, quick to start a fight, and always yelling or crying. His father seemed upset too.

After she dropped Scott off at school, Anita cleaned and cleaned, organizing her small family's possessions over and over again. The contents of the Arnows' drawers were probably the neatest in Encino.

One day an old friend from back east came by for a visit. Over coffee Anita bleakly described her days as so empty that her entire gratification in life came from cleaning the bathroom. She was pleading for someone to help her put her life back on course. She desperately needed help.

Anita began to take her first tranquilizers to calm her nerves. However, an occasional Valium couldn't fill the void in her life. Her apathy toward everything increased, and functioning normally on a daily basis without letting others in on her pain became more and more difficult for her.

As an adult, Anita's son, Scott, described that period in their lives. "My dad was the one I had more quality time with. My mom and I didn't have the type of relationship where we spent a lot of quality time together. She was too bitter and didn't have a purpose. Even as a little boy I saw it."

Scott wasn't the only one caught up in his mother's misery. Friends noticed how bad off she was and tried to help cheer her up by keeping her busy, taking her places, and introducing her to new people. But nothing seemed to work.

Besides being discontented, Anita continued to grow more distant from Roger. As the couple grew apart emotionally, they began to see the world differently. Roger thought their life was okay: they had friends, their child was healthy, and Roger made enough money to provide for his family.

For Anita, this wasn't enough anymore. She was twenty-eight years old, and it felt like her life was almost over. Unable to separate her marriage from her own personal dilemma,

Anita felt safer blaming someone else for her unhappiness. Roger was the most convenient.

The stomach problems she would suffer from for the remainder of her life were already acting up. Whenever she spoke about her life, her stomach was in knots.

"What should I do?" Anita asked friends sitting around the pool, not really expecting that their answers might give her a reason to go on.

The women stared at her. Anita's pain touched them all, reminding them about how difficult finding fulfillment can be when you're busy raising a small child.

"Try getting a job," one friend suggested lovingly.

"How would I do that?" Anita asked. "Who would want to hire me? What can I possibly do? Besides, I have to be home for Scott when he returns from school each day."

This was the first time ever that Anita had shown her California friends how apprehensive and timid she was. Until then, she had always presented herself to them as sophisticated and self-assured. The appearances were a facade that protected her vulnerability. The women wanted to help.

"I can ask my boss if he's looking for someone," answered Barbara Wolpow, a neighbor and friend. "He's flexible about hours."

"Gee, that would be great," Anita exclaimed. "You'd do that for me?"

Her friends noticed that she was surprised someone would help her and that she seemed excited about the prospect of working.

Only Anita and Phyllis knew the secret she was hiding, and Phyllis didn't know the half of it. Anita's anguish was more than just boredom and disenchantment. She had considered getting out of her marriage and she had a plan. Anita was wise enough to know you don't get out without having something or someone else to go to.

Anita told friends, "I know I'm destined for better things." With Roger, the prospects of getting those things looked slim.

Anita found herself caught up in the never-ending cycle of consumerism from which many in the Valley suffer. With so many expensive restaurants to choose from, dozens of costly places to go, and miles of glitzy boutiques to shop in, it was a lifestyle that was easy to get used to. Anita wanted it all.

Anita told her friends back east, "Everyone in California is rich. You should see the cars, Cadillacs, Porsches, Mercedes. There are more Rolls Royces here than in England." It seemed the upper-class communities like Encino, Beverly Hills, and Bel Air were the only communities Anita looked at. She never saw the poorer neighborhoods like Pacoima, East Los Angeles, or Compton.

Anita also complained, "I don't feel like I fit in anywhere." She wasn't the only one in Los Angeles who felt that way. Almost everyone she met in the San Fernando Valley came from somewhere else. Nobody knew who anybody was anymore. Family names didn't mean a thing and didn't assure one's standing in the community. People used money to buy their positions in the community, and money was, in Anita's mind, a sign of power. She told one friend, "Having money means you're good at what you do. That obviously makes people stand up and listen because your success impresses them." Power was always very important to Anita.

Anita Arnow recalled the respect her family received back home. Now, in Encino, she was just a face in the crowd. Without her parents' support, Anita didn't have the money she believed she needed to make a statement about herself.

With her friend Barbara's help, Anita went to work part-time in Melvin Green's accounting office in 1974 as an office assistant doing a variety of low-level jobs. Though it wasn't the bright lights of Broadway or a prestigious position of power, working in Mel's office helped Anita's self-esteem, and she was optimistic about her future.

Anita like working and was delighted that her rich and powerful boss was pleased with her progress. Anita knew Melvin Green could teach her a lot about making money, and she was determined that she would make herself indispensable to him.

That's exactly what she did. Within months, the new part-time office assistant was keeping the same hours as Melvin Green. It seemed he was just what she was looking for.

Later, when her oldest friends, Phyllis Baltin and Nata

Preis, a friend from childhood, reflected on what happened to her, they both were convinced that greed is what ultimately got Anita. It wasn't only greed for herself though; she wanted the money to make a statement to the temple.

Nata said, "I don't think she was impulsive. I think she was very calculating and never acted, but always reacted. I mean, the plan was well established before she found the men who were going to fill that plan. I don't think it was Mel. It was his money. I don't think it was Steve. It was who he was in the community. They could have been anybody."

Phyllis added, "In the end, Anita was less materialistic, but by then she wanted money not so much for herself but for the temple, and to secure her place with Rabbi Jacobs. She wanted to build his dream temple. Melvin's money gave her that power. Foolish, foolish lady, she gave up her life for that."

11

The Cruel Covenant

From the minute she stepped through the door of Melvin Green's accounting office, Anita headed straight to the top. She worked hard and learned quickly. Her new colleagues marveled at how adept she became in learning Mel's complicated business.

Anita, who never knew she had ambition, was astonished. She had not expected to take to the working world since she vividly remembered hating her first job after trade school. But now she greeted each day as a new adventure and looked forward to arriving at the office every morning. Though her job was with a small firm employing only a handful of office workers, the instant camaraderie of new friends was much more stimulating than staying home with only the soaps for company. Anita enjoyed listening to the stories of her colleagues' lives and adventures. Her earnest attentiveness toward others and her willingness to always lend a hand proved beneficial, and Anita was soon accepted as one of the team.

The pace of her new life was grueling. In addition to her growing responsibilities at work, Anita had a house and child to care for. But she rarely complained. She was that grateful about having some place to go in the mornings. Each day Anita would eagerly drop Scott off at school and hurry to arrive at the office by nine. After putting in a full morning with perhaps an hour off for lunch, Anita would rush back for Scott. Then she would cook and clean, and finally return to the office in the evenings after Roger came home to watch his son. She was tired but radiant.

"Anita, you've blossomed like a flower. It seems you've taken to working like a bee takes to honey," Irene Sherwyn told her. Anita's friends could not get over how good she looked, so confident and full of purpose.

Colleagues couldn't maintain her pace. Anita was just too energetic. Yet none were jealous. Anita did not seem to be brownnosing to get their boss's attention. Besides, few ever wanted Mel's attention. They were happy that he had someone else to keep him busy.

Anita felt sorry for Melvin. She wondered why people were so frightened of him. She knew he could be a bully, but she assumed all bosses acted that way. Besides, as long as she did whatever Melvin asked her to do, he was a pussycat. Anita supposed he was lonely and miserable. She saw all the signs because she was all too familiar with them. He had low self-esteem, a volatile temper, problems communicating, an obsessive need to hear how wonderful he was, and a keen desire to remain in absolute control.

Anita saw Mel as an enigma. At times he was a tormentor, yelling at his staff and telling them exactly how he wanted their work done. Soon she noticed that even outside his employees' presence Melvin was domineering and overbearing. He was most certainly into control. He had to govern his wife, his kids, and even his parents. Why, he even tried to push around his clients by forcing them into decisions that some were not ready to make. Anita found that odd. Why would clients remain so loyal and devoted toward a man who treated them so horribly?

At other times Mel was a delight to be around. He could be charming, articulate, and entertaining—a complete paragon. Anita could listen to him for hours. He fascinated her with his witty stories and parables. Mel appeared so worldly. He seemed to know everything there was to know about whatever anyone was talking about.

Even if Anita was not seeking out special attention or treatment, her efforts and attention did not go unnoticed by her powerful and often frightening boss, Melvin Morton Green. Taken with Anita's charming ways and alluring smile, and clearly impressed with her abilities, Mel began to pay more and more attention to her. He gave her more responsibilities, like bookkeeping, and often spent most of the day teaching her how to accomplish specific tasks and showing how he liked things done. Anita smiled to herself knowingly; she still had what it took to attract a man.

Melvin noticed that not only were his employees fond of Anita, his clients were too. Many looked forward to seeing her when they came into the office, and some even began to bring in their friends to meet her. People were simply drawn to Anita. She made them feel special and important. It was a trait that came naturally to her and Mel wanted it.

It wasn't long before Mel realized that this trait was something his firm had always lacked. Some people saw him as arrogant and egomaniacal. He knew his complex personality made it difficult for people to trust him. Clients automatically trusted Anita. She had brought congeniality into the firm. It worked wonders on everyone, including Melvin.

It all started innocently enough. Melvin would call Anita into his office when a client was there. They would talk, and Mel noticed that often the clients, especially the male clients, seemed comfortable with Anita. She had a natural way of putting people at ease.

Soon Mel began to show Anita how he liked his papers done and how to read an audit. He felt comfortable with her too. He trusted her. Mel soon saw that Anita had a real head for numbers, and, unlike many of his employees, Anita did not cower whenever he was around. She seemed impressed by both his knowledge and his power. She didn't mind his bullying, and her acceptance of it made Melvin act nicer to her than to others.

By this time in his life, Melvin was frantic to find someone to love and accept him. Somewhere locked inside of him was a normal person waiting to live life. Mel figured Bernyce lacked the key to let that person out. They had been at it again last night, fighting over his temper and his lifestyle, and he was tired of it. He wanted the respect he so rightfully deserved.

"I'm sick of your yelling, and I'm tired of staying home alone all of the time. Why aren't you ever home? Why don't we go anywhere together?" Bernyce asked tearfully.

"We went to temple together two nights ago," Mel replied. "What more do you want from me? You know how busy I am."

"Come off it, Mel. I don't mean temple. You go there for your own reasons anyway, and, as always, its only to get clients."

His wife was right. For Mel, the Stephen S. Wise Synagogue was the socially acceptable place to be. He put on his four-inch gold, diamond encrusted *chai* necklace, the Jewish symbol for life, and walked around like he owned the place. He always found clients there. Who was she to complain? Bernyce claimed he was using religion to his own advantage. Hell, everyone used people and situations to their own advantage. That's the way the world worked. Melvin was sick of his wife's put-downs. Bernyce just never understood that his business was his life.

As far as friendships and a social life were concerned, the Greens' were virtually nonexistent. Melvin sang in the Stephen S. Wise choir. Bernyce did her own thing. They didn't go out very often with other couples for dinner or a movie. Melvin was far too busy and besides he just couldn't handle it. He was simply incapable of being a friend. He was always suspecting that something sexual might take place. Melvin could never understand how a man and a woman could be friends without becoming lovers.

Bernyce grew more frustrated. She tried to show an interest in his business, but Mel refused to let her in on it. The office was to remain his private domain. She tried another tactic and asked him about his new clients.

"What new client? How do you know I have new clients? Are you being a snoop?" Mel hollered.

"No, your father mentioned you picked up a new client. That's all. I wanted to know what they did," Bernyce answered. "Who referred them?"

"Stop being so nosy. It's none of your business."

"Let's just forget I ever asked. But please don't tell me that I don't care."

Living with Melvin was like living on the edge of a volcano. Bernyce never knew when he would erupt. Her husband was two different men. He was smart and articulate, and at times could be wonderful to be around. That's what had initially attracted her to him. But whenever she tried to get close, he would attempt to take over and control her every move. When she protested, he grew mean. His temper could be explosive and he was very abusive verbally. Bernyce grew frightened of talking with him and at times avoided any interaction whatsoever.

Bernyce grew lonely. She was tired of being bossed around by a bully and even more tired of her sons being tormented by one. She stopped trying to reach out to Mel and began to fight back.

Bernyce had instinctively handled her husband's bullying in two ways that resulted in opposite reactions. If she stood up to Mel and fought him, he enjoyed the process and would often get meaner. Ignoring Mel seemed to be a more effective way of getting his attention and of controlling his outbursts. Melvin Green hated being ignored more than anything in the world. Bernyce had a powerful weapon, and she used it often. It was a trait Anita would master in later years.

Anita was having problems of her own during these months. Staggering from the amount of work at Melvin's office, coupled with raising a child and running a house, she continued to feel severely depressed at home and very confused. The more devoted to work she became, the more she fought with her husband, Roger.

He would ask, "Why isn't there any food in the house? Where are Scott's clean clothes? How come you missed your son's soccer game again? Don't you care about your family?"

Of course she cared, but she was tired of taking a backseat to the world. Her life was holding her back. Anita felt trapped. "You don't understand; I need to do this."

As time passed and Mel and Anita spent more time together, Anita concluded that her boss's moodiness reflected his growing unhappiness with the world. Anita felt a kinship with him. She thought of how she was acting at home and toward Roger. Anita and Mel were both suffering from depression and lack of fulfillment in their personal lives. It was not the healthiest way to start a relationship. But the two of them needed each other.

Anita's childhood friend Nata recalled, "Money and power were always aphrodisiacs to Anita. She couldn't resist Mel's. She used to brag that he threw money around like it was just paper. He acted like a drunken sailor with his money, and she always loved that. She liked being his trophy wife, his prize."

Anita also adored Mel because he believed in her. He saw that she was a good worker who had a talent for motivating others. She liked his mind and admired what he had done with it. They began to spend more and more time together. Anita literally worked her way into Mel's life.

Anita had her share of experience with men. In her teenage years, she'd been able to attract whoever she wanted. Needy, lonely men like Mel were the easiest. If she played her cards right, he'd be eating out of her hands in no time.

Anita coyly began to ask Mel questions about his unhappiness, making it appear as though he was the only person in the world who mattered to her. They would linger over lunch after the other women went back to the office, and they would talk for hours. This was just what Mel craved, someone sympathetic and attentive to listen to him. Mel loved to talk and devoured Anita's questions.

Mel complained that Bernyce didn't understand him and didn't recognize that he was such a good businessman. He confessed to Anita that in his mind his wife wanted to control their marriage to emasculate him. Anita confided that she too had become unhappy in her marriage. Her husband, Roger, was wishy-washy, not strong and forceful like Melvin. In fact, she was so unfulfilled that she had looked for a job. Perhaps fate had brought them together.

Melvin was completely smitten. It wasn't often that a woman paid him compliments. It had been quite awhile since Bernyce had had anything positive to say about him. Besides, this woman was a good worker, and if they worked together to build Melvin Green, Incorporated, there was no telling how far he could go. He took the bait.

Melvin thought he was one step ahead of Anita and calling all the shots. Anita thought she was in control of the relationship.

Anita and Mel had their own agendas for their relationship. "Both had motives and both knew exactly what they were doing. I don't know if they ever really fell in love. Perhaps he did with her, but I don't think so. I mean, look at their prenuptial agreement. But I doubt she ever loved him. I asked her once and she replied, 'We have a very loving relationship.' Shit, you can have a loving relationship with a dog," Phyllis Baltin explained.

Anita and Mel became the talk of the office. Hearing the rumors and seeing the signs, Barbara Wolpow rolled her eyes. She couldn't imagine what Anita saw in him. She wondered if his pocketbook had anything to do with it. Anita had always wanted Roger to be more successful. Barbara tried to contain her anger because she was very fond of Roger. The two families had grown close over the years. She begged Anita to stop what she was doing, but eventually she turned her eyes. Anita refused to listen, and Barbara thought she had lost a good friend.

Mel moved out of his house in Bel Air and would spend the nights on the sofa in his office. Each night after she put Scott to bed, Anita would sneak back to the office to be with Mel. She would explain to Roger that she still had more work to do. He wanted desperately to believe her.

A few months after he moved into the office, Mel filed for divorce. At the time of his filing, he was making a solid six-figure income and lavishing gifts on Anita. She was charmed. He was so generous.

Bernyce didn't think so. Because she had forced Mel to leave after finding out about Anita, he fought her tooth and nail for every penny in the divorce settlement. It wasn't really a matter of money, but rather control. Mel needed to have the final say in every decision.

In the end, Mel paid off their Bel Air house and gave Bernyce a generous sum of money. But rather than pay it as alimony, Mel required Bernyce to go on disability so he could save money on taxes.

How Mel handled Bernyce made Anita sick and frightened. Sure, it saved them money, but her new love interest always had a way to beat the system. How could everything he was doing be considered legal?

Mel was now free, but Anita wasn't, and Mel didn't like that. He pressured her daily to do something. "Don't border on the brink of indecision," he said. "Choose and move, or suffer the consequences of indecision and repent on what might have been."

"Mel, what are you saying? Why do you keep quoting that to me? Are you threatening to leave?"

"Get him out of the house or things are over between us," Mel hollered. "I'm tired of sleeping in the office. I want to move in with you."

"I know you do, honey. I just need a little more time."

Melvin obsessed about Anita and Roger's living arrangement. He began to drive Anita crazy. Day after day he worked on her. He told her that it was either Roger or him. When she answered that she preferred him but she needed more time, Mel would storm around the office. He said she didn't love him. He called her an egocentric, rapacious, self-centered person. When she insisted that this wasn't the case, he threatened to take away her job. Anita grew tired of arguing with him. She promised to get rid of Roger as soon as possible.

When Roger broke his leg playing basketball, Anita responded by throwing him out of the house. She simply didn't have the time to take care of him, and she didn't want to be bothered by missing work. Besides, Melvin needed her now. As soon as her husband moved out, her boss moved in.

By the time Anita's parents, Riva and Joseph, arrived in California a month later, Roger had gone home to New York to be with his parents so they could take care of him.

Riva sighed; that was exactly what her daughter should be doing. What kind of a wife wouldn't take care of her injured husband? Roger had stood by Anita during her long and difficult pregnancy.

Anita had arrived at the airport to pick up her parents with her new boss tagging along. He was a heavy, obnoxious man who was overly solicitous of their affection. He seemed to be trying desperately to get them to like him. Why would he care what his employee's parents thought of him? Riva and Joseph despised him immediately.

When they arrived at their daughter's home, a heartbroken Scott led his grandparents out to his father's little blue Toyota.

"Mom says its just for a little while, but I know he's not moving back home. Why, Grandma?"

"Your mommy and daddy fought too much. Maybe he'll be back one day, sweetheart."

Scott's words broke his grandmother's heart. Riva thought about the man Anita had just introduced them to. She already could see that he was a terrible person. She would have to have a talk with her headstrong daughter. She just didn't understand what could be happening.

Meanwhile, Barbara Wolpow continued pleading daily with Anita to reconsider. She tried everything, to no avail. In time, Anita filed for divorce. To this day Barbara feels guilty and somewhat responsible. She brought Anita into Mel's office and destroyed two marriages in the process. That was a total of three children's lives she had unknowingly tampered with. Barbara, a caring and loving woman, had no idea at the time how deep her guilt would grow.

At first, after she divorced Roger, Anita seemed a little leery of marrying again, preferring her freedom. Instead of marriage, Anita agreed to live with Mel. But Mel desperately wanted a marriage certificate, and he would not wait for it indefinitely. After five years together, Mel had to do something.

Sensing Anita's hesitancy, Mel finally bought her a beautiful house in the heart of Encino. Although Anita was to contribute a little toward the house's down payment, the majority of the money for her dream house came from Melvin.

The house was located on a semiprivate street in the midst of half-million-dollar homes. It was new, luxurious, and immaculate. There were six bedrooms and six bathrooms and an enormous master suite. The yard had a pool and a Jacuzzi. Anita couldn't resist.

Mel's only two requirements were that she marry him and that she sign all the documents he had prepared for them. Anita agreed to both demands. He promised her she would never regret it.

Anita wrote a letter to her parents explaining the changes taking place in her life. She told her mother about the house and the upcoming marriage, begging her, as usual, not to tell Daddy. As always, Anita wanted her father's approval, and since her parents' recent visit, she suspected how much Joseph already despised Melvin Green.

Despite warnings and protests, and, obviously, with a few of her own reservations, Anita Arnow, thirty-two years old, married forty-five-year-old Melvin Green on New Year's Day in 1981. Her son, Scott, had just turned fourteen.

A few days before the small ceremony, Anita's future mother-in-law phoned her and said, "I love you, but what are you doing? You don't need him. You'll live longer without him." June Green knew her only child better than anyone else did.

The ceremony was held at Anita's temple in Rabbi Steven Jacobs's study. Mel took an immediate liking to the rabbi. He thought his speaking skills were admirable and that Rabbi Jacobs was a good listener. Mel liked to talk and appreciated when people listened to him.

Anita and Mel's children from their previous marriages witnessed the union. Not one of the teenage boys seemed at all pleased by their parent's decision to remarry. Rabbi Jacobs talked lovingly to all three boys, and both Anita and Mel were touched by his kindness.

The only other people in attendance were the bride and groom's parents, Rebecca and Joseph Rice and June and Hyman Green. They too wore frowns.

What guests remember most about the postceremony reception is Mel's singing to his new bride. "He was loud, obnoxious, and completely inappropriate. I mean, here we were at Chasen's, and he was making an ass of himself. We wanted to die. Imagine how his bride felt," said one of Mel's former clients.

Anita was indeed embarrassed. This was the chic, expensive, and famous Chasen's restaurant, known for attracting movie stars and glamorous people. Here she was with her new husband, and he was carrying on and making a spectacle of himself. Certainly it was his wedding too and he was entitled to have a good time, but Anita wondered why he always had to be the center of attention.

The next few days, during the honeymoon, she tried to put the wedding incident behind her. She told herself that Mel loved her and merely had trouble finding an appropriate way to express his feelings toward her. But finally she asked him why he had sung like that.

"Because I wanted to," Mel shouted.

"Weren't you even a little embarrassed?"

"Hell no. I paid good money for that room. My money is the same as any movie star's. I don't care what people said."

Anita did. It was the beginning of the end for both of them.

12

Love and Betrayal

Anita and Mel Green's marriage teetered on the edge of collapse from the very beginning. Perhaps this was because their union was never really a normal marriage, but more of an arrangement. Mel agreed to provide for Anita in grand style, and in return, she agreed to make him happy. To do that she had to work for him and keep her mouth shut. She was also expected to give up any part of her life that he deemed no longer appropriate. Anita was to be above all, "Mel Green's wife." Their problems erupted because they both had different definitions of the meaning of wife.

"Anita was his trophy wife. Mel was so big and fat, and though she wasn't classically beautiful, she could be very sensual. Anita was his declaration to the world that he still had it in him. He acted like he owned her," said a former client of Mel's who chose to remain anonymous.

Mel was extremely jealous of Anita's friends and resented it if she spent any time with them. Not wanting to make things any more difficult for Anita, many pulled back.

Anita was by nature a social person who loved to go to parties and have a good time. Her friends meant a lot to her. She did not want to lose them. She hoped that her husband would soon feel comfortable with them and would stop worrying about why she was friends with them.

"Why is she your friend? You're not at all alike. Do you have the hots for her husband?" Mel would ask. About another friend he'd comment, "She's a loser. I don't want you to associate with the likes of women like that."

Most of the time Anita had no idea of what Mel was talking about. Perhaps he knew better than she did what types of people they should associate with. He traveled in a class far different from what she was used to. Anita also felt sorry for him. She knew how insecure Mel's weight made him.

The first time they went to one of her friend's parties together, Anita had a wonderful time despite the fact that her new husband was unhappy. She danced and talked until midnight and she felt like Cinderella. She was so happy and proud to be married to a wealthy and successful man like Mel.

Mel was miserable. He complained about the music, the food, the bartenders, and, most of all, the "lowlife" Anita associated with. He tried to dominate all the conversations and got angry when people were turned off by his obnoxious and inappropriate actions.

Anita was shocked. She had wanted her friends to like her husband and him to like them. Why did he have to put everyone down? Mel, never a mixer, had pretended to be an expert on everything. He was boastful and pompous and she had been embarrassed. When they got home from the party, Mel had bellowed at her, "If you must waste our time at these stupid affairs with these scummy friends of yours, why don't you make it worth our while?"

"What do you mean, Mel? How can I make you happier?" Anita asked. Her husband was fuming, "You can't be that stupid. Don't you realize that all your friends have their taxes done? Why haven't they brought their business into you yet? We've been together for several years. What kind of friends are they? They must think you're pretty stupid or they would be coming to us already."

"I never knew you expected me to bring all of my friends' tax work into the company."

"Of course I expect it. What's the matter with you? That's one of the reasons I married you. The primary reason, if you must know the truth. Your job is to make me happy and to bring business into my firm. Do you understand?"

"I'm sorry, Mel. I'll try harder."

Anita's newest responsibility as Melvin Green's wife was to bring all of her friends, and relatives' tax work into the firm. Within a year of their marriage, most had complied. Melvin was ecstatic. Those who hadn't were no longer their friends; they had rejected Melvin's expertise, and he took rejection personally.

One devastating casualty to Anita was her childhood friend, Nata Preis. Nata's husband had been solicited by Anita. He had even gone into the office to meet with Melvin, and the two had gotten into a major confrontation about Mel's dishonest practices. From the minute the Preises refused to give Mel their tax work, they were no longer allowed to associate with the Greens.

Melvin's family walked around on edge, never knowing when he would attack them next. Anita grew sick of him. There were times when she just had to escape. She began to pursue her own interests out of necessity. Her very survival depended on getting away from the man she had married.

Their marriage began to disintegrate even more rapidly, because by having interests other than him, Anita was defying Melvin's need for total control over her. Once she began to look for a life of her own, conditions in their house only got worse.

Melvin panicked. He tried to regain control, and, in the process, stopped seeing Anita as a life partner or even as a business partner and began to consider her even more his own personal property.

The only reason Mel had allowed Anita out to go to temple in the first place was because he had seen it as a socially acceptable place to find clients. By this time, every aspect of Mel's life was centered around his work, and any chance to attract and woo new clients was encouraged.

Mel grew busier than he had ever anticipated, and the stress seemed like it was pushing him over the edge. But, in Encino, stress was the norm. The busier your business was, the better your neighbors thought of you. For Mel, this was glaringly important. As long as he made a fortune, people would say, "He's weird, but he must be doing something right. Look how much money he makes."

The temple not only provided the Greens with instant clients, but with instant friends as well. There were parties, dances, and classes that all the members automatically received invitations to. There was always someone to talk to at shul, and one never needed to feel lonely. The temple was the Greens' life.

Just two years into Anita and Mel's marriage, eight of Rabbi Jacobs's most fervent followers from Temple Judea broke off and started the Shir Chadash temple. Anita and Mel were part of the group. At that time, both of them were devoted to the project. Anita seemed especially elated. This project gave her a purpose in life. She had never felt so important before. The only problem was, in a small new shul, she would not be able to hide her husband's ever-escalating temper.

On a particularly lovely weekend, the new temple's pioneers held a religious retreat at a trendy resort in Marina Del Rey to get the temple started. It was an inspiring weekend filled with animated discussions that kindled passions in people. The prayer sessions were equally moving. The weather was lovely. The night sky was filled with stars. Anita was overwhelmed by the beauty and power of the retreat and filled with hope for the future. She swayed to the music and hugged her new friends. They were all so wonderful to be with. They shared so many of the same values and thoughts on life. Anita took great pride in being part of such a group. The others seemed to feel the same way about her.

Melvin found it all slightly unsettling and made his feelings known to Anita.

"Why do they hang on you so?" He hissed into her ear. Melvin seethed. Why did people think what she had to say mattered so much? He was articulate, knowledgeable, and infinitely more worldly about these sorts of things. Why, he probably knew more about building a shul than anyone else present. Yet, in his mind, no one was listening to him.

And he was right. To the temple founders, Melvin Green came across as arrogant, angry, and egomaniacal. He had tried to dominate the evening's discussion and people were turned off.

Melvin had the social grace of a shark. He actually came up to people and tried to force them to listen to him. He would attack verbally if he felt he was being ignored. People had finally given in and listened. But few really cared about what he had to say because they were so angry that he had forced them all into listening. Anita had watched the discussion and had tried to tell Mel how to go about getting his ideas across to others, but he only attacked her for trying. She left the meeting room, crying softly to herself.

"What's the matter, Anita?" a new congregant asked in the ladies' room after the program.

"Nothing. I'm fine. I'm just so happy to be here."

"We all are. Is there anything I can do for you?"

The woman could actually feel Anita withdraw. It was as if she did not want to let anybody know what was going on between her and her strange husband.

"I'm fine. I'm looking forward to working together. I'll see you in the morning. Good night."

Anita exited and joined Mel, who was pacing in front of the ladies' room.

"What took you so long?" he hissed.

"I was just going to the bathroom. Leave me alone. Can you please stop picking on me?"

As they walked back into the meeting area, Anita noticed all eyes upon them. She smiled to her friends. Another couple took the hint and joined the Greens. The four adults walked to their rooms together, laughing and talking about how special the day had been. The Seewacks noticed that they had rooms next to the Greens and commented on it.

Anita smiled politely and prayed that Mel would behave. Perhaps she should have their room changed. She sensed that Mel was going to be a problem tonight. The two couples bade one another good night.

Not an hour passed before the Seewacks heard shouting. Then they heard crying, which they soon realized was Anita's. The Seewacks had no idea at the time that the Greens' shouting match was a relatively mild incident.

Rabbi Jacobs grew very close to the eight couples who had left Temple Judea to build him his dream shul. The Shir Chadash founders and early members were almost exclusively from wealthy communities like Encino, Calabasas, and Tarzana. These founding members were more like cult members than congregants, and they quickly found a way to pay the rabbi what he needed.

One Los Angeles rabbi described Steven Jacobs's followers. "They were all in love with Rabbi Jacobs. Sometimes we jokingly refer to him amongst ourselves as the Jim Jones of the rabbinate. I think that they would have followed him to the ends of the earth if he had asked them to."

Certainly, Anita would have. She grew more mesmerized by Steven Jacobs daily. The rabbi could do no wrong. She even told her mother how wonderful the rabbi was.

Riva recalled Rabbi Jacobs from Scott's bar mitzvah at Temple Judea and from Anita's wedding. She didn't like him and couldn't imagine what her daughter saw in him. She thought the rabbi was an insincere phony and not the least bit rabbinical.

"He's an actor, Anita. He's not a rabbi."

"Oh, Ma, give him a chance. You'll like him."

Others felt the same way as Riva. But apparently the rabbi saw nothing wrong with being compared to an actor. When one congregant at Temple Judea mentioned after a funeral how moving the rabbi's eulogy had been, Steven Jacobs smiled and said, "I can make the telephone book sound moving."

Shir Chadash grew quickly. Many of the rabbi's followers left Temple Judea to join him at Shir Chadash. The founders made up the core of the temple's leadership during the eighties, and their visions directed the path of the temple. It was a tight group to break into, and they remained Rabbi Jacobs's inner circle of close confidants.

Anita began to spend more and more time with Rabbi Jacobs working on temple projects, and less and less time at the office. She liked the sense of accomplishment that came from being a well-respected temple voice. People listened to her ideas, and she was given freedom to implement them. It felt good and she was proud of herself. She was making a valuable contribution to the world. One of Mel's cousins, Sue Artoff, said "Anita felt guilty about some of the things Mel made her do at work. She knew he often hurt people. The temple was morally good work and it made her feel better about herself."

But increased self-esteem and confidence were not the only benefits of temple life. There had always been a deep emptiness at the core of Anita's world. She had never had a purpose before, and being trapped with Melvin made the hollowness in her life all the more apparent. The temple filled that void now and gave Anita a reason to go on.

"Other people had their jobs, their children, their spouses, and perhaps a hobby or two. Not Anita; she lived for Rabbi Jacobs and for Shir Chadash. It was very important that her new friends see her as the strong, independent woman she had grown to be," her friend Nata recalled.

Anita had by now grown to hate Mel's frequent outbursts and violent temper so much that she not only ran away to the temple, but she began to hide things from Mel as well. Little things, like an occasional smoke, or a date for lunch with a "forbidden" friend. Then there were the big lies: the affairs, the trips, the large donations to charities he despised, and the numerous and lavish shopping binges.

Of course, her deceit only angered him further. Mel decided to regain control of his marriage. He was tired of being a "charity to the world."

On August 17, 1985, at 6:52 P.M., Anita and Mel sat down to write a nuptial agreement. The purpose was twofold: to show Anita how serious Melvin was about her towing the line, and to delineate how their possessions were to be divided in case of a divorce.

Mel wrote the eleven-page document and forced his exhausted wife to sign it. In her emotionally battered and weakened state, she had neither time nor energy to fight him.

The nuptial agreement between Anita Molly Green and Melvin Morton Green was later used by the district attorney in Mel's trial to show how controlling an individual Mel could be.

One juror said, "If any one document helped me decide that Mr. Green hired someone to kill his wife, it was the nuptial agreement he forced her to sign four years into their marriage. It showed that there was no love in that marriage."

At Mel's trial, the prosecutor compared one page in the document that exemplified Mel's attitude to the maniacal husband character in the movie *Sleeping With the Enemy*.

And Mel wasn't done yet. He wanted to regain total control over Anita's personal habits as well. In the long document Mel ranted on and on about the sorry state of Anita's and his marriage.

Anita further agrees in writing under oath that she will never again smoke a cigarette as long as she lives. If she is caught smoking at any time it is immediate grounds for her dismissal terminating the marital relationship, and immediately forcing this event to occur, specifically the dissolution and her termination businesswise. The reason for this being Anita had consistently promised to quit smoking. It was the basis for Mel and Anita moving in together or Mel moving into Anita's place, for their engagement, for their buying a house together, and their marriage.

Since no employee is allowed the privilege of smoking with the exception of in their office or the smoking room, which is the waiting room and Anita has abused this so many times and fouled up the confines of the one ladies bathroom only and has asked other people to cover for her, it is clearly understood that smoking is permanently and irrevocably forbidden.

Therefore, Mel has the right to invade her privacy any time he chooses, but if he invades the bathroom and any stranger might have caught a glimpse because of his thoughtlessness than he forever thereafter has no further right to inspect. In any event her purses and everything else are open for inspection because of her lies, mendacity, and deceit.

Though Anita thinks this is a bunch of bullshit Mel is so much against smoking that if this agreement is not signed no later than one hour from the time it is complete the marriage and the business relationship are over.

Each page was initialed by Anita and Mel. On the last page, underneath Mel's signature, were the words *husband and community entity*, as well as *separate entity*. Underneath Anita's signature were the words *community entity* only.

During the next five years Anita and Mel Green's marriage continued its downward spiral, a descent into living hell for both of them.

13

The Rise of Queen Anita

By the time 1987 began, the members of Shir Chadash had cause for celebration. They had finally found the place to build their new home, and their leaders had designed an innovative plan that they hoped would make the temple a reality.

The congregation leased a large parcel of land from the Los Angeles Community College District. The plan was for the temple to use part of the land and sell the remaining portion for single-family homes. The profit Shir Chadash expected to make on the land would help pay the costs of carrying the land and, hopefully, defray the eventual construction cost.

In order for the bank to lend the congregation the money, $1.5 million at first and later another $1.5 million, thirty-one member families had to sign on as personal guarantors of the loan. This was extremely risky, but the guarantors knew that once the land was sold, they would no longer be on the line financially. Since the temple was to be located on one of the Valley's few remaining pieces of undeveloped real estate, it was likely that the land would move very quickly.

In the 1980s the San Fernando Valley went through a major housing boom. All over the Valley construction crews worked night and day to finish the sprouting luxury homes and planned communities.

Yuppie families from Los Angeles migrated to the Valley's suburbs at an alarming rate, seeking the security of life away from gangs, and because the homes in the Valley were more affordable by Los Angeles standards than anything comparable in the city proper.

During most of the eighties, affordable new homes in the Valley were in such demand that often builders opened their doors months before the completion of a project and would sell out in the first day. Home buyers would literally camp at the gates of communities before a housing project opened. Numbers were passed out and homes were sold by lottery.

Los Angeles builders made a killing as home prices doubled and tripled in just a few years. Many people made a fortune on their homes. They would turn around and buy newer, even bigger homes.

Builders began to scour the Valley and even farther out, in communities like Agoura, Westlake, and Thousand Oaks, for more land to build on. Besides the developers fighting for land, just about everyone in the Valley was building a home or knew someone else who was. It was an easy way to make money at a time when money was where it was at. There was a shortage of land to feed the ever-growing hunger of these new real estate moguls.

The temple's building committee was comprised of several amateur and professional real estate experts who got caught up in the frenzy of the time. They were optimistic that one of the Valley's leading builders would soon buy up the temple's excess acreage.

Given their excitement and the state of Los Angeles's economy in general, it was not too difficult to convince temple members to agree to the plan to put up their assets and, in a sense, their houses as collateral to the bank. These families, with varying amounts of money, placed from twenty-five thousand dollars to hundreds of thousands of dollars on the line to ensure that the temple would be built. What better way to show Rabbi Jacobs your commitment to him than to offer your own home as security.

Being a temple loan guarantor soon became a mark of status for some. In Encino and other wealthy Valley communities, your home was your finest possession. If you were ready to risk it all for the synagogue, that meant symbolically you were a more religious and charitable person than someone who would not make a sacrifice like that, even if they had the means. This was just the type of thing that was important to someone like Melvin Green.

As soon as the land deal came through, Mel began boasting that he was putting up his house as security. Nobody took him too seriously. It was part of Mel's personality to brag about what he was going to do for them. Unlike Anita, who really followed through once she became committed, there was always a big gap between Mel's promises and his actions.

Secretly, Mel drove Anita crazy about the proposal. On one level, he wanted to do it so he would appear to be as generous and magnanimous as the others. But at the same time, he told Anita that the rabbi had gall. It was a little like God asking Abraham to sacrifice his son. What if something went wrong? One could never predict the future. How far would these people be expected to go for the rabbi?

Melvin wondered how the temple's leaders expected to sell leased land. Mel was a smart man, and he saw that what they were planning did not make sense. When the rabbi was questioned further, he answered perhaps the temple would keep all the land and build the Shir Chadash Village, an elaborate temple, recreational area, and school. To Melvin, who was a businessman, it all sounded preposterous.

Anita was heartbroken. Her greatest dream was to show her new extended family her commitment. Like Melvin, she had a certain image she was trying to project to the temple members, an image that could only continue if she could do what all of Steven's other wealthy supporters seemed to be doing. Anita felt obligated to make this sacrifice for the rabbi, because she hoped he might later be equally obligated and responsive to her. This preoccupation with appearances may have pushed Mel over the edge and cost Anita her life.

"What's it worth, Anita? Will you start working again?" Mel had asked.

"It's worth more than anything right now. I have to do this. I'm a temple leader, and I have to set an example for others."

After much debate, hours of fighting, and many tears, Mel relented. Once again Anita had given her soul. She was now instructed by her husband to work hardest for Mel's company and to stop spending so much time at the temple.

When Mel finally agreed to attend a meeting to learn about the proposed land deal, he asked more questions than anyone else there and drove the banker crazy. When he finally agreed to be a guarantor, his tone was self-congratulatory and pretentious. After signing the papers, he walked around like he was better than everyone else, including those who had made the same decision for far larger amounts.

In the end, Anita and Melvin Green put up three hundred thousand dollars to keep the temple arrangement afloat. Melvin later said, "Had I known that they were probably already screwing, I would not have been so generous. I really had the wool pulled over my eyes. No one supported that temple more than Anita and I did."

Anita was delirious with joy about being one of the loan guarantors. She told Phyllis that Rabbi Jacobs was both happy and grateful for what they had done for his temple.

"He's so proud of me, Phyllis."

"Proud of you? You sound like you live for that man's approval. What does it matter to you what he thinks about you?"

"I can't explain, but it does matter. I'd do anything for him. I want to please him."

Anita's devotion was apparent, and she did not need to tell anyone how much she wanted to please the rabbi. They had by now grown quite close. She had finished a term as the congregation board's secretary, and her work had been exceptional. She was a talented and giving leader.

One fellow board member recalled with wonder and awe the copious notes Anita would take as secretary. Each page was placed in a plastic cover and then in a three-ring binder for preservation. Her energy and enthusiasm for temple projects appeared to be endless.

Four years had passed since the temple's inception, and Anita had worked tirelessly to get the building started. She proved to be a reliable, intelligent, hard-working leader. She was sensitive yet strong. She was always ready to lend a hand and do more, especially when building the synagogue was the goal. This was the aspiration that took over her life, and it took precedence over everything she did. Anita was no longer a balanced person.

Her son described it best. "In one aspect I was proud of her. She was doing something great...something that she liked. It gave her an outlet and a life. At the same time, I felt like it did take away from her personal time, from my time. I thought she was getting into it too much. People were calling her constantly. That's why I got my own phone. She was on the other phone day and night. To be honest, it forced me to grow up alone, not really alone, because she loved me, but on my own."

Melvin could not stand Anita's increased commitments to the temple. By winter of 1987 their life together had turned into one long fight, mostly about her temple meetings and about her increased absences from work. Anita expected a major blowup at any moment.

At this same time, Anita's beloved father, Joseph Rice, became extremely ill. He lay dying in a hospital in New York while Mel hassled Anita about flying home to be with him.

"Don't subordinate your position to me. Just who do you think you are? I don't want you to go anywhere."

"I'm going today and I'll be gone for as long as he needs me."

"At least fly home on weekends, take care of business, and then go back. I'll pay for it."

"No, Mel. I will not do that. My father is dying." Anita didn't want to believe that anyone could act this way, especially toward someone they supposedly loved.

She stormed out of the office. Anita arrived in New York the next day. It was good to be home. Though her father was already quite sick, his presence filled her with wonderful memories of her childhood.

Her parents were grateful that she had made it home. Her loving support was very important to them both. On this trip she grew closer to her mother than ever before. They both shared a deep love for her father, and only they could understand one another's pain at his illness. As they watched Joseph suffer, they leaned on one another for support and comfort.

Mel called twenty times a day. Why the hell wasn't his wife coming home yet? He finally forced the issue and Anita arrived on the next plane.

As soon as Anita was back home, her father passed away. Because her parents had bought a condominium in Los Angeles before Joseph's death, her mother decided to go ahead with the move. She had her husband's body shipped to California for burial.

Anita went into mourning. Mel freaked out. He had had enough! He wrote himself one obsessive note after another. "Mourning? She is mourning as an orthodox Jew, which she is not. Bacon is one of her favorite dishes. Shellfish is one of her favorite dishes. She does not keep kosher. She's not even marginally conservative, virtually not only unorthodox, but totally reformed. When I needed help she wasn't there. I have had enough of this garbage. I can't depend on her, and I have to fend for myself. I'm tired of it."

And if Anita was really in mourning, why was she already back at the temple? Her mother remained in their house, sitting *shiva*. Yet Anita, who had refused to go in to work to help her husband, was at a temple meeting. It was already late, and Melvin was still waiting for his wife so they could go over some paperwork. He left his office to find her, with the intuitive feeling that she would not be home. He had had enough, and when he found the garage was empty, he exploded.

Speeding down the street toward Ventura Boulevard, Melvin drove to the temple to reclaim his wife. In a fit of rage, and despite his fear of heights, Melvin scaled the wall and dropped down the security drop to get into the temple's offices. He was not injured.

He pounded on the door.

"Who is there?"

"Melvin Green."

"State your business."

"I'll kick the door in if you don't open it."

The door opened. There was silence in the room as everyone stared at him, their shocked expressions impossible to hide. Anita walked out looking sheepish.

"I thought you were in mourning. What the hell are you doing here?"

"Never mind. Can't I even say goodbye?" Anita asked.

"Good-bye," Mel answered as he dragged Anita out of the building. He looked at his wife. He was distraught. "If you can work for them, you can work for me. Here's the mail. You've ignored it long enough with all your stupid funeral excuses. Take it to the post office, if you please."

"Mel, I don't want to go to the post office. It's late."

"Drop it off, Anita, or suffer the consequences."

For the remainder of the summer, Anita and Mel fought this way. But Anita wouldn't get out. She wanted the love, acceptance, and power that she got at the temple and from the rabbi, but she also wanted the financial security of a life with Mel. His pocketbook guaranteed that she and Scott, as well as the temple building fund, would be well taken care of. What Anita took a long time to understand and accept was that her goals were impossible to attain without angering and hurting her husband.

In 1988 Anita achieved a dream come true. She was chosen to serve as president of Shir Chadash. Despite her lack of education, her limited knowledge of politics, and her embarrassing husband, the temple members elected her to lead them into the nineties. Anita had finally been completely accepted by her peers.

For the next three years, Anita had almost no life of her own. A conscientious president, she refused to abandon her board members while they did the work she delegated. Anita remained involved in all aspects of temple life, and the synagogue's committees and programs thrived under her tutelage and direction.

Anita's presidency had more responsibilities than ever because the synagogue was now trying to build a home. There were months at a time when Anita worked well into the night and on weekends. She never seemed to have any energy or time left for Melvin. Even if she had, she would not have spent it with him. By this time Anita and Mel shared a loveless marriage that neither was willing to take the time to get out of. Anita told people she still loved Mel, but by now Mel said he felt nothing but hatred toward her. Both walked around complaining constantly about how awful the other one was.

During Anita's presidency, she and the temple suffered serious setbacks that affected her morale and the congregation's as well. The temple's massive building project was further delayed by legal and financial technicalities that caused costs to soar.

The Woodland Hills Homeowner's Association began fighting the temple to stop the building, and though the congregation eventually emerged victorious, the battle took several years and hundreds of thousands of dollars to win.

Anita had to pacify many frustrated temple members who wanted to see something for the money they were donating other than the sign on the temple acreage that read: FUTURE HOME OF SHIR CHADASH—THE NEW REFORM CONGREGATION. Apathy was at an all-time high and the building fund was almost depleted. Anita called upon the rabbi, and the two restructured the entire building fund-raising committee and programs.

Anita's problems with Mel escalated. He could not handle her presidency and the power it gave her. He hated that Anita now traveled openly with the rabbi and that no one seemed to care. He wanted to be "let off" the temple's debts, and he felt used because his wife was still writing more checks to Shir Chadash. Melvin's records indicated that he paid out a total of $192,000 in checks to Shir Chadash, in addition to being a guarantor on the land and having made a huge building-fund pledge. In reality, Melvin's total cash contribution to the temple was $50,000.

In the summer of 1989, Anita developed a tumor on her salivary gland that was caused by excessive smoking. The painful condition was further aggravated by her inordinately high level of stress. When Anita underwent surgery to correct the condition, the surgeon asked about her bruised neck and cheek. Anita told him it was nothing. She had just had a bad fall.

While she lay in the hospital recovering from the operation, many temple friends came to visit. On one side of the bed sat the rabbi and on the other sat Mel. Riva and Scott didn't know what to do. Temple members were there around the clock and Scott could not get his mother's attention. He finally left in frustration.

One night in July of 1989, Anita pulled into the garage after a late temple meeting and saw Mel's massive body standing in the window. When Anita entered the house, Mel began to scream.

"Where the hell have you been? I'm a fucking joke around there now, unless you need me to be at a temple dinner so you can look good."

"I never look good when you're around," Anita hollered back. "Do you know what a joke you are?"

"Who thinks I'm a joke? Tell me now. Which one of your damn whore friends told you I was a joke?"

"They all think it, idiot," Anita replied.

Mel had had enough. He grabbed his gun and began brandishing it wildly over the stairway banisters. Anita backed away.

"Why not kill me, Mel? Would that make you feel like more of a man?"

"I'd rather divorce you and leave you penniless. See if your temple cronies will still love and accept you when you're on welfare. Who will pay the damn building-fund pledge then? Think about that, Anita."

Anita began to cry. She ran to the bedroom, passing Melvin as she went by. He shoved her, knocking her hard into the wall and leaving a large bruise on her shoulders. It would be another week of long sleeves.

The two increased their threats of divorce throughout the year, but they continued to stay married to one another. They were entrapped by their own neurotic codependency. As the year drew to a close, Mel began a descent into a personal despair from which he would never emerge.

Mel's mother, June Green, had always been a good woman. She loved her son very much but had never been able to get through to him. His temper had scared her. As she lay dying, succumbing at last to the cancer that had ravaged her body for fifteen years, June valiantly tried to tell her son that he did not treat people properly. But she was too weak, and his hatred toward others was too strong to make a difference.

During the final days of her illness, it was her daughter-in-law, Anita, and her elder grandson, Michael, whom June would call for and derive comfort from. Anita was completely devoted to June and did everything she could to make her mother-in-law's last days comfortable and calm. On the morning June died, Anita and Mel had just left her. Her grandson, Michael, whom she had cared for and supported emotionally for many years, and her husband stood by her side.

Two days after her death, Rabbi Jacobs officiated at June Green's funeral, while Cantor Doug Cotler sang Anita's and June's favorite melodies and prayers in the background. In the middle of the funeral, Mel stood up and went to the podium where he gave a moving eulogy describing his mother as the greatest influence in his life.

After her death, Mel, always a jealous person, became furious that his son, Michael, was with June at the time of her death. Mel had always resented that his mother favored Michael, and he began resenting poor Michael even more after his mother passed away. Instead of being appreciative of all that Anita had done for his mother to make her comfortable during the end, Melvin seemed angrier with her than ever.

By the end of January, at least one person had had enough. Anita's twenty-two-year-old son, Scott, announced that he was moving in with his girlfriend, Clarissa, whom he intended to marry the following summer.

"Why are you doing a thing like that?" Anita asked.

"Because I love her."

Anita spoke in the voice of the stern parent. "She isn't Jewish and she's Hispanic. I'm not prejudiced, but you know our background. Think of your grandmother. What will this do to her?"

"She will understand. She always has in the past."

"Have you thought this all through? Aren't you too young to get married?"

"Mom, I want to marry her. She makes me feel good about myself." Scott seemed genuinely happy.

Anita and Mel made one attempt at functioning as a family as the two sat down to talk with Scott. Scott refused to budge and began to pack his belongings.

A few days after his announcement Scott received a curious letter from his stepfather. The letter was Mel's attempt at being loving. Perhaps he had remembered a lonely part of his life when he had turned to a woman for comfort. Whatever his reasons, Mel tried to reach out to Scott to explain why Anita was upset with him.

She is concerned that your passions are ruling you and maybe your need for identity and independence. She feels that you are marrying someone from a disparate culture and this might create any differences that will be less than a successful marriage or not as successful as it should be, and it will create in you a series of hardships that you will be obligated to face because you made a commitment to someone and it's not up to you to walk away from that commitment. She has had two marriages that were less than successful and she is hoping better for you.

She wants you to have the good life and achieve and marry someone preferably of your own culture, your own country, and your own religion. When you marry you consider just the moment but what you should consider is, can you grow old gracefully together and be committed to each other happily, not out of obligation and not because you have made a choice that's irrevocable.

Mel's letter seemed reflective of his own inner turmoil. If only he had married for the right reasons. Clearly he was implying that he and Anita were stuck in an irrevocable fate. Whatever was to happen would happen.

So, in early February, a few days after Scott moved out, Anita and Mel stopped being man and wife in the literal sense. It ended quickly; their attraction had long since waned. They made one last attempt at intimacy, but it filled them both with a deep sadness and melancholy.

Anita moved into Scott's old room and Mel went slowly insane. As he bordered on the brink of madness, he began to make more and more calls to Anita's friends to see what dirt he could dig up on her.

By this time Mel hated his wife so much that he openly solicited people to listen to his problems. He didn't care who he aired his dirty laundry to. When he could not find anyone who would listen to him, he would write long letters to his lawyers, his business associates, and to himself, explaining how much he hated his wife.

1990 was the year Mel's letters began in earnest. He wrote more and more, detailing the causes of his unhappiness. In one letter he wrote, "Anita waited until the rabbi's divorce was almost final to file for her own divorce. Once Steven was available, she had to file or she risked losing him."

14

The Groundbreaking

October 7, 1990

The longest summer of Anita's life had finally passed, and the High Holy Days had come and gone. The large congregation seemed uplifted and inspired by Rabbi Jacobs's wonderful services. At the close of Yom Kippur, the rabbi had called the congregation's children onto the bimah to be blessed. The room was filled with magic, and there was not a dry eye in the congregation. Anita was filled with hope for the future.

The temple held their High Holy Day services in the elaborate ballroom of the Woodland Hills Marriott Hotel. Earlier in the day, Anita and the rabbi checked into the room they would share for the holidays. During the service Rabbi Jacobs told one of his favorite stories, a story that perhaps best illustrates his ends-justify-the-means philosophy. It was a simple story.

One *Shabbat*, while a revered orthodox rabbi is studying Torah with a young student, a notorious gangster drives up to the small shul and hands the rabbi ten thousand dollars. Without saying a word, the rabbi takes the money. "For the *kinder*," the gangster says and then drives off leaving the student angry and bewildered.

The student can not hold his anger and finally questions the esteemed rabbi. "Rabbi, don't you know who that was? How he comes by that dirty money? How can you take it on *Shabbat* no less?

"I know," replies the rabbi. "I also know that for one

moment, maybe it was his mother's *yahrzeit*, he was for an instant trying to be a pious Jew. Who am I to discourage him?"

It seemed Rabbi Jacobs did not mind breaking the rules as long as he made someone feel good in the process. After concluding services, Steven and Anita went up to their room. Anita felt better than she had in ages, and he seemed euphoric. They discussed how wonderful the new year would be for both of them and for the congregation. Anita later expressed regret to Phyllis, at their last lunch together, that she and the rabbi had not been able to make love that day because Steven's children were staying in the adjoining room.

The awe of the High Holy Days and the response of the congregation told the temple leaders that whatever they were doing was working. By October, everybody was ready to work together toward building their common goal, a temple of their own.

This was the day, October 7, 1990, that the entire congregation had been waiting for. The groundbreaking ceremony would symbolize the beginning of the building of the new synagogue. The congregation had spent many years sharing quarters with the Woodland Hills Community Church, and it was time to move on. So, though the temple's board did not have the funds to build yet, the ceremony would take place.

Anita had confided to Phyllis that if the synagogue's members were inspired to raise building capital by the groundbreaking ceremony, then Steven would certainly marry her. Everyone knew she was the moving force behind the group that had brought the congregation to where it was today.

Phyllis remembered thinking, "All she wants to do is build a monument to that turkey."

Anita was compulsive and driven and had worked tirelessly to solve the congregation's horrendous land issues and other numerous problems.

Even in a town as tolerant of people's differences as Los Angeles, not everyone wants a temple in their backyard. The Woodland Hills Homeowners Association had fought the building of the temple. The legal battle was finally over, and Anita would be the one remembered for getting the job done. The rabbi knew it was true. Melvin couldn't take that away from her. Nobody could.

A formidable task lay ahead. Today's ceremony was only the beginning. Members would have to part with more of their money. The eighties were over, and the Los Angeles economy was already beginning a downward spiral.

Though many in the congregation were wealthy, the richest members were feeling the strain. They were carrying the financial burden for the majority of the congregants. The costs over the past few years had been astronomical, and the almost two million dollars that had been raised to build the temple had been spent instead on the high cost of carrying the land lease, property taxes, and unexpected legal fees. In addition, thirty-two families were guarantors to the loan. They shouldn't be asked to give more.

Anita knew that everybody would have to give and give generously. She also knew that some members were frustrated because they had nothing to show for their often generous previous contributions. Not a single brick had yet been laid. For these people, giving more money, especially in difficult times, might prove impossible.

On the morning of the ceremony, Anita dressed and left Steven, making the twenty-minute drive from the rabbi's rented house in Northridge to her new apartment in Encino. Anita wanted to shower and she was meeting her mother there. She hurried down Balboa Boulevard, wanting to arrive at her apartment before her mother.

The day was perfect, the air crisp and cool. Taking advantage of the empty roads, Anita rolled down the top of her cherry-red Corvette, turned up the volume in the cassette deck, and sped happily down the streets. She hadn't felt this good in months.

Anita pulled into her apartment's underground garage. She showered quickly and was drying her hair when her mother entered. Walking into Anita's bedroom, Riva stared at her elder daughter's reflection in the mirror. Anita was radiant, her face glowing with happiness. Riva was momentarily stunned. It had been years since Riva could remember seeing Anita this happy.

Riva exclaimed, "You look better than you have in months, darling. I'm so proud of you for finally leaving him."

Anita didn't answer, but kept smiling. She seldom discussed her personal life with her mother; her approval was far too important to risk. It was easier to have Riva think that she was glowing because she was finally rid of Melvin, rather than because she was elated over being with Rabbi Jacobs. Her mother had never liked Steven Jacobs.

Riva Rice sensed what was going on. She had suspected all along that Anita was seeing the rabbi. But her daughter had insisted that they were just good friends. Now Anita looked like she was falling in love. Riva did not want it to happen again so quickly and once again with the wrong man. As a mother, she could not face watching her daughter suffer once more.

"Why don't you just be alone for awhile. Don't get involved with another man. You have so many friends now, and a lot of respect in your community. Take some time for yourself, to live."

"Oh Ma, I will." Anita laughed and added, "Don't worry so much!" Then, wondering to herself just how long she could hide her secret from her perceptive mother, Anita and Riva headed to the temple's land.

Mother and daughter went to the groundbreaking service together. It was a rare occasion on which Riva would join Anita at temple. But today Anita had insisted. A shovel reclaimed from Auschwitz was to be used to break ground, and Riva and other holocaust survivors, along with Anita and the rabbi, were to have the honor of turning the earth.

Exiting her car, Anita walked briskly to the temple's leased land with her mother at her side. Located directly across the road from the sprawling Pierce College campus in Woodland Hills, the land was part of a semirural haven surrounded by high trees and several farms. Centrally located, the temple would attract members from all areas of the Valley. The western part of the San Fernando Valley was made up of several small, tightly knit communities, each with its own history and character. The temple's land was located almost exactly in the center of the west valley, in the middle of Woodland Hills, and equal distance away from Encino, Calabasas, and Hidden Hills, where the Valley's wealthier Jewish populations lived. Encino, Tarzana, and Woodland Hills supported about ten congregations of varying size. By 1990 Shir

Chadash–The New Reform Congregation had grown in size to almost six hundred families.

The Jewish population in these communities was large, politically active, and temple-going. Parents here wanted their children to receive formal Jewish educations, and affiliations of Jews in temples was higher than the national average.

Today, the raw earth had been transformed by the temple's groundbreaking committee. It was freshly graded, and the weeds that had been growing rapidly throughout the summer had been removed. The dirt was covered with green Astroturf that was comfortable to walk and sit on. A large, flower-covered podium stood behind a strip of dirt where the groundbreaking shovel rested beside a microphone. Rows of Astroturf surrounded the dirt, and hundreds of rented white party chairs were arranged in rows around the Astroturf.

Anita couldn't believe that the groundbreaking committee had set up a huge party in the middle of an empty dirt lot. Brightly colored blue and white Shir Chadash balloons filled the sky, lending a festive touch to the setting. Anita watched them floating in the air, making a large arch visible in all directions over the San Fernando Valley. She smiled, knowing that everyone for miles would finally see Shir Chadash was here to stay.

On the stage, behind a stunning flower arrangement, were chairs reserved for various clergy members, politicians, guests of honor, and herself. Anita looked over the typed list of dignitaries' names and was proud to be part of such a group. She had come a long way financially and socially since she had married her first husband, Roger Arnow, back in Queens.

When Rabbi Jacobs arrived, he too looked surprised by the setting. Perhaps he had expected to walk onto a dirt lot, as opposed to the inspiring outdoor setting that had been created from the raw landscape. The rabbi walked over to where Anita and the others stood and surveyed the scene. He seemed amazed by the power of the moment. Nobody said a word as they looked out at the vacant earth and waited for the con-gregation to begin arriving.

By eleven o'clock the land was packed with over five hundred congregants, guests, and friends, all clearly moved by the inspirational service. Anita and her mother were among

LEFT: Anita Rice, eighteen months old, smiles for the camera. A bright, curious child, Anita lit up the lives of her parents. *Courtesy: Rebecca Rice*

RIGHT: Anita Rice on the way to the beach. Outside her new green-and-white house on Chester Street in Long Beach, New York. August 1952. *Courtesy: Rebecca Rice*

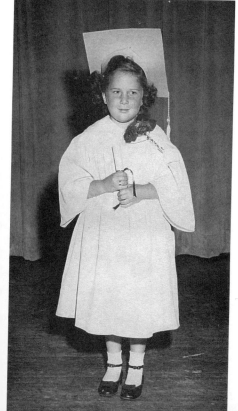

Anita at her kindergarten graduation. She was six years old and already a handful. *Courtesy: Rebecca Rice*

Anita Rice's high school senior portrait taken in April 1965. Anita was headstrong and sophisticated by then and "boy crazy."
Courtesy: Rebecca Rice

Melvin Green, a jock and an honors student during high school, was also a recluse and a bully. His interest in girls had not yet developed.
Courtesy: Melvin Green, Cory Green

Melvin Green and June Green, the mother whom he adored, celebrating his twentieth birthday on the beach in Monterey, California, June 27, 1954. *Courtesy: Melvin Green*

Melvin, who joined the army in 1953, thrived on the regimentation of army life and to this day has never been happier. *Courtesy: Melvin Green*

TOP: Melvin and Anita became involved sometime after she began working for him in the mid-seventies. This picture was taken in 1977, on one of their first dates. *Courtesy: Melvin Green*

CENTER: Melvin Green, in 1978, recites the kiddush, the traditional Jewish blessing over the wine. *Courtesy: Melvin Green*

BOTTOM: Melvin and Anita Green, a year after their marriage, at a birthday party for friend Phyllis Baltin. Anita was thirty-four years old, and Melvin was forty-seven. *Courtesy: Phyllis Baltin*

TOP: Cary, Melvin, Anita, and Scott attend a bar mitzvah at Shir Chadash in May 1985. *Courtesy: Phyllis Baltin*

CENTER: Anita and Mel Green at the reception dinner after the bar mitzvah. Mel wore the superman tie, his favorite, that Phyllis had just given him for his fiftieth birthday a month earlier. *Courtesy: Phyllis Baltin*

BOTTOM: Anita and Phyllis at the bar mitzvah of Phyllis's sons. Anita, at thirty-seven, was already showing signs of stress. She was very unhappy in her second marriage and told Phyllis in many ways it was far worse than her first marriage had been. *Courtesy: Phyllis Baltin*

Melvin Green in his accounting office in May 1989.
Courtesy: Los Angeles Police Department

FACING PAGE

TOP: Anita and Mel at a family party in July 1988. She was under a lot of stress and had aged considerably. Mel had put on another 150 pounds.

CENTER: June and Hy Green, Mel's parents, in 1985. June was a warm and loving woman who suffered immensely from Mel and Hy's treatment of her. She loved her daughter-in-law, Anita, and had warned her several times to stay away from Melvin. *Courtesy: Phyllis Baltin*

BOTTOM: Encino movie marquee announces high holy day services for the New Reform Congregation in 1984. *Courtesy: Michele Samit*

Anita Green in August 1990. This photo, the official temple photograph of Anita as president, was taken after she left her husband and just a few months before her murder.
Courtesy: Rebecca Rice

Rabbi Steven B. Jacobs in the early fall of 1990, the year his life would change drastically. His relationship with Anita was in full swing by then. *Courtesy: Miriam Jacobs*

the first to dig into the earth with the shovel. There wasn't a dry eye as everyone linked arms and sang the traditional prayers. Rabbi Jacobs filled a small container with earth to be placed in the cornerstone of the new sanctuary when it was completed.

Music played as parents shared the beauty of the day with their children. Then religious-school students burst into song. "We're standing on the shoulders of the ones who came before us," Rabbi Jacobs told the children. "We are the heirs of yesterday and the architects of tomorrow."

On the sidelines, watching, one woman stood alone. Ginger Jacobs, the rabbi's first wife and the mother of his four children, carefully studied the faces in the crowd and on the podium. She had heard the rumors and had confronted Anita and had gotten a partial confession. In addition, Melvin Green had been hounding Ginger for months. Though her ex-husband had denied the rumors, she told some she knew they were true.

Long after the congregants had left, Anita stood watching the clean-up crews. She couldn't tell whether it was hours or minutes before she got in the car and drove to her apartment. She was filled with happiness and wonderful memories of a beautiful day, yet at the same time she felt a deep sadness. She wanted her marriage to end so that she could start her new fantasy life, but she had not yet figured out how to escape the nightmare alive.

IV

The Investigation

October 1990–April 1991

15

The Doctor Who Prayed

"Something terrible has happened. There's been a tragic accident and Anita's been shot." The message traveled quickly throughout the tight temple community.

"What do you mean, *shot*? Who would shoot Anita?" were the shocked responses.

Within hours, "Who shot Anita Green?" became the "Who shot J.R." gossip game of the Valley. Everyone suddenly had an opinion and a conspiracy theory. The killer was a hired gun. Many knew Mel hated Anita. Some of Mel's clients and business associates had shady pasts. Did Mel pay one of them to shoot his wife? Neo-Nazi hate mail had been received during the bitter two-year court battle to build the temple. What about the community college district? The rumors continued to fly. Nobody seemed to know what was really taking place.

A few minutes before the end of his ten-hour shift, a weary Dr. Phil Hassen listened to the emergency-room scanner; a paramedic was calling with news that a female, code-three gunshot victim was en route. Dr. Hassen, dressed in a wrinkled white coat, took off his glasses, rubbed his eyes, pulled on his mustache, and listened to the scanner in disbelief, fighting the exhaustion taking over his senses. Was he hearing correctly? A gunshot victim at 10:30 in the morning?

North Hollywood Hospital serviced a poorer section of the Valley, as well as the middle-class residents that surrounded it. Many of the patients seen in the emergency room came in with ailments that mirrored urban society's increasing ills. Though a small community hospital, it had one of the busiest emergency rooms in the Valley. That week alone, in addition to drug overdoses, the emergency-room doctors had seen a fourteen-year-old suicide attempt, a baby who had been burned by her parents, and a rape victim. Now they were about to receive a gunshot victim.

Anita Molly Green was wheeled into the hospital in the midst of a full cardiac arrest. She was dying, and Dr. Hassen's first concern was to resuscitate and stabilize her. He began CPR. The battle had begun.

Her pulse rate was 174. Her blood pressure was 70 over 35, and she remained unconscious and unresponsive. Anita was suffering from a rapid, irregular contraction of the heart muscle. Her blood pressure was fluctuating constantly from the tremendous loss of blood.

The emergency-room doctor skillfully inserted a chest tube into Anita's trachea so breathing would be easier. He carefully avoided the gaping wound in her neck; he would deal with that later, after he got a cardiac rhythm going again.

Upon first examination, what worried Dr. Hassen the most was that Anita's brain had been without oxygen for some time. She could be brain-dead already, but that determination would not be made until after the acute stage was over. They had to give her every chance possible to pull through.

A hospital *Code Blue* demanded the very best from an emergency-room doctor: split-second decisions, physical stamina, absolute concentration, and the ability to let go when the battle had been lost. For gunshot victims, the tension is even more apparent, with the added pressure of dealing with the often massive injury itself, as well as treating the results of it, such as heart and other organ failure. Some doctors thrived on the excitement of it all, saying there was no experience quite like it. According to other doctors, Dr. Hassen wasn't one of them.

Dr. Hassen's immediate objective was to pump Anita full of life-giving fluids. The gunshot wound was quickly draining her body of blood and other fluids. The doctor hoped replacing them would bring her blood pressure back up, which would, in turn, jump start both her heart and lungs.

A nurse wheeled in the defibrillator and Hassen grabbed the paddles. Skillfully positioning them against Anita's torso, the doctor pressed the trigger buttons. No response. He repeated the procedure.

After what seemed like an eternity, someone shouted, "Blood pressure rising; we've got a sinus rhythm."

Dr. Hassen looked at the monitor and saw the pattern was returning to normal. After stabilizing her breathing, the doctor made a quick examination of the rest of Anita's body. He noted that the main injury was a gunshot wound to the neck, which had exited through her cheek. Positive the wound would require surgery, the physician called the head-and-neck surgeon on duty, Dr. Warren Line.

Before noon, Dr. Warren Line joined Dr. Hassen and the nurses hovering over Anita. Dr. Line stood over six-feet tall, with broad shoulders and large hands. A man in his late thirties, with a strong physical presence, the other doctors moved away from the patient when Line began his lengthy exam. Despite his size, the nurses noticed his gentle manner with Anita. Though she remained comatose, the doctors talked to her throughout his entire exam.

The surgeon noted that the bullet had perforated the back of Anita's neck, injuring the left vertebral artery, before exiting through the left check. Her condition was critical. Line ordered an angiogram to tell him where the internal damage was, so he could plan his surgery accurately.

While he was in the emergency room with Anita, Dr. Line, a calm and thoughtful man, was approached by a top hospital administrator. Taking the doctor aside, he whispered, "Do whatever you can to save her. The hospital is making everything available to you. This is an important woman, and we'll be watched closely by the community."

"I do whatever I can for all my patients," he answered. Although known around the city for his surgical skills, he was even more highly regarded for his avoidance of politics. Warren Line treated the poorest uninsured patient the same as the wealthiest dignitary.

A surgeon trained at Los Angeles County Hospital, Dr. Line had firsthand experience with gunshot-wound victims. Often surgery did the trick. The compassionate doctor wasn't about to give up.

Today, Line found himself surrounded by other doctors,

administrators, and the police, all offering their opinions. The tension in the emergency room was almost unbearable. Line couldn't remember ever seeing people work themselves into such a tizzy. Who was this woman? he wondered.

At about 1:00 P.M., Dr. Line wrote the orders to have Anita Green moved from the busy emergency room and admitted to the hospital's intensive care unit. At the time, he wasn't certain of the extent of Anita's brain damage. He wanted another opinion, and was grateful Dr. Hassen had already called in a neurologist to consult with them about the brain damage that concerned them all.

Dr. Line went out to talk with the family, who by now should have been notified. As the surgeon entered the ICU waiting area, he prepared himself for the dreaded conversation, carefully choosing the words he would use. These meetings never got any easier for him. When you graduate from medical school, you are called a doctor. These meetings made you feel like one. Line felt so much for the families. They always looked to him to do something. Deep in thought, he almost bumped into the short man who was talking with one of the nurses.

"Here's her doctor now, Rabbi," the nurse answered.

"I'm Dr. Warren Line."

"Rabbi Steven Jacobs. How is she?"

The doctor looked at the visibly shaken clergyman. He looked scared. He didn't know how much the rabbi could tolerate to hear, and at this point wanted to break the news as gently as possible.

"She's had a horrible injury. We don't know if she's going to survive it yet. Her condition's critical and we're taking her to the ICU. There's some brain damage, but we're not sure at this point how extensive it is. Only time will tell. I'll be praying with all of you."

"Can I see her?" the rabbi asked.

Line led the rabbi toward the ICU, where the head emergency-room nurse, Ellen Morrison, had just taken Anita. The room was guarded by two police officers. The rabbi stared at them.

Watching, the doctor explained, "When I worked at County Hospital, gunmen often posed as visitors and went in to finish off their jobs. This is normal police procedure for a gunshot victim." Then he tried to prepare Rabbi Jacobs for Anita's condition. "The bullet tore her apart. She's lost quite a bit of blood. She looks terrible."

When the two men entered the room, they found Anita surrounded by doctors and nurses busily attempting to stabilize her. While one nurse checked her vitals, another closely monitored the fluids flowing into her, both keeping meticulous notes of everything.

Dr. Line signaled them to leave so the rabbi could be alone with Anita. He looked closely at the rabbi. As he did, he noticed the police staring in their direction. They never took their eyes off the rabbi, glancing away only when someone else approached.

The rabbi took Anita's hand and began to stroke it. He started to pray. The doctor watched in silence. Rabbi Jacobs was tender and caring. Obviously she meant a lot to him. Line could feel the rabbi's pain.

Anita looked awful. She was bruised, and her head was completely bandaged, the blood still visible. There were dozens of tubes attached to her, life-support equipment and intravenous fluids, including bags of blood.

To the doctor it appeared that Rabbi Jacobs handled the sight before him better than most. The doctor knew clergymen routinely counseled and visited with gravely ill patients. Many detested the job and averted their eyes. Rabbi Jacobs never took his eyes off Anita. The doctor turned away, not wanting the rabbi to see his tears.

The rabbi had been the first to arrive after his secretary had told him where Anita was. Melvin Green had called her with the news that Anita was in the hospital and things were serious.

"But I just talked to her on her car phone a few minutes ago, Mel," Sylvia Holste-Lillie, the rabbi's secretary, exclaimed. "She was pulling into the driveway. What happened?"

"She is very ill, and not likely to make it." That was all he would tell her.

After the ominous phone call, Sylvia called the hospital to find out what had happened. She beeped the rabbi, who returned her call and then phoned the hospital himself. The rabbi arrived as soon as possible and was waiting for the surgeon in the second-floor waiting room adjacent to the ICU.

He had already spoken on the phone with the police, and they had made an appointment to question him in his house at 3:00 P.M. As far as the police were concerned, Rabbi Jacobs was the last person who had seen Anita Green before the shooting.

The North Hollywood Police Department's homicide coordinator, Mike Coffey, arrived at the hospital at a little after 2:00 P.M., when he had finally finished at the crime scene. Entering Anita's room, Coffey found the rabbi with her, praying. Observing the rabbi's behavior, Coffey noticed he was distraught, a normal response given the circumstances.

Rabbi Jacobs left the room to use a telephone. One officer told Coffey that the rabbi was constantly on the telephone. On one phone call, the officer overhead him say, "I just know Mel's involved. She was so frightened of him. I'm frightened for my safety as well." The officer told Coffey what he had overheard.

Meanwhile, the hospital staff was also worried about safety. Anita, admitted under the alias of Ruth Bell, was well hidden from the outside world. But family members and friends were beginning to arrive. Hospital security had been alerted, having been informed by homicide detectives that family members are always first in the line of suspects.

Concerned security personnel asked the police to remain with Anita at all times and to approve everyone who would enter her room. Detective Coffey was told by the hospital administrators that Melvin Green was a great risk to Anita and was not to be allowed into the room. Coffey wanted to know why the hospital thought Melvin posed a security risk. Who was providing them with information?

Coffey watched the rabbi reluctantly leave Anita's side when the doctors and nurses resumed their work. The rabbi walked slowly, head bowed. Coffey knew he was leaving to meet detectives at his house.

To Coffey, he seemed like an okay kind of guy. And he was a rabbi, the perfect "Mr. Citizen." But did he know something? After all, Jacobs had been the last person to see Anita Molly Green before the shooting. Melvin Green had already told the police the rabbi was "screwing" his wife. Coffey didn't have to be brilliant to know they needed this guy on their side.

An hour later, Detectives Sonny Medina and Gary Arnold interviewed the rabbi in his Northridge home. As the detectives asked the rabbi questions, he appeared to be struggling with something. It was obvious he wasn't comfortable when they questioned him about his and Anita's personal relationship.

Jacobs reluctantly told the detectives that Anita had spent Wednesday night at his house. They had watched a little television together. Mostly they talked. The rabbi explained that Anita and he were very good friends.

"What did you talk about?" Media asked.

"Mostly about problems, about life, nothing specific. I knew she was going to see Melvin," the rabbi added. "Before she went to sleep, Anita told me she was supposed to meet Mel at his office in the morning to do some work."

When questioned further, the rabbi said he did not know what time she left in the morning because Anita had not awakened him. He woke up a little before his secretary called him with the information that Anita had been taken to the hospital and was seriously ill, at a little after 10:30 A.M.

"What else can you tell us that might help out our search for the shooter?" Arnold asked.

To the detectives, the rabbi appeared rigid and uncomfortable. Though he was obviously distraught, he was very controlled, never letting his emotions get the best of him.

"I performed Anita and Mel Green's marriage about fourteen years ago," he incorrectly stated. "The marriage began to deteriorate about five years ago. Anita and Mel are members of my congregation. Anita is very active in the temple and devotes many hours there. She is the temple president and has been for three years."

"Does she work at the temple all day long?" Arnold asked.

"No, but she's in contact with us all day long." The rabbi explained that Mel resented the time Anita spent at the temple. "Mel Green is a very jealous person," Rabbi Jacobs said. "Anita is not permitted to go anywhere or do anything with another male without being accused of adultery."

Detective Medina never missed a beat. He looked directly at the rabbi. "Did he accuse you of committing adultery with her?"

The rabbi sighed. He tried to answer the question with another question and then tried to avoid it altogether.

The detective repeated his question. The rabbi stared straight at him, started to answer, and then turned away and gave him another evasive answer.

"Yes. Mel would call me on the phone and make annoying accusations about what Anita and I were doing together. I'm a rabbi, she was my president; we had to spend a lot of time together. We weren't sleeping together," the visibly shaken rabbi added.

The detectives knew they had struck a nerve and their questioning was making the rabbi uncomfortable. "We understand this is difficult for you. It always is."

Detective Arnold chose his words carefully, not wanting to offend the clergyman. "Were you involved with Anita?"

The rabbi became indignant. "Of course not. Mel accused me of sleeping with Anita. It isn't true. We were just close friends."

"Why did Anita sleep here Wednesday night?"

Again the rabbi's story just didn't sound right to the detectives. "We spent a lot of time together. She was afraid of her husband, so she came here," he explained.

To both detectives, Steven Jacobs's answer was, at best, evasive. He was trying to hide something.

"Was last night the first night she slept here?" Medina continued.

"She's slept here a couple of times since she left Mel's house in June. She never felt safe around Mel. I warned her that he was dangerous, especially since she told me of his assaulting her several times. That's why I occasionally let her stay here. She was scared, and perhaps she was lonely."

Rabbi Jacobs went on to tell the detectives that Mel had been his accountant for many years, but he'd fired him in August, because his taxes had not yet been prepared and returned.

The detectives wondered what the rabbi still knew. They would have to question him again at a more appropriate time.

Back at the Medical Center of North Hollywood, the angiogram confirmed active hemorrhaging into the left side of the neck. The results were sent off to Dr. Line while Anita was at her CAT scan.

Sometime after the scan, Dr. Richard Mendius, a prominent Valley neurologist, examined Anita Molly Green. Dr. Mendius was a short man who resembled Sigmund Freud, complete with a little goatee, a round, pudgy face, and wire-rimmed glasses. Mendius looked like a typical psychiatrist or neurologist, scholarly and a little eccentric. A respected man in his field, the other doctors were curious as to whether or not he'd be able to pinpoint the amount of brain damage that had occurred.

Dr. Mendius concluded Anita's estimated time of ischemic injury to the brain—the time the brain was without oxygen—at about ten minutes. The maximum time for the brain to be deprived of oxygen without injury was unknown, but most doctors believed the magic time was about four minutes. Dr. Mendius knew from experience, however, that things could go either way. Only time would tell the condition of Anita's brain. He wanted to give her time to declare herself.

The neurologist's immediate concern was to relieve and monitor the pressure in her skull. Dr. Mendius sought a neurosurgeon to put an intercranial-pressure monitor in Anita's head. Known as a Burr-hole, the surgical procedure was quite effective in these situations. Dr. Mendius contacted Dr. Loren Hooten to do the surgery later in the evening, after Anita's neck surgery was finished.

Anita was brought back to her intensive care room to be watched over by Ellen Morrison, the unit's head nurse. Ellen showed a remarkable understanding of wounds and the complications that can arise from them. The ICU doctors and surgeons felt fortunate when Ellen was assigned to their patients. Her talents at detecting problems early on were remarkable.

In just a few moments, Ellen noticed Anita's neck was expanding, rapidly filling with blood and other fluids. Calling Dr. Line, she informed him, "Your patient's dying, doctor. I think you'd better get here right away."

Dr. Warren Line rushed over, glanced at Anita's neck, and reevaluated the situation. Calling his partner, Dr. David

Aroesty, he said, "Get here immediately. I'm ready for surgery and I need you to assist." The doctor then requested the next available operating room.

Meanwhile, a few miles away, at about 4:00 P.M., Riva Rice reached for the ringing telephone.

"Are you sitting down, Riva dear? We've been trying to reach you. Anita is gravely ill," Mel's secretary, Irene Sherwyn, said.

"What do you mean, gravely ill? What happened?" Riva asked.

"I don't know; just go to her. She's at the Medical Center of North Hollywood," Irene blurted, quickly hanging up the telephone.

As she grabbed her purse and telephoned her neighbor, Jackie Meister, to accompany her, Riva knew something terrible had happened. Anita's doctors weren't located at North Hollywood Hospital. Surely if Anita were merely ill, she'd go to the hospital where her doctors were on staff. Riva was sure her daughter had been in a terrible car accident. She'd always hated that goddamned sports car Anita loved to drive.

The two women entered the hospital at a little before 5:00 P.M. "Where's my daughter, Anita Green?" Riva worriedly asked at the information desk.

"There's nobody here by that name," the lady at the desk replied.

"I know she's here. I'm her mother. I've got to see her."

"I'll try to find out if she's here. Please sit down," the receptionist said.

One of Anita's ICU nurses was contacted by the front desk. Ellen Morrison went downstairs to prepare Riva. A sweet, caring woman, with a reputation for being one of the most supportive crisis nurses on staff, Ellen knew she'd have to tell Riva to see Anita before she was taken to surgery, in case she didn't survive the operation. How could she prepare the elderly woman for what she was about to face?

Approaching Riva, Ellen searched for the right words. "Your daughter's been shot. We've admitted her under another name to protect her. The doctors are preparing to take her to surgery in just a few minutes," she said, her warm voice filled with compassion and empathy. Ellen watched for signs that the information was more than Riva could handle.

Riva began to shake. "Anita's been shot?" she asked tearfully. "What do you mean? What happened? I want to see her."

"That's fine. I'll take you to her." The nurse's heart went out to Riva. "I want to prepare you. She looks awful. You can expect the worst and then some. I want you to take a few deep breaths before we go upstairs. Try to brace yourself. I'll be by your side the whole time."

Knowing what she was about to face would be horrendous, Riva hugged her friend, Jackie, and left her downstairs. She then went upstairs with Ellen Morrison to see what was left of her elder child.

Riva exited the elevator at the ICU area, where Anita lay in the small corner room. Several uniformed police officers were standing in key locations.

Rabbi Jacobs sat in the small ICU waiting lounge with two temple staff members. He had spent the last hour periodically checking with Anita's doctors. Glancing at Riva, his eyes filled with tears and he rose to greet her.

With the young nurse beside her, Riva went to see Anita. From her first glance Riva Rice thought it unlikely her daughter would survive. The doctors were just about ready to take Anita to surgery. Riva was grateful they weren't giving up yet, but as she stared at Anita, she knew not to expect miracles.

As she looked at her daughter, Riva began to shake. "This isn't her. This can't be my baby. What happened? Can somebody tell me what happened?" Nobody answered her.

She remembered looking at the faces of the police, the doctors, and the rabbi, all of whom had seen this kind of thing before. Every one of them was crying with her.

Anita's surgery began at a little after 5:30 P.M. Minutes melted into hours as the family awaited some word of her condition. Riva and the rabbi had returned downstairs to join the others in the hospital's main waiting room.

During the long wait Riva was haunted by the memory of the last time she had seen Anita. It was nine days earlier, Tuesday, October 16, 1990, at about eight in the evening. Anita had come to visit and to borrow twenty-five thousand dollars, because she said Melvin hadn't given her any money since she had moved out in July. Anita looked terrible, and Riva knew she was terrified of something. When Riva questioned her, Anita just hugged her mother and said she was upset about the divorce.

Riva's memories were interrupted by the entrance of her twenty-two-year-old grandson, Scott Arnow, running toward her. He was screaming, his voice carrying across the hospital. "He did it. He did it. I just know he did it." Scott was very upset.

Nobody asked Scott about his suspicions, but they knew instinctively that he was referring to Mel. Riva turned to Scott's wife, Clarissa, not knowing what to say to Scott. Clarissa turned away.

The rabbi attempted to calm Scott. Indeed, he had expressed the same thoughts as Scott to several others, but now was not the time for accusations. The rabbi explained to Scott what had happened and that his mother was currently in surgery. Riva heard him add, "Things aren't hopeless yet, Scott."

Riva was relieved when Scott's father, Anita's first husband, Roger Arnow, arrived a few minutes later. She hadn't seen her ex-son-in-law in quite awhile, but he had remained close to his son.

Scott and Roger had the sort of relationship that many adult children wish for. They were good friends who enjoyed one another's company. They were always there for each other during crises. Scott had called his father as soon as he heard about the shooting. Riva knew Scott would need Roger's love more than ever.

Uniformed police officers and detectives in street clothes remained stationed throughout the small community hospital. Some observed the family; others talked to doctors.

Lily Lopez arrived at the hospital around 6:30 P.M. Mel's shocked receptionist hugged Riva. "I never thought it would end this way. All the bickering. I'm so sorry, Riva." Her words would haunt Riva for months to come.

A little later, while his estranged wife was still in surgery, Melvin Green arrived at the hospital and greeted his friends and family members. Nobody was glad to see him. He gingerly placed a kiss on his mother-in-law's cheek. Glancing at Scott's angry expression, he decided not to approach him. Mel paced up and down the room, not knowing who to talk to.

Melvin was unaware of his stepson's accusations which had been made just minutes earlier. He had only begun to hear some of the circulating rumors. All of his wife's visitors seemed angry at him. These were people who meant a lot to him as well. Did everyone suspect that he was involved just because he and Anita were having a few problems with their divorce? Didn't they know he wanted the divorce she was asking for too? Why was everyone so eager to abandon him in his time of need?

Melvin felt alone and angry. Seeking conversation, he sat down next to Roger Arnow. Roger worked up his nerve and turned to him, demanding to know what was going on. At that point Melvin became even angrier. He expressed his outrage at being questioned by the police and wanted to know if Roger thought their questioning was appropriate.

Roger was shocked. Someone had tried to murder his wife, and Mel was sitting next to him showing no concern. All he seemed to care about was himself.

Mel continued complaining to Roger. "They think I did it," he said. "I've always hated cops. You know they're Anti-Semitic." He then proceeded to carefully explain his morning to Roger, outlining his every move before the shooting. He kept going over where he was sitting in the office, what he thought when he heard that someone in a red car had been shot. "I tried to help her," Mel added, "but it was too late."

Roger thought Melvin's confession odd, but he had always known Mel to be odd. Still, he was not prepared for Mel's next question.

"Do you have keys to her apartment?" Mel asked.

"What?" Roger replied, unbelieving. "I don't even know where she lives." This man is nuts, Roger thought. Why is he asking me this?

"She lives exactly one mile away from our house. I've clocked it many times. However you go, it's one mile on the odometer," Mel added.

Roger thought Mel's remark was very strange and felt he had to get away from him. "Mel, can you excuse me? I want to be with Scott," Roger said. He slipped away quietly, leaving Mel alone.

Meanwhile, the surgeons working on Anita's neck found the vascular damage was extensive and the bleeding was still out of control. After giving it their best shot, the doctors agreed that there was nothing else they could do to save her. Knowing the police wanted to find a bullet, the doctors explored her neck further to see if they could locate one, but they were unsuccessful. Finding only a few minute fragments in the tissue of the jaw, the surgeons felt certain that the bullet had either shattered into hundreds of tiny pieces or had exited from her cheek. They had done all they could for Anita. Dr. Line volunteered to break the news to the family.

Anita's surgeon, Dr. Line, and the neurologist, Dr. Mendius, entered the lobby. The two doctors compassionately told the family Anita's condition was worsening. One doctor contended that even if Anita did live, she could remain in a vegetative state. He was preparing them for what was beginning to happen. Dr. Line did not want the family to lose all hope, but at the same time he didn't want to give them false hopes.

When Rabbi Jacobs turned away from the doctors and walked toward Scott, he passed Roger and whispered, "It would take a miracle."

Then he turned to Scott and, more upbeat, said, "They're still trying to stabilize your mom. We'll see her early in the morning. There's nothing any of us can do now except pray."

Next, the rabbi spoke to an emotionally distraught Riva, who had remained strong throughout the surgery but now, realizing the situation, was bordering on shock. "I'm calling Linda; she needs to get here."

Rabbi Jacobs phoned Riva's younger daughter, Linda, in Philadelphia and told her the news, asking her to arrive as soon as possible. The rabbi then remained on the phone, calling everyone who had beeped him asking him about Anita. He told each person that the only thing left to do was pray.

Walking slowly, her head bent, Riva Rice left the hospital to try and get a few hours of sleep. Riva knew that Mel Green had made her daughter suffer for many years. The extent of that suffering was about to be revealed to her, whether she wanted to hear it or not. She felt frightened and helpless. These feelings haunted her and kept her awake through the long dark night.

16

I Wanted Her to Leave Me Alone

Before noon on the day of the shooting, while doctors fought valiantly to save Anita Green's life, homicide detectives were already hard at work to find clues that would lead them to Anita's shooter.

The fact that Anita Green was a popular community leader and a well-loved woman didn't make their jobs any easier. Within hours, the heat was on the police to find and apprehend the gunman.

Detective Coffey needed help. However aggressive and tenacious, Coffey had many cases under his immediate direction, and they all needed his supervision and guidance on a minute-by-minute basis. He was swamped. He would need a strong detective to handle what appeared to be a complex case.

Coffey assigned the case to Ray Hernandez, a dedicated detective with the experience and ability to handle a difficult and unusual crime like this one. Since Hernandez was industrious and hardworking, Coffey knew he would aggressively pursue all leads.

While several officers photographed the crime scene and others waited at the hospital, Melvin Green was interviewed at the station. The police quickly learned he was a likely suspect, the estranged husband going through a bitter divorce. Though they knew he wasn't the gunman, his odd actions at the crime scene indicated to the police that he merited further investigation.

During his first interview, the atmosphere in the questioning room was neutral, since it had not yet been determined whether Melvin was a victim or a murderer.

Because Ray Hernandez had not yet arrived, Detective Jorge Armenta interviewed a calm and confident Melvin Green. He didn't seem to be at all traumatized by his wife's shooting or particularly concerned about her condition. Armenta found Green rude, disrespectful, and not the least bit remorseful.

"My wife moved out July 15 and filed for divorce July 16," Mel said matter of factly.

"Is she seeing anybody right now?" Armenta asked.

"Yes, Rabbi Steven Bennett Jacobs," Mel shouted. He proceeded to repeat the name four times and then spelled it out slowly two more times for the detectives. "If I cry, I cry; that's about it," Mel bellowed, not looking like he was really about to cry at all.

"It's perfectly normal to cry," said the detective.

"How long have Anita and Mr. Jacobs been seeing each other?" Armenta asked.

"Minimum, a year, probably a lot longer from what people have told me once they knew I was separated from her."

"Is this the cause for your separation?" Armenta asked.

Mel's voice was filled with sarcasm and anger. "I don't know. I don't think it was that alone. I'm sure it was the precipitating factor once I was aware of it. I was just fed up with her. She was getting lazy, not working, not being a wife. That's about all I can say. We were just going in different directions and I didn't want any part of her anymore. I just wanted her to leave me alone."

Armenta tried not to let Mel know that his answers were painting an interesting story for the police. The detective asked, "Aside from today, when was the last time you saw Anita?"

"I'd have to look at my calendar," Mel said. "I'm guessing sometime last week when she came in to do some work. She works for me periodically, when she's in the mood."

"Anything unusual that day? Any arguments?"

"Just the usual: When are you going to give me some money? When are you going to work? I asked her. It was just a pissing contest at this point. I said, fine, we'll let the attorneys handle it. We'll go to court and settle it. I loved the woman. I didn't particularly want to hurt her. I just was hurting myself, but that's about it. This is not what I wanted to happen."

In a "think session" later with Coffey, the detectives admitted they doubted the truthfulness of Mel's last statement. Armenta noted he had never seen a husband act this way. Mel wasn't concerned about his wife's medical condition at all, but instead was accusing her of infidelity for at least a year. Armenta said he had sat on the edge of his chair during the talk, staring at Melvin, as he waited for him to continue.

"What happened today?" Armenta asked.

Melvin Green's nervousness was now firmly under control, the hostile tone gone. He answered in a calm and deliberate manner, which was unusual for him. "I came into work at around 10:00 A.M. Anita was due to come in at 10:30 or thereabouts."

The detective's ears perked up. Without realizing it, Melvin Green had just told them that he knew exactly when Anita was scheduled to arrive at the office.

"And," Melvin kept talking, "I'd prepared some tax work for her to take home. I was putting it out for her when the doorbell rang."

Armenta scribbled some notes onto a paper. Melvin Green continued talking, explaining that when the business doorbell rang, a female ran in and claimed that a woman in a red car had been shot in his parking lot. Melvin accompanied the woman outside and observed his wife slumped over in the driver's seat of her red Corvette. "I tried to help her, until the police asked me to stop."

Detective Armenta asked Mel another question. "Is she only seeing Rabbi Jacobs, or is she seeing somebody else?"

Mel laughed. "I can start crapshooting if you want me to do that."

Then Melvin Green proceeded to tear down his wife's reputation, matter of factly telling the police that Anita Green was "screwing" numerous male acquaintances: Alan Lebowitz, Hal Mitchell, and Rabbi Steven Jacobs were just a few.

Melvin had still more. He accused the Woodland Hills Homeowners Association of being responsible for his wife's shooting because of a dispute over temple property around Pierce College in Woodland Hills. Armenta didn't believe him.

Although they had never implied to him that he was a suspect in the shooting of his wife, Green took it upon himself to steer the detectives toward other people. Mel knew the police were fishing, and he just kept tossing them fresh suspects. The police were certain Melvin Green wanted to keep them busy questioning others so nobody would have time to focus on him.

Later, when he went over the interview, the experienced Coffey felt just like he had when he was at the crime scene, that Mel was giving them names to confuse and delay the detectives coming to investigate.

As Coffey listened to the tape of Mel's interview, he wondered, Who was this guy? More importantly, who was Anita? So many prominent people were already calling with leads, they must be an important family. Yet Coffey, who must have jogged past Mel's office hundreds of times, had never heard of the Greens.

Unless this shooting was simply a random act of Los Angeles violence—a possibility Coffey considered highly unlikely, given the method of the shooting—someone had set it up. To Coffey it was crystal clear that the shooting had been arranged by someone who knew Anita Green. They had known her well enough to want to kill her. And they had known where to find her to do it.

The detective in charge of the investigation and the man most obsessed with finding the answers was Ray Hernandez. Hernandez, an overweight forty-one-year-old cop with dark hair and a neatly trimmed mustache, spent most of his waking hours working on homicide cases.

His real name was Raymond Hernandez, Jr., but at the station he was known affectionately as Boom Boom, nicknamed after the sound of a shooting gun.

Hernandez was a California native, born and raised on the streets of Los Angeles. He had been a police officer for more than seventeen years and a detective for almost that long. Ray joined the force when he was twenty-six, not because he had a passion for police work, but because, at the time, it was the only relatively high-paying job he could find. Very quickly he realized that he liked using his brains more than his brawn, and since he had always loved solving puzzles, he decided to give detective work a shot.

For twelve years the homicide department had been Ray's home. A career detective, he always got his man, no matter how the investigation interfered with his family life. Perhaps that was why Ray had separated from the same woman three times—the separations always coinciding with his toughest· cases. Known throughout the police department as a people person, Ray's tough interrogation skills made even the most reluctant witnesses talk.

Hernandez arrived at the crime scene at 1:30 P.M., when Anita had already been taken to the hospital. Mel had already been interviewed at the station and the Corvette had been towed away. ·

Hernandez was frustrated and disappointed. Anita's blood on the sidewalk was the only clue he had seen with his own eyes. He would have to rely on his colleagues' work to put the pieces together. Ray cursed and swore never to play golf on a weekday again.

Hernandez rolled up his sleeves and, despite the hellish heat, began combing the neighborhood surrounding Mel's office, looking for witnesses and gathering statements. He followed up on a tantalizing clue that the other detectives told him about. Across the street from Melvin and Anita's office was Rohan Glass, a shop where both Anita and Melvin conducted business. Ronald Barkley, an employee at the shop, reported seeing Melvin walk out his office door and look toward the street at around 10:30 A.M. Seconds later, Barkley saw Anita drive her red Corvette down the street. She was closely followed by a person on a motorcycle.

His sighting was confirmed by the shop's owner, James Rohan. "Ronald turned to me and said, 'Look, there goes Anita.'" Thirty minutes later a police officer came in with the shocking news that Anita Green had been shot.

"We're both shook up about this. About what we saw, about someone we know having been shot at and all, especially when it all happened so close to where we work."

In reality, what the men reported was very interesting to

Ray, because it could have meant Mel knew when Anita would be shot and was waiting excitedly for it to happen. Why, he was even waiting at the front door, a place Ray was told he seldom appeared, when someone informed him of the shooting.

Finishing his search, Ray went to the hospital to watch and talk to Anita's family. After spending only a few minutes there, the detective was called back to the station to conduct another interview.

Driving back, Ray expressed frustration to his partner. "I missed Green. Why didn't they ask him where he was before, during, and after the shooting?"

Ray didn't have time to lament about missing the action. Melvin Green's younger son, Cary Green, was waiting at the front desk. Cary had something that he needed to get off his chest. Hernandez knew that in homicide investigations the first place to look for answers is the immediate family. He would be glad to listen to whatever Cary Green had to say.

Hernandez led the boy to an interview room, thanking him for coming forward. Cary Green was scared, but like his father, arrogant and self-assured. He had come to the detectives today with a minor problem. When Cary went to his father's office after school, he found his dad flushed and emotional. His father explained to him that his beloved stepmother, Anita, had just been shot by an unknown blond guy on a blue Suzuki motorcycle.

Cary Green secretly owned a blue Suzuki motorcycle. No one in his family knew it existed because they were all opposed to motorcycles. He didn't want his father to find out about it.

Hernandez looked the boy square in the eyes. "Why are you telling us this?"

Cary fidgeted with his hands, searching for the words. "For two reasons. First, to offer my cooperation. You can let anybody you want see the motorcycle. I want to alleviate your fears that I am not some agent and that this is not a master plan to kill anybody."

"Well, hold on. How did you go to school? How were you dressed for school?" the detective asked, sitting forward in his seat.

"I was dressed in white shorts, running shoes, and a jersey

that says *Sun Devil* on it," Cary said, almost indignantly. "I was in a running class. The teacher took roll. It's kind of a coincidence because he never takes roll," Cary added.

Hernandez stood up. He walked right over to Cary and looked him in the eye. "Do you own a motorcycle helmet?"

"I did own a helmet, but not now. My friend ruined it. I probably still have it in my car."

"What color is it?" asked Ray.

"Black."

Ray sat back down and jotted down some notes. "We're going to go to your apartment together to see the bike. I hope you don't own an army jacket or a handgun."

Cary, sounding more and more upset by the minute, voiced his objections. "You're talking to me like I'm guilty or something. I only came to you because I don't want my family to know I own a motorcycle."

"Everything will be fine. As long as you don't have an army jacket, you have nothing to fear." Hernandez watched Cary to gauge his reaction.

Cary Green's visit puzzled the experienced detective. If he were involved, it was very unusual that he would come forward to the police. Still, Hernandez considered him a suspect. After he searched Cary's residence and came up empty-handed and after the roofer didn't identify his motorcycle, Hernandez decided just to keep Cary's name filed in the back of his mind.

As the afternoon rolled by, more and more people began to come forward with information about Melvin Green. A lawyer named Janis Marie McDonald was the next person Ray interviewed. McDonald practiced in Century City, a prestigious strip of high-rise office buildings filled with entertainment executives and high-priced attorneys. Hernandez soon learned she was Anita's divorce attorney. She had begun to represent Anita the previous May, after Anita had been referred to her by another attorney and friend, Janet Frangy. Janet Frangy was Anita and Mel's attorney, and she had become Anita's friend.

McDonald told Ray there were three things about her client's husband that she thought they should know. First, Melvin was abusive, both physically and verbally, often pointing loaded firearms at Anita. McDonald knew this was the reason Anita was deathly afraid of her husband. Second,

Melvin was obsessed with destroying Anita financially, physically, and mentally. He would often send McDonald letters that illustrated the extent of his hatred toward his wife. He did not want Anita to get "his" money. Last, and perhaps most frightening of all, Anita had told McDonald that she had grown increasingly concerned about her husband's business improprieties. When she had mentioned her concerns, Mel became obsessed that she was out to ruin him, swearing that she would never live to do so. He had become so violent that she had finally pushed for a divorce and moved out.

The divorce papers had been served in July. Anita had asked McDonald not to file a restraining order because she said she feared getting one would make Melvin even more violent.

When Hernandez questioned the other attorney, Janet Frangy, Frangy confirmed Anita's knowledge of Mel's secrets. Anita had even told Frangy that she could make a lot of trouble for Melvin if she wanted to.

Frangy added one more surprising twist. Recalling the time she had handled a case for Melvin and Anita in 1985, she claimed Melvin had boasted that he could have someone "taken care of" permanently. She understood that statement to mean that Melvin could have someone killed and that he knew people who would do such a thing.

Frangy had not believed that Melvin was capable of hurting Anita. But now that Anita had been shot in the front seat of her Corvette, at Mel's office, she wasn't sure what to think. Mel knew exactly when Anita was coming to see him. It was a strange coincidence. He had admitted his abilities before and even boasted of them.

Given the scope and tone of the lawyers' interviews, Hernandez was even more convinced that Anita's shooting was a professionally planned hit and that her strange husband might have had something to do with it. It was clear that whoever shot Anita had done so with the definite intention of killing her. Robbery had quickly been ruled out by the police as a possible motive. Also rape. There was simply no evidence to support a sexual encounter. Melvin certainly had motives.

All things considered, Ray felt that keeping an eye on those who knew Anita best couldn't hurt. By early evening, the detective was back at North Hollywood Hospital. He was horrified by the way Melvin treated Anita's family and by his obvious lack of interest in his wife's precarious medical condition.

Mel's inability to care struck Hernandez as odd. Though he often appeared to others as the stereotypical hard-nosed detective with no emotional involvement in his cases, Ray Hernandez felt himself getting pulled into this one. He felt so badly for Anita's family that he knew he was hooked. Ray found himself growing more and more fascinated with the Green case hour-by-hour.

17

Melvin's Hell

A few hours after his wife had been taken to the hospital and before he went there to be with her, Melvin Green called his divorce attorney, Marian Stanton, with the information that his wife had been shot a short time ago.

Shocked, Marian quickly headed down the hall to speak with Arthur Alexander, a well-respected criminal attorney. One thing was certain, even if her client had nothing to do with the shooting, just the fact that he was in the process of getting a divorce at the time made him a suspect. Marian wanted him to have the best advice possible.

Marian Stanton's firm was located in the heart of Encino, in a prestigious office building. It was a block away from the temple offices and less than a mile from both Anita's apartment and the home she had once shared with Mel.

Following Marian to her office, Arthur remembered when he had first met Melvin Green in Marian's office only a few short weeks ago. He had sensed immediately that something was different about this man.

While Mel talked to the two lawyers on the telephone, they took notes. Arthur told him, "Come in right away, Mel. You have no idea of what you're about to go through, even if, as you say, you've done nothing." Arthur was insistent and Marian agreed. Melvin felt cornered.

That was how Melvin Green found himself retaining one of the Valley's most respected criminal attorneys less than four hours after his wife's shooting.

A half hour later, an angry Mel Green arrived at Arthur Alexander's office. He was visibly shaken. Adamant, he shouted, "I didn't do it. How can the police think it was me?" He was shaking his head in total disbelief.

"I have to prepare you, Mel," Arthur responded. "You will be the suspect, just because of where it happened, how it happened, and because you're going through a divorce."

It took a while, but Alexander's words finally sank in. Agitated, Mel pounded his fist on the table. "There is no way the police can suspect me of any involvement. I was in my office, with Lily." Mel felt he had an ironclad alibi.

"Why not, Mel?" the veteran attorney asked. "I doubt they'll suspect anyone else. You're too easy a target. So you didn't shoot her; they'll say you set it up." The lawyer wanted Melvin to see just how serious a situation he was in.

Arthur Alexander had seen the inner workings of the Los Angeles Police Department. In his opinion, the department's treatment of witnesses and suspects was appalling. More often than not, the police would only check out the easiest leads during an investigation. Alexander knew they would put a red star by Melvin's name as soon as possible.

"I know you've already given a statement to the police. I know they'll be back, and they'll keep coming back. Just remember these words: 'My attorney has instructed me not to talk to you.' Can you do that?" Alexander asked, his voice filled with compassion.

Arthur had seen it all before—the denial and disbelief that occur when someone is accused of a serious crime. Melvin was beside himself.

"Absolutely," Mel said, proceeding to write the words down so he would never forget them.

Watching, Arthur knew something was wrong with Melvin Green. Here was a bright, articulate man writing down a simple phrase. Even the dummies Arthur saw didn't need to write down the words.

As he watched his new client leave the office, the attorney hoped that no one in his own family was ever accused of a serious crime. He did not even know any of the particulars, just that Mel was in for a rough time. In the current climate, it was really tough to be up against the police.

Walking into his office, Mel told his staff that he didn't want to talk about what had just happened, and he didn't want to hear them talking about it either. There were enough accusations flying around.

Melvin was sweating and his face was flushed. He prepared one of his liquid-diet drinks and after downing it felt a little better. He had just been through a traumatic experience. He didn't know which was the greatest indignity: the parking lot, the police station, or his trip to Arthur Alexander's.

Calming himself, Mel typed a letter to his staff, outlining his new attorney's instructions. They were to tell everybody who inquired Anita was gravely ill in the hospital. No details were to be discussed with anyone. Her condition remained guarded and grave. All of Mel's appointments were to be deferred unless he had no choice.

Not wanting to appear casual or indifferent in the letter, he instructed people to send donations to the Shir Chadash building fund in lieu of flowers. He opened the door, passed the letter to Lily and his secretary, Irene Sherwyn, and disappeared into his office once more.

Lily and Irene looked at one another. They knew there was nothing strange or out of character about Mel's reaction. He appeared to be back at work, taking care of business, hours after his wife's violent shooting. Others might think it strange, but that was the way Mel always was. His work had always allowed him to escape from his problems.

Lily got up, walked to Mel's office and knocked, waiting for him to answer. "Mel, I'm going to pick up my kids. Afterwards, I'm going to the hospital to check on Anita. Please meet me there," she called through the closed door.

"Go ahead, maybe I'll join you later," he said. "I have some calls to take care of. Have Irene call Riva with the news. I can't bear talking with her now."

As Irene called Riva, Melvin used another line to dial Phyllis Baltin. He reached her answering machine. Very matter of factly, he left a message. "Phyllis, this is Melvin Green. I hate to relate this to you this way, but there's no other choice. Anita's been shot. The police officer Coffey may be investigating the situation. I told him about Alan Lebowitz and Hal Mitchell, so if they question you about this, tell them what you know honestly. Thank you, thank you, dear." Hanging up, he felt confident that his old friend Phyllis would come through for him.

Mel Green dialed another number and reached Anita's son Scott's answering machine. Also nonchalantly, he left a message on that machine, telling Scott his mother had just been shot. Mel recited the news in a monotone, as if the message were unimportant. He didn't want his voice to alarm Scott about the severity of the situation. Mel then decided he too would go to the hospital to see what was happening, but first he had a few more things he had to take care of.

Melvin decided to go home, change his clothes, and pick up his mail and messages. Wearily he drove to his house, all the while wondering how he had allowed himself to get into this mess.

He pulled into his garage at a little before 7:00 P.M. Melvin was famished. He went into the kitchen to prepare one of his diet shakes. The drink seemed to do the trick. He wasn't able to think clearly without it. Melvin wondered if his diet, with its severe caloric restrictions, was affecting him.

At about 7:05 P.M., just as he was about to set off for the hospital to see Anita, his roommate, Joseph Corrado, arrived and walked into the kitchen.

Joe was surprised to find Mel home so early and even more surprised when he heard Mel's reasons. On weeknights, Melvin seldom arrived home before 10:30 P.M. "What are you doing home so early?" Joe asked.

"Anita's been shot," Mel told a shocked Joe.

"What happened?" Joe asked.

Melvin went on to explain. "She was shot by a motorcyclist who came from the freeway, Joe. She probably cut him off. You know how Anita drives that sports car."

Joe thought the story sounded farfetched, even for Mel. "What freeway are you talking about, Melvin?" he asked. Joe wondered why Melvin was having this conversation with him anyway. His wife had just been shot and he should be sitting at the hospital with her. The more he thought about it, the more implausible Mel's story seemed. "What freeway would she be taking, Mel?"

Melvin looked more upset by the minute. Why didn't Joe

Anita and Melvin Green's accounting office in North Hollywood, California. Anita was shot in the rear parking lot on October 25, 1990, as she pulled her Corvette into a parking place. *Courtesy: Los Angeles Police Department*

Anita's car in the exact location where she was shot, a few minutes after she was rushed to the hospital. *Courtesy: Los Angeles Police Department*

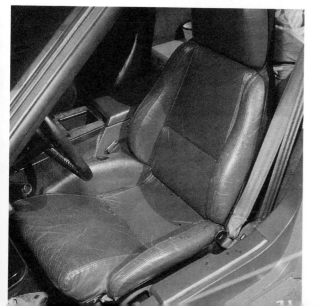

Close-up of the inside of Anita's blood-splattered car, minutes after the shooting. Anita had just had the car's registration changed to her name alone. Her shoes are splattered with her blood. *Courtesy: Los Angeles Police Department*

TOP LEFT: Melvin Green's many diplomas adorn his office walls. Most are fake or mail-order diplomas from non-accredited programs. *Courtesy: Los Angeles Police Department*

TOP RIGHT: Melvin Green at Anita's funeral.
Courtesy: Lori Valesko/Los Angeles Daily News

BOTTOM: The entire community gathers gravesides at Anita's funeral,
October 30, 1990. Rabbi Jacobs leads the service while an ostracized Melvin
Green stands defiantly alone. *Courtesy: Lori Valesko/Los Angeles Daily News*

Rabbi Jacobs married Miriam Leah, formerly known as Mary Louise, in May 1991, less than a year after Anita's tragic death. *Courtesy: Miriam Jacobs*

The new rabbiness and the rabbi's three sons from his first marriage. His daughter, Tammy, missed the wedding because she was in Spain when her father unexpectedly pushed his wedding date up and married before she could return. *Courtesy: Miriam Jacobs*

Melvin Green also planned to marry. He announced his engagement to Alexandra Leeds at a dinner party in early April, just days before his arrest for the murder of his wife Anita. He had eluded the police for six months and had lost another one hundred pounds.
Courtesy: Alexandra Leeds

After spending $2,500,000, all that the Shir Chadash congregation has to show for it is a vacant lot with this sign standing on it. *Courtesy: Jay Samit*

UPPER LEFT: Gerry Chaleff led Mel's million-dollar defense team. He was the heavy hitter who Mel thought guaranteed him an easy victory in court. *Courtesy: Gerry Chaleff*

UPPER RIGHT: Arthur Alexander was Mel's original defense attorney and the attorney he remained the fondest of. Art was responsible for keeping Mel's temper under control, a difficult job at best. *Courtesy: Arthur Alexander*

BELOW: Prosecuting attorney Kent C. Cahill called the Green case his most challenging ever. The judge's decision in the case surprised many in the district attorney's office. *Courtesy: Ernie Pava, The Picture Place*

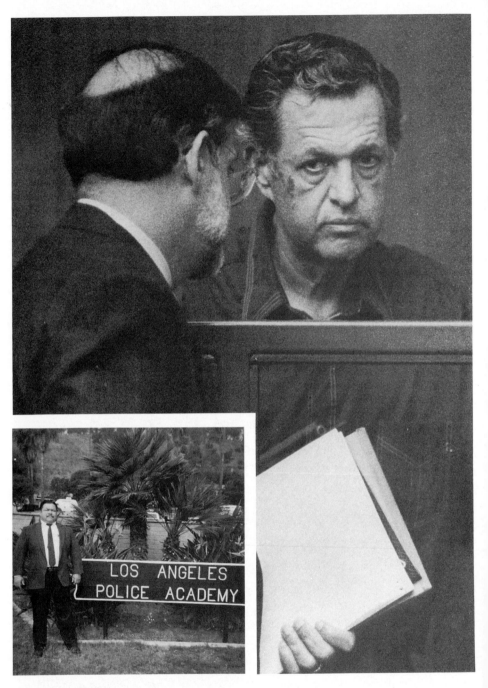

A beaten Melvin Green and his attorney Arthur Alexander at his arraignment April 11, 1991, after Mel's first sleepless night in jail.
Photo: David Crane/Los Angeles Daily News
INSET: Ray "Boom-boom" Hernandez, the detective whose relentless pursuit of Melvin Green resulted in an arrest that no one expected to stick. After Ray arrested Mel, he thanked God the "son-of-a-bitch" would never again walk the streets.
Courtesy: Michele Samit

A stern judge George Trammel sentencing Melvin Morton Green, May 27, 1992. During the trial it became apparent that though fair, the judge disliked Melvin. *Courtesy: Lori Valesko/Los Angeles Daily News*

In the courtroom during his sentencing, a dejected Melvin Green looks over to his family and friends for support. *Courtesy: Lori Valesko/Los Angeles Daily News*

An angry and defiant Melvin Green gets up to proclaim his innocence one last time to the judge, his supporters, and God before being sentenced to life in prison without the possibility of parole. *Courtesy: Lori Valesko/ Los Angeles Daily News*

understand what he was saying? It was all so clear to Melvin. He knew how things must have gone down. Perhaps if he tried again, Joe would buy his version of the events.

Melvin knew his biggest personality flaw was his violent and explosive temper. He forced himself to take a deep breath and to remain calm. "Anita was on the freeway, and she exited at Oxnard and traveled westbound before turning right onto Wilkinson," Mel said.

Joe looked at Mel. "I always come to your office on surface streets and I usually travel eastbound on Oxnard. What makes you so sure Anita wouldn't go that way?" Joe questioned Mel further, to prove to him how unlikely his story was.

Melvin pounded his fists into the kitchen table. He was vehement. "I know I'm right, Joe. She had to be coming that way." Joe knew Melvin could be irrational at times, but he'd never seen him this insistent.

Mel spent the next half hour trying to convince Joe that this mystery shooter had followed Anita on the freeway. Joe decided he had listened long enough and tried to get away. Mel followed him from room to room, explaining the scenario over and over again.

Exasperated, Joe threw his hands up into the air. "How can you be so sure it happened that way?" he asked Mel. Joe Corrado was having a tough time understanding why Mel was telling him this crazy story anyway. How would he know which way his wife was traveling? And why would he care?

Mel went on to explain that he talked to a witness, a roofer who had seen the whole event. The roofer told Mel exactly in which direction Anita was traveling. Explanation finished, Melvin left Joe sitting alone in a darkened kitchen, as he rushed off to visit Anita in the hospital. As he drove, he made a mental note to talk to the roofer in the morning to confirm the story he had just told Joe.

Melvin finally arrived at the hospital, where family and friends had spent most of the day, about nine hours after Anita was shot. Melvin found his family waiting for some news on her condition. Someone told him his wife was in surgery where the doctors were diligently trying to save her. No one else said anything to him. He approached his mother-in-law, Riva Rice, and gingerly placed a kiss on her cheek.

Then he began to angrily pace up and down the halls, gauging people's reactions to him. Mel felt nauseated and tired. As time passed, the doctors came out with an update on Anita's condition and a report on the progress of the surgery itself. Much later, when Mel tried to enter his wife's room, a uniformed officer approached him. "I'm sorry, you can't go in there." Mel was attempting to see his wife, who had been moved to a recovery room.

Mel's face filled with anger. "What do you mean I can't go in there?" He took a deep breath and moved forward, as the officer grabbed his arm. "I want to see my wife."

"No. I'm telling you that you're not welcome in there right now. Hospital security. We'll keep you informed about her condition," the officer added.

Mel Green began to bang hysterically on the hospital door.

"Just who do you think you are? Why are there people in there with her now? I have every right to visit my wife. I need to be by her side." The officer wouldn't budge.

Since it was already late and there was nothing else he could do about it, Melvin Green reluctantly went home. As Melvin drove his Cadillac home to Encino, he passed the temple's offices. Parking in front of the building, he stared at the bricks. He could not remember ever feeling as sad as he did at this moment. This was the place where his life had literally begun to fall apart. Melvin Green began to cry, for the life he had lost, for his children, and for Anita, whom he had loved so much, and whom he had lost so long ago.

18

The Community Speaks

Within a day after the shooting—by early Friday morning, October 26, while Anita's unconscious body continued to breathe—a number of people had voluntarily gone to the police. Ray Hernandez's phone rang off the hook. Anita's friends and colleagues were overcome with feelings of guilt. They were finally speaking on her behalf.

Many people felt partially responsible. Perhaps their silence about Mel's threats had led Mel to believe that his anger was acceptable. Some people lamented that they hadn't pressured Anita into getting out of her marriage earlier; many had seen the writing on the wall. Though most claimed they hadn't known about her affair with the rabbi, many weren't surprised, and some admitted they had suspected it all along.

Anita and Mel Green's friends lived in a comfortable world where shootings didn't occur. Nothing like this had ever happened before, and they were frightened. They wanted to help the police in any way that they could, but they were worried about their own safety. Would Melvin Green go after them because they had gone to the police?

Ray Hernandez arrived at the North Hollywood station at a little after 6:30 A.M. the day after Anita's shooting. He hadn't slept well, his mind filled with questions. After visiting the hospital the night before, he was already certain that following Melvin Green was the way to go, and he steadily built his case from that point.

A few minutes after arriving, Hernandez received his second call from Anita's divorce attorney, Janis McDonald.

McDonald confirmed to Ray that Mel was a frightening character and that she, herself, had personally witnessed his threats
toward Anita. Janis told Ray about an assortment of letters
Anita had collected that were filled with Melvin's threats and
rantings. "He's been saying he'd kill her for years now, and
that's what I think he's done. I've never met anyone like him."
Before hanging up, McDonald promised to locate both Anita's
and Melvin's checking and savings account numbers.

Hernandez wasted no time checking out the leads, assign-
ing the best of the North Hollywood detectives. Normally
nine-to-fivers, the team was working round the clock.

Several Shir Chadash board members came forward with
information that Mel Green had waited outside a temple board
meeting a few months ago looking for his wife. They said he
had bragged that he was carrying a gun. Anita later mentioned
to two board members that she was very frightened of Melvin
and if anything ever happened to her, they would know who
was involved.

One temple member told the police that Mel boasted he
could have anybody he wanted eliminated. According to this
congregant, the rabbi had even told him that he feared Melvin
Green would shoot him while he was standing on the pulpit.

Other temple members confirmed Mel's bizarre behavior,
saying he always had to be the center of attention. He sat in the
front row during services, he sang the loudest, and he was
always very abusive toward his wife.

In another call, Hernandez learned about the temple's
problems with the Woodland Hills Homeowners Association.
A temple employee assured the police that Anita had resolved
the problems peacefully for the congregation. It wasn't likely
they had anything to do with the shooting.

A good friend of the Greens', Phyllis Baltin, told Ray
Hernandez briefly about a bizarre message Melvin had left on
her machine the day before, telling her the shocking news and
instructing her on how to talk to the police if they came asking
questions. Phyllis claimed that Melvin had recently asked her
which car Anita was currently driving, claiming he wanted to
make sure Rabbi Jacobs wasn't using his Corvette. "I paid for
that car, and I'll be damned if he's going to get to drive it," he
had shouted.

Phyllis indicated to Hernandez that she had more information about the Greens that would help the case. "Just give me a few days to gather my thoughts. Right now I want to be here for the family. Make sure to set aside a lot of time. I could fill books."

Hernandez could tell Phyllis Baltin had a remarkable memory for detail. Since she had been friends with the Greens for years, it was likely Mel trusted her. Mel's phone call to Phyllis after the shooting proved he considered her a close personal confidant. The detective thought that, with a little luck, perhaps Mel would fuck up with her. He knew a guy with a fat lip and a loose screw like Melvin Green couldn't keep quiet for long. Mel was a walking time bomb, and Ray Hernandez was now convinced he would confess something to someone soon. Ray thought that Phyllis Baltin might be that person.

Mel's current roommate, Joe Corrado, called Ray to set up an interview time, stressing that the police were not to tell Melvin that he was talking. "I don't know what he'll do to me when he finds out." Others said the same thing. "Can you protect us from him?" Ray Hernandez couldn't remember when he had last had so many requests for protection.

The stories fascinated the North Hollywood detectives. It appeared that everyone who called was frightened of Melvin Green: his kids, his clients, his wife's friends. What kind of a hold did this man have on people?

Besides information on Melvin Green, the police were receiving other leads that needed following up. The manager of Anita's apartment building, Greg Adler, thought he had the key piece of information. According to Adler, Anita had a "long-haired" boyfriend who drove a motorcycle and frequently parked it at the apartment building. Adler suggested that the police contact Mel Staples, the building's security manager, to get the motorcycle's license-plate number.

Meanwhile, at about the same time as Adler's phone call, the people living in the area of Mel's office began to talk with the homicide detectives. Several confirmed hearing a motorcycle; others had actually seen a man speeding away on one. One elderly neighbor recalled, "He was in a big hurry and looked upset." The information indicated that this didn't seem like just any motorcycle driver, but rather a panicky one trying to make his getaway.

With the avalanche of witnesses coming forward with

information, it was impossible to investigate everything. Hernandez, who often got tunnel vision when he was honing in on a suspect, couldn't concentrate.

"Shit, I've got to get off the phone. Can you handle the calls for me, guys?" Hernandez asked two detectives.

"Glad to, Ray. We'll write everything down." The two men looked at him. They had seen him get like this before. Ray was famous for it; he became totally obsessed. "Look at him. He's going into his battle trance," they joked. "Hey Ray, are you getting ready to talk to Green?"

"Sure am. As soon as I grab Coffey. He won't want to miss this." The two detectives noted that Ray had leapt to his feet as soon as they asked about Melvin.

Later, when Hernandez and Coffey returned to the station after attempting to interview Melvin Green, there were several message books filled with scandalous tips. The two detectives joked to Ray that he was investigating the Peyton Place of the Valley.

While his colleagues handled the phones, Hernandez had focused his energy on Melvin. He had prepared himself for meeting Green by talking with all the officers who had had any contact at all with Melvin the day before: Armenta, Sullivan, and Coffey. None had anything favorable to say about him, and all indicated that Mel was hiding something.

Ray Hernandez and Michael Coffey finally arrived at Mel Green's office at a little after 9:30 A.M. with the intent of giving Melvin a polygraph examination. As soon as they walked in the door, they were ushered back to Mel's office. The detectives found Mr. Green hard at work. Coffey let Ray do the talking.

"Hi, I'm Detective Hernandez," he said, extending his hand to Melvin.

To Melvin, who had made the decision to have absolute faith in his new attorney, even an innocent visit by the police might be dangerous. He found himself in an uncomfortable situation. He hoped his mouth would not get him in trouble. At the same time, he didn't want to offend the detectives by appearing uncooperative. He began to pace around the small room like a caged tiger.

Melvin answered Hernandez's handshake with the obviously rehearsed statement, "I am instructed by my attorney not to speak with you. I'm sorry," he added hesitantly. "I'd like to help."

"You have an attorney? What for? Who is he?" The fact was, as far as Ray Hernandez was concerned, hiring an attorney was practically an admission of guilt. "What kind of attorney do you have?"

Melvin was adamant. "I've been instructed by my attorney, Arthur Alexander, not to speak with you. I have the right as a citizen not to cooperate with you."

"Arthur Alexander? He's your new attorney?" Ray asked incredulously. Ray knew Alexander was a criminal lawyer. Detectives know all the good ones. He was intrigued. "What do you have to hide?"

Melvin wanted the detectives to trust him. He thought carefully about the topics he could talk about. Rising from his chair, Mel decided to show Hernandez and Coffey how much weight he had recently shed. Mel thought Hernandez looked like he could afford to lose a few pounds.

Mel started to walk toward the kitchen area adjacent to his office. The detectives followed. Ray whispered to Coffey, "I don't like it. I have an eerie feeling that he's our man. I mean, his refusal to talk, his hiring of an attorney, his stated animosity toward his wife, and look how he's acting. It has to be him." Coffey nodded.

Mel came out of the kitchen with a large belt. At first Ray Hernandez thought it might be a weapon, but after looking closer, he realized it was just a belt.

"Look, this used to fit me," Mel told the detectives. Mel took his shoes off and dropped to the ground for a push-up. "My stomach used to hit the floor first, Ray. What do you think?"

Hernandez didn't know what to think. This guy was bizarre. He watched as beads of perspiration began to form on Mel's forehead.

"Detective, detective! Sit down! Sit down!" Mel shouted.

Hernandez was getting angry watching this spectacle. He turned to Coffey and then back to Mel.

"No, Mel. You sit down," Ray answered, trying to regain

control of the encounter. "I've had enough of your shit." The detective got the distinct impression that Melvin Green was trying to weasel into his head.

"Listen to me, Mel. You don't want to speak to us?" Hernandez asked.

"No," Mel said. "I'll talk to you about diets, the weather, taxes, anything but what happened in the parking lot. Hey guys, it isn't my job to figure it out. You're the experts. That's what the city pays you for, isn't it?"

Ray Hernandez was shocked. No one had ever talked to him this way. What could be more important than helping the police find his wife's shooter? Maybe sitting with his dying wife at the hospital, but this guy wasn't crying at the hospital. He was just continuing to sit at his desk and act important. Hernandez looked over at Coffey and shrugged his shoulders. Perhaps Mel didn't understand the seriousness of a homicide investigation.

"You see, Mr. Green, what I guess you don't know is, I'll be back. I won't leave you alone," Ray Hernandez said forcefully. Both detectives watched Mel for his reaction. They studied the uncomfortable expression forming on his face. Coffey saw Mel's skin turn pale, and to Hernandez, he appeared scared.

Watching, Ray Hernandez was certain that Melvin Green was at least partially responsible for the shooting of his wife. He was not certain if Mel has orchestrated it, or been in on it, but he'd done something. Hernandez knew why Arthur Alexander was telling his client to keep his mouth shut.

The stuff Mel said while his wife lay dying was incriminating enough. When the detective added to that what everyone else was already saying, he was certain. Melvin Green was an arrogant man who thought himself above the law. Ray Hernandez promised himself right there on the spot that he'd nail the son of a bitch.

Disgusted and frustrated, Hernandez got up to leave. Coffey could tell how upset he was. He knew immediately that Ray would be obsessed with the case, and would probably crack it if it didn't crack him first. At that instant, Coffey knew he had picked the right man for the job. Glancing back only once, both detectives noticed that, as they left, for the first time all morning, Melvin Green looked relieved.

Exiting Mel's office, Ray Hernandez felt more frustrated than ever. He was trying to put together a jigsaw puzzle when over half the pieces were missing. He could easily fit together the pieces that he had, but they alone would not make a picture. Ray could guess at what the hidden picture revealed, but how could he expect a prosecutor or a jury to do the same.

"You know, Mike, this guy is smart. He's trying to control us. Throw us off. We've got to stick with him a little longer."

"If he'll let us, " Coffey added and then pointed across the street. "There's the roofer I was telling you about. He's still working on the same house."

"I'm going to talk with him," Ray stated, as he began walking toward the man who had heard the shooting and observed the getaway the day before.

"Mr. Foss? I'm Detective Hernandez. Can you recount the circumstances of the crime you witnessed?"

"Sure," the man answered nervously as he glanced over toward Melvin's office. "But first, I think there's something you need to know. The lady's husband is strange. He approached me today and he was real upset. He asked me which way his wife was traveling when she pulled into the driveway. After informing him I wasn't supposed to talk with him, I told him that I never witnessed the approach." Foss went on excitedly. "You know that I didn't lift my head until after I heard the gunshot?"

"We know that. Did he leave you alone after you explained?" Hernandez asked.

"No, not hardly. He acted like he was possessed. He kept trying to convince me that what I saw wasn't really what I saw. We got into an argument about it. Finally I told him he was nuts." The roofer added, "I mean, I know what I saw. Can you keep him away from me?"

"We sure can," the detective answered. He pulled a picture of Cary Green's motorcycle out of his pocket.

"Can you jog your memory for me? Was this the bike?"

Shaking no with his head, Foss answered, "That's not it. The color is similar, but it isn't the same bike."

"Are you sure? Could it be the same bike?"

"No, I'm sure it isn't," Foss replied. Hernandez barely masked his disappointment.

"I'm sorry, detective."

"Don't be. Thanks for your help. We'll be in touch."

Before driving back to the station, Michael Coffey and Ray Hernandez combed the neighborhood and located two other people who had heard the motorcycle and the shooting. Though neither had actually witnessed the incident, both assisted the detectives by showing them the direction in which they believed the motorcycle was traveling. Separately, each confirmed the police's suspicions. The motorcycle had left Wilkinson and turned onto Erwin Street, which fed directly onto the freeway.

As soon as he returned to the station, Hernandez followed up by talking with Mr. Robert Riley, a truck driver who worked for the Department of Water and Power. Riley had seen a motorcycle driver speeding away from the crime scene. "I almost hit the guy. He lost his balance and actually fell off his bike."

"Can you tell us what he looked like?"

Riley described a tall, blond, white male. The man's bike had a black motorcycle helmet hanging on the handlebars. The detectives had a police composite drawn from Riley's description, so the suspect could be identified in the future.

Before noon, the two exhausted detectives set off for Anita's apartment to search for evidence. The rabbi had already called about getting into Anita's apartment for a few things. The cops agreed to meet him there. Ray Hernandez wondered what he wanted.

When they arrived, the rabbi was waiting impatiently at the front door. Coffey and Hernandez began their search in the kitchen. Taking Anita's message pads, answering-machine tapes, and personal papers, they examined everything carefully. The rabbi eyed them and finally asked if he could go into the bedroom for a moment. Hernandez instructed him to wait in the apartment's entryway with Anita's maid, who not knowing of the shooting, had let herself in to clean. Ray Hernandez found Steven Jacobs to be extremely uncomfortable and very anxious to get into the bedroom.

Hernandez noticed a pair of airline tickets lying next to the kitchen phone. The airline tickets were made out to Rabbi

Steven B. Jacobs and Anita M. Green. He turned to face the waiting rabbi. "Were you planning a trip together?"

"Uh, yes we were," Rabbi Jacobs answered nervously. He began to pace back and forth in the apartment's small kitchen.

Wanting to know if Mel's accusations had any validity, the detective pushed further. "Why? Are you two lovers?"

Rabbi Jacobs looked away as he gave the same answer he had earlier provided. "We're only good friends. I'm the rabbi, she's my president. We take a few trips together, always on temple business." He began to run his fingers through his hair. His face reddened. Ray continued to probe.

"What kind of business?"

"The usual. Meeting with colleagues, interviewing potential temple employees, whatever needs to be done," he explained. To Hernandez, Jacobs appeared to be growing more uncomfortable each minute.

Steven Jacobs went on to explain that temple board members were all part of his extended temple family. Travel together was not unusual. Ray Hernandez didn't believe a word of what the rabbi was saying. The detective knew he had him cornered.

Slowly, Ray entered Anita's bedroom. Rabbi Jacobs followed, trying desperately to pass the detective. Hernandez pushed him back and asked him, "What kind of person is Anita?"

"She's the neatest person I've ever met. She's so meticulous," Jacobs responded.

Hernandez slowly opened Anita's top dresser drawer. He watched the rabbi's face. The drawer contained her panties, neatly folded, and her nylons, rolled one by one in a row. In one corner of the drawer sat the prize: a red foil box in the shape of a heart that had once contained See's Valentine chocolates, but now held a myriad of letters and cards.

"May I have those?" Rabbi Jacobs asked the detective nervously. "They mean a lot to me."

The rabbi had managed to remain extremely secretive about this aspect of his life. He had hidden it for so long, and now this one detective was about to ruin him. Rabbi Jacobs couldn't hide his anger. Once again he pleaded, "May I please have those?"

"No, you may not. I'm logging all of them as evidence," Ray

Hernandez replied. "Rabbi, you're still a suspect. You realize that, don't you? You were the last one seen with her."

Rabbi Jacobs recoiled, visibly appalled. "Just who do you think you are? Do you really think I could be responsible for an act as horrible as this? I'm a rabbi. I could never hurt anyone."

"I don't know what to think right now, but I'm not about to dismiss any possibility yet."

Ray Hernandez knew anything was possible. The hardened detective certainly wasn't about to let up because the rabbi was getting uncomfortable. Ray hated that Jacobs had the gall to hide behind the cloak of the clergy. Besides, this guy certainly wasn't acting like a rabbi.

"Be straight with me; are you two involved?" Hernandez pressed as he continued to stare at Jacobs.

Clearly in agony, Rabbi Jacobs answered, "No."

"Yeah, yeah, knock it off. I want the truth," Ray Hernandez said, shutting the bedroom door behind them. "You're not free to go until you tell me the truth." The detective stared at the clergyman until finally Ray asked him, "Did you ever have sex with Anita Green?"

The rabbi turned red. He was very angry and appeared to be forcing himself to remain calm. He seemed to be thinking about the question in an overly conspicuous way. It was as though he was playing the part of a smart, calm, reflective rabbi. He had mastered the role. After all, thinking carefully is what a rabbi is supposed to do. Ray thought that Jacobs should have done that before, especially since appearances seemed to be so important to him.

"Did you have sex with Anita Green?" Hernandez persisted. It was a question Steven Jacobs could no longer ignore.

"Well, yes... on just a couple of occasions. Maybe two times or something like that," the rabbi whispered softly. Ray Hernandez thought he seemed ashamed.

"Did you have sex the night she stayed at your house? Um, let's see, Wednesday night, the night before she was shot?"

Rabbi Jacobs did not answer right away. He looked defeated. Slowly he nodded his head, finally replying, "Uh, yes, I suppose we did. But we only had sex about two times. She was already separated and I'm divorced. We were two adults, just beginning a relationship. I know nothing about what happened to her. Really."

By now, Hernandez didn't believe anything Jacobs said. Coffey wasn't sure what to believe, but he knew the rabbi had something to hide. Besides, it didn't really matter to Ray how many times they had done it or how long they had been lovers. The only thing that mattered was the night it had happened and that it had happened at all. Hernandez had what he wanted.

"You're free to leave. But remember, you're a suspect. You cannot leave the country. You need to be available to answer any of our questions. I trust you'll be able to help me out."

Rabbi Jacobs nodded unhappily. Hernandez thought the rabbi couldn't wait to get out of the apartment. Before Jacobs left, he removed a personal photo of Anita and himself and another of Anita.

"May I take these?" he asked calmly.

"Of course, Rabbi," Hernandez answered. "Thanks for all your help. We'll keep you informed on the case. Please tell anyone at the temple who knows anything to come see me."

"He's a lot less arrogant than when he got here," Ray said to Coffey as they watched the rabbi exit the apartment. "He looks a hell of a lot older too. Probably thinks he'll lose his rabbiship or whatever they call it."

"Be easy on him, Ray. He seems like an okay guy," Mike Coffey added. Poor man, the detective thought. He got caught with his hands in the cookie jar.

Ray Hernandez left with the knowledge that the story Mel was circulating about Anita and the rabbi was true, though none of the temple members he had talked with were brave enough to admit it. Ray supposed they had gossiped about it among themselves. But when he asked them about it, they were silent. It was as if they wouldn't dare confirm anything. They were protecting their beloved rabbi's reputation. It appeared to the detective that they were as afraid of the rabbi's wrath as Mel's acquaintances were of his.

It was an interesting thought to ponder. Both Mel and the rabbi exhibited tremendous control over their followers, and both faced similar problems. In some ways the problems Rabbi Jacobs faced, as a moral leader who was having an affair with his temple president, mirrored those Melvin would encounter if his clients found out about his shady business practices. Both men would end up with ruined reputations.

Hernandez did not know that there is almost always a strong political component to synagogue life. No temple can ever rid itself of the factionalism that controversy can create in a congregation. When Rabbi Jacobs was rumored to be having an affair while still a rabbi at his other congregation, Temple Judea, the factionalism manifested itself in bitter and conflicting opinions about the talented and popular rabbi.

At that time, talent and popularity weren't enough to overcome the negative effect his social indiscretions had on his reputation. Since many Shir Chadash board members came from Temple Judea, they were fearful that their new congregation could not survive another round of rabbi rumors, especially during a building campaign. That was probably why they chose to remain silent.

Hernandez's gut reaction was that the rabbi wasn't involved in Anita's death. He was merely involved intimately with her life. Still, since he admitted to being the last person Anita was with, they had to investigate him as a possible murder suspect. Besides, the guy wasn't too eager to volunteer information. This was what Ray had on him to keep him in tow. When you're a possible murder suspect, you had better cooperate with the police. Ray Hernandez always found a way to get what he needed most from people.

When he arrived home the rabbi was upset. He consulted with a few temple members about hiring a lawyer. They told him not to, yet. Then the rabbi called in his political connections. They were sorry, but they couldn't help. Finally, Rabbi Jacobs called Ray Hernandez's superiors and sought refuge from the lieutenant. How could Detective Ray Hernandez accuse him, Rabbi Steven B. Jacobs, of being a suspect?

Ray Hernandez's lieutenant, Ron LaRue, respected Ray's abilities and usually trusted his decisions. "I'm sorry. I stand by Ray's decisions. He is an excellent detective."

LaRue was right. Ray did not give a damn about titles. He would have arrested a priest or the pope if he had to.

Not only was the rabbi upset about the detectives' questioning, worried about Anita, and concerned that his affair would soon be public knowledge, he was also fearful for his own safety. Immediately following the shooting, the temple hired two off-duty police officers to serve as the rabbi's personal bodyguards. He began wearing a bulletproof vest, and as an extra precaution, Rabbi Jacobs began driving a rented car.

Once back at the station, Michael Coffey decided to call back Melvin Green's attorney, Arthur Alexander, who had been leaving messages since early morning. Melvin wanted to see his wife. Apparently the security department at North Hollywood Hospital wasn't letting Melvin into Anita's hospital room, and Coffey's officers were following their orders. It appeared that someone had mysteriously and cryptically told hospital security that Melvin was a prime suspect.

Coffey suspected the culprit was the rabbi. Rabbi Jacobs had probably told hospital administrators that Melvin was dangerous. Shit, Coffey thought. Mel has just as much a right to visit his wife as Jacobs has. At this point, they were both suspects. Anyone who knew her well enough was a suspect.

Coffey agreed to meet Mel and his lawyer at the hospital. The guy might be a weirdo, but he was a weirdo who was going to visit his wife. "I'll have to stay with your client to make sure he doesn't try anything funny," the detective added.

"Of course," Alexander answered. "I'll let him know."

At the hospital, Coffey was struck by how calm Mel seemed. He wasn't shaky or jumpy, not on the defensive. He wasn't upset about what his wife was going through. He wasn't sad and he wasn't angry. It was as if Mel was a ventriloquist's dummy, going through all the motions, always with his attorney or someone else telling him how to act. Melvin Green thought he was a damn good actor. But others thought he should have been showing more concern. His indifference was inappropriate.

Only when Coffey searched Mel for weapons did he get upset. But that wasn't out of the ordinary. Not many people relished being frisked.

"Art, about the only thing they didn't do was go up my ass," Mel later complained.

"Don't let them upset you," Alexander answered. "I told you it would be like this."

Melvin held his head high as he entered Anita's room escorted by Detective Coffey. Arthur Alexander remained outside and waited.

Coffey turned to Mel. "Look, I have one rule for you. She's been through a lot; don't touch her." After all, the woman was in intensive care. She was hooked up to dozens of machines.

Mel agreed, then asked, "Can I place a hand on her bed while I pray?" Coffey nodded in agreement.

As Anita Green lay in her hospital bed with tubes attached to her for life support, Melvin Green stood at the foot of her bed, next to a police officer, and placed a keepah, a small skull cap used in prayer, on his head and a prayer shawl around his shoulders. Detective Coffey remained at the side of her bed, never taking his eyes off Melvin. Melvin began to pray, swaying and chanting loudly.

After a few minutes, Mel looked at his watch and turned to Coffey. "I'm finished."

Surprised, Coffey exited the room with Mel. Jeez, thought Coffey. The man had made a big fuss considering he only spent about five minutes with his wife. It seemed like he couldn't wait to get out of there. Coffey watched as Mel began to walk away.

Just then, a doctor approached. "Mr. Green, your wife isn't getting any better."

"You're saying she won't recover?" Mel asked. The doctor nodded.

"You're sure?" Mel pressed on, making the motions of wiping a tear from his eye.

Coffey stared at both the doctor and Melvin. He left the hospital as convinced as Ray Hernandez was about Melvin's involvement. "I never saw him shed a tear," the detective told others back at the station. "He was just his obnoxious self, even when he talked with her doctor, which I guess is normal for this guy. I have never seen anything like it."

Meanwhile, the San Fernando Valley was filled with rumors about the shooting. Since Anita was a well-known community leader, the rumors were spreading at a rapid rate. It seemed everyone had a theory.

Ray Hernandez spent some time checking into the most likely theories. There had been a dispute with the Woodland

Hills Homeowners Association over the use of the temple's land near Pierce College. Some homeowners were not too happy about having a temple for a neighbor and had expressed concern over potential noise and traffic. Hernandez discovered that Anita and Robert Gross, the president of the Woodland Hills Homeowners Association, had resolved the issues after many months of heated debates and there were no longer any problems.

With the land issues cleared up, Hernandez decided to visit the other men that Mel Green had told police were screwing his wife. The detective hoped they could shed some light on the situation.

After interviewing both men for several hours, Ray Hernandez found that once again Mel was giving them false leads and that the men were merely friends of Anita's and Mel's. Frustrated, he returned to the station. By seven that evening, Hernandez found Coffey had eliminated the guy with a motorcycle who had parked at Anita's building. He was the boyfriend of another resident who had already moved out. Besides, his motorcycle had been impounded several months ago.

Ray's interviews and follow-up calls ended at about 7:30 P.M. He was exhausted by the physical and mental effort he had expended and frustrated by what he wasn't finding. Where was the gun? Why couldn't they find the bullet? If the shooting was indeed a hit, what money had Mel used to pay for it? Why did Mel have so many damn bank accounts? Were there any life insurance policies? How was he supposed to guess which leads were legitimate and which, like the parking-lot motorcyclist, were a waste of time?

Hernandez realized that what he did have was good: Anita's set appointment at Mel's office, the planned execution-style hit, and Melvin's own atrocious behavior. He thought that the people at the temple probably would not talk because either they really did not know anything else, or they didn't want to talk about what they did know. But Ray Hernandez knew someone, somewhere, had to know more about what had happened. Ray would have to gain the trust of someone who was close to the Greens.

And so, despite his exhaustion from working a fourteen-

hour shift, Ray Hernandez went to observe the people closest
to Anita and Melvin Green: their temple family. He wanted to
talk to them before they talked with each other, or their
statements would not be worth a damn. In this case, he wanted
to catch them before they compared notes about what not to
talk about. Ray set off for the temple where *Shabbat* services
were already in session.

The Shir Chadash congregation held services in the sanctuary of a small community church located in a residential part
of Woodland Hills. On *Shabbat* and whenever else the temple
used the facility, a large Israeli flag was placed over the cross
that adorned the sanctuary wall. A portable ark housed the
congregation's three Torahs, including one that had been
rescued from the Holocaust and brought to America.

Tonight the sanctuary overflowed with congregants. Rabbi
Jacobs seemed drained and exhausted. He had spent a frantic
day rushing from his house to Anita's apartment, to the
hospital, to the temple, all the while with a phone in his hand.
He informed confidants that he had to remain strong for his
congregants, for his children, for Ginger.

Though stressed and clearly worried about his own safety,
Rabbi Jacobs was actually holding up well. He always stayed
calm during a crisis, and he wanted to do as much as possible
for the many people hurting from this tragedy, just as Anita
had always done everything for everybody.

As the rabbi watched his followers stream into the church's
sanctuary, Ray Hernandez knew he was probably praying that
his congregation would stand by him. It appeared that they
would, for now, more than ever, the congregants needed to be
together to experience the power of community. Jacobs was
their leader. They needed his spiritual guidance to help make
sense of this tragedy. Ray had seen it before. He called it the
"Jimmy Swaggart phenomenon." For these people, no explanations were needed.

As the congregants joined together to pray for Anita, many
were moved to tears. They were angry, they were outraged,
and they were scared.

As Ray Hernandez stood anonymously in the back of the
sanctuary, he noticed Melvin Green sitting in the front row
with another woman. Ray saw that the other congregants

avoided looking at Mel and few offered him their prayers. It seemed to him that Melvin Green had become the community pariah in just twenty-four hours.

It must have been strange for many in attendance, being at a religious service, praying for a well-known and well-loved congregant's recovery, knowing that the woman, the victim of a shocking shooting, might have been shot at her husband's request. The whispers filled the room. "Her husband is involved, you know. The police are certain."

It was after ten P.M. when Ray Hernandez pulled out of the church parking lot, but he still had one more place to visit before calling it a night. He had to get to the hospital to see what was going on. Once there, the detective found Anita's family bleary-eyed from lack of sleep, eyes swollen from crying. Her sister, Linda Borsen, had arrived earlier in the day from Philadelphia. She stood by Anita's side, softly talking to her big sister.

Family and friends were beginning to realize that it might be better if they lost her. It was all so sudden and horrible, and they were overwhelmed by pain. The shell of a person in the hospital bed was not their Anita. They wanted to remember the laughing, loving Anita, always so full of life, the lady who would often do the unexpected.

Ray Hernandez was moved to tears. It was not often that he got this way. These people had no idea of the pain they were about to face when they found out about the dark sides of Anita, Mel, the rabbi, and the many others who would soon be exposed by the investigation to follow. No matter how good a person Anita was, there were secrets lurking in her past. Ray knew that these secrets would have to be made public to trap her killer.

19

May You Go to Another Place in Peace

Two days after the shooting, most of Anita's bodily functions had shut down. Machinery kept her lungs working and her heart beating. For more than forty-eight hours, the ICU specialists had given it their all. Six IVs dripped life-giving fluids and medicines into her body. A seventh transfused blood. She had received fifty-four units in all since the shooting. An intercranial bolt measured the pressure surrounding her traumatized brain. Machines monitored her cardiac function.

The head emergency-room nurse, Ellen Morrison, had already called several Code Blue emergencies to resuscitate Anita early Saturday. Each time her heart stopped, the ICU staff would swing into action, administering drugs and trying every trick they knew to get her stabilized. It was exhausting and frustrating.

Ellen Morrison was badly shaken from Anita's last cardiac arrest. Although Anita had pulled through, her heartbeat was now even weaker. Having seen enough seriously ill patients to know this one wasn't going to get better, Morrison asked the family, "Why don't you let her die with dignity? We can stop the Code Blue orders at any time."

The nurse remembered the family as having been badly shaken by her suggestion. Her foreboding words took away their last bit of hope. Nevertheless, after discussing the situation at length, they agreed it was what Anita would want.

186

Anita's twenty-two-year-old son, Scott, appeared to take the news the hardest. When the family returned to his mother's room after their decision, Scott stared at his mother. He couldn't believe what was happening. She was really dying. Crying, he knocked his head on the equipment hanging from her bed and fainted.

Ellen had seen all this before. She turned to Scott's father, Roger Arnow, and said, "I was waiting for something like this to happen. He's been so strong." The nurse revived Scott quickly with smelling salts and water.

As Scott returned to his mother's side, he was joined by another visitor. Melvin Green walked into the room and stood on the left side of Anita's bed with Linda and Riva. His son Cary was with him, standing in the back of the room. No one said a word to either one of them.

Scott and the rabbi remained on Anita's right side. Roger stood by the door. Four uniformed officers stood in the room to make sure Melvin didn't try anything. Rabbi Jacobs shielded Anita's body from Melvin's touch. The irony of it all made Scott sick; now that it was too late to make a difference, everyone was trying to protect his mother.

Melvin Green looked at his wife. As if on cue, he put his chin down and placed his hands over his eyes. After just a minute, he raised his head. Those around the bed noticed there wasn't a tear in his eyes.

Then, while standing at his wife's deathbed, Melvin took out a small blender, prepared his diet shake, and drank it. After finishing, Melvin proceeded to walk around the hospital room and explain to everyone present how the life-support equipment that was in Anita's room worked. Michael Coffey couldn't believe it.

A few minutes later, Anita died.

As her family and friends went back into the room to say their own private goodbyes, they noticed a nurse had drawn the shades, leaving the small room in a kind of perpetual twilight. Anita looked like she was sleeping, and against the light, her beauty shone through despite her horrible injuries. Now, in death, Anita Green had at last found peace and sanctuary.

Melvin Green, not the rabbi, began to chant the *Shema,* the watchword of the Jewish people. Anita's family and friends at first pretended not to hear but then bowed their heads in prayer. At the close of the prayer, a nurse finally pulled a sheet over Anita.

The rabbi noted that Anita Molly Green died on *Shabbat*, at 3:35 P.M. He later said at her funeral that she died as the Torah portion was being read in shuls across the nation. "The *Sedra*, the Torah portion *Lech Lecha*. May you go. *Lech Lecha*. May you go to another place in peace."

Later that day the family decided the funeral and *shiva* would be held at the rabbi's house because he insisted on it. Riva Rice offered to have it in her condominium's recreation room, but the temple members quickly talked her out of it. Anticipating a huge crowd of mourners, they felt Riva's building wouldn't be able to accommodate them all. Too weak to argue, she agreed to do whatever the others thought best. She just insisted that nothing be held at Mel and Anita's home in Encino. In fact, she wanted as little do with Mel as possible.

The next day, Sunday, Scott, Anita's sister Linda, and Phyllis Baltin set off from the rabbi's house to go to the cemetery to make arrangements for the memorial service and funeral. The rabbi allowed Linda and Scott to pick Anita's coffin, with the one stipulation that it be an oak wood, similar to the dining-room set Anita and he had just purchased together. His comments were perceived as strange, and they made everyone present uncomfortable. But Anita wound up in an oak casket.

After the small group's trip to the funeral home, Rabbi Jacobs phoned the coroner's office and was told that since Anita had died on a weekend, the autopsy wouldn't take place until Monday morning. The funeral could be held Tuesday afternoon. The rabbi then called the temple staff with the information. A group of volunteers stood ready to make all the necessary phone calls.

On Monday morning, Detective Ray Hernandez sat in on Anita Green's autopsy. Autopsies of gunshot victims determine the actual cause of death. It is important during a subsequent trial that the police should be able to testify as to whether the gunshot wound killed the victim, or if the person died from a heart attack following the shooting, or from something else as a result of it.

To Ray's astonishment, Anita's body looked completely different from the photograph that he had studied carefully, trying to get a picture of her in his head. Here on the slab, her head shaved, her body filled with fluids and swollen beyond recognition, Ray saw exactly what the bullet had done to Anita Green. As he stared down at Anita, he was more troubled than ever about Melvin Green.

The medical examiner, Dr. Susan Selser, worked for the Los Angeles County Coroner's office, performing autopsies on people who died sudden, unexpected deaths. A forensic pathologist, she'd performed over three thousand autopsies and now held a supervising position in the coroner's office.

Selser confirmed that Anita had died from a gunshot wound to the posterior neck. The wound caused multiple-organ system failure. Her brain showed evidence of infraction or ischemic injury. She had developed pneumonia, a common secondary symptom of a gunshot wound. A large bruise was found on Anita's arm. All of this was a chain reaction from the gunshot wound.

Because Anita's hair had been shaved around the entry wound, there was no visible soot or stippling from the bullet on the surface of her skin. Upon further examination, under a dissecting scope, a small fragment of lead could be seen. There were no obvious gunpowder particles present and no bullet was ever recovered. Selser noted that hospital records indicated the presence of gunpowder residue, which, if correct, would indicate the killer had shot her from an extremely close range.

On Tuesday afternoon, October 30, 1990, the body of Anita Molly Green was laid to rest next to her father's grave at Groman Eden Memorial Park in Mission Hills, California.

Nearly five hundred people gathered to mourn the death of their friend, role model, and leader. The large chapel overflowed with mourners. Chairs had to be set up outside to accommodate the crowd. Everyone was furious that such a young, vital woman had been shot down, execution style, in the prime of her life, in what was obviously a planned killing.

Wearing the traditional black mourner's ribbon on his vest to symbolize that a loved one had been torn from his heart, Melvin Green stood alone watching the crowd coming to honor his fallen wife. He thought they were making her into a hero.

What people remembered most vividly about the funeral was the shocking tone of the rabbi's sermon. It was obvious that Rabbi Jacobs's moving speech was not just a eulogy but a passionate memory of a lover now gone. So intimate was its tone that many were caught off guard.

The rabbi recalled "stopping to gaze at her, her makeup put on fastidiously, with baggy shorts and a sweatshirt. Or elegant, in one of her many outfits with her jewelry and her rings. Admiring or just staring at her beautiful nails and her gentle hands; holding those hands, her skin so very soft, so reassuring, those beautiful hands."

This was not the grieving husband recalling his wife's soft skin and beautiful eyes, but the spiritual leader of the community. The gossips, who for months had rumored about Jacobs's most recent affair, felt vindicated. It appeared the rabbi was now baring his soul to all who had gathered to honor Anita.

At the conclusion of the service, each mourner filed past the coffin before going out to the grave site. The rabbi stood in front of the coffin with a huge Samoan bodyguard behind him who watched everyone as they filed by. Four plainclothes policemen were also present, taking notes for Detective Hernandez. While walking to Anita's grave, people clung to one another for support. Many could barely stand.

At the grave site, the rabbi read Anita's High Holiday message to her congregation, written just a few weeks earlier. "Our span on Earth is brief. We do not write our names in sand. Rather we carve them in everlasting memories, always with the hope that they will hold meaning for those who follow."

As Anita was buried, a handful of earth taken from the temple's land at the groundbreaking ceremony was placed inside her grave. The rabbi said he positioned the holy earth in the grave to sanctify the ground and to link Anita symbolically to the congregation forever.

As Anita's coffin was lowered into the ground, the mourners began to chant *Kaddish,* the traditional Jewish prayer to honor the dead. At last Melvin Green emerged from his silence, brazenly chanting with an exuberance ordinarily reserved for celebrations. He even began to clap his hands.

In the Jewish tradition, as the funeral came to a close, mourners lined up to place a shovelful of earth over Anita's coffin. Mel threw his shovelful into the open grave and stared down at it. Then he began to rain dirt over the casket in what seemed like a frenzied attempt to cover more than just the coffin. The onlookers recoiled in shock until one woman intervened, gently calming Melvin by taking the shovel away.

Long after the last mourner had left, and after she had returned home, Riva Rice sat in her living room with her only living child and did what she seldom did. She cried and cried. First, for the spectacle the rabbi had made at the funeral; his words during her daughter's eulogy had embarrassed her so. Second, for what she feared she was about to find out. And finally, for the loss of her beloved daughter.

20

Outlining the Puzzle

On October 30, while hundreds of people mourned Anita at her funeral, the homoside investigators were hard at work. One thing still bothered Ray Hernandez, the question of the temple's land. Though the temple's staff said Mel was wrong, that the land was no longer a problem, Hernandez wasn't certain. Why hadn't the congregation built yet? Was someone or something preventing them from getting the project started? Over the years, Ray Hernandez had seen people murdered for all sorts of strange reasons.

To ease his nagging suspicions, Detective Hernandez questioned Robert Gross, the Woodland Hills Homeowners Association president. The reality was, despite Mel's story, it didn't seem plausible to Ray that this group had anything to do with the killing, and Gross seemed very upset about what had happened to Anita.

Armed with that knowledge, Hernandez left Woodland Hills and went back to his office frustrated and tired. Several hours had passed and he was getting nowhere. Each time he questioned one of the people Melvin had accused, he found them to be normal, law-abiding citizens whom Melvin had merely decided to point a finger at. The detective assumed that Mel would probably keep coming up with his own theories as long as he was worried about what the police might find on him.

Meanwhile, the homicide desk was taking dozens of calls about the murder now that the suspect's composite picture had run in the newspaper and on television. When Hernandez entered the station, the detective at the desk handed him several messages on a yellow pad. Smiling, she said, "Good luck. Looks like you'll need it on this one."

Ray glanced at the calls and returned just one, to Anita's divorce attorney, Janis McDonald. McDonald informed him that she thought several insurance policies existed on Anita that might still be in effect.

Hernandez put a police department investigator right on it. The detective knew that if Mel carried a great deal of insurance on Anita, he would have a significant financial gain by getting rid of her. Financial gain was always a great motive for murder.

He was still mulling over this possibility when a man entered his office. "Are you Detective Ray Hernandez?"

"I am," Hernandez said calmly. "If you're here to talk to me about the Green murder, I'm ready."

Gilbert Mershon was a certified public accountant who had known Mel for three years. A tall, lanky man with a nervous air about him, Mershon sat down next to the detective. "I called you on the phone. You have no idea of the kind of man Melvin Green is."

"I think we're beginning to get the picture," Ray replied, thinking, here come more Mel Green stories that are sure to be outrageous. But how were all these stories going to lead to answers? Hernandez leaned across the interview table. "Do you have anything specific?"

"Oh yeah, tons," Mershon answered nervously, as he readied himself to spill his guts. Hernandez thought this guy was about to explode.

"He said that if Anita ever decided to divorce him, he would hire a hitman to blow her head off."

Ray Hernandez tried to remain calm. He listened attentively before asking, "What else did he tell you?"

"He just told me if Anita ever left him, he would kill her." Mershon replied. "Mel was very matter-of-fact about it and made the threat to me at least nine times."

"Nine times?" Hernandez asked incredulously.

"Yeah, nine times," Mershon said. "Mel has severe personality disorders."

"What kind of disorders? Can you describe them to me?" Ray was trying to mask his excitement. His initial impression was that though Mershon obviously did not like Melvin Green, he was telling the truth.

"Well, the first time I got really nervous about Mr. Green was when he pointed a loaded gun at me."

"Was he moody, irrational? What do you mean he got you nervous?"

"I mean, he became violent all the time. He was very abusive, very cleverly abusive." Gilbert Mershon was getting all worked up talking about Melvin Green. "He liked to yell and scream and carry on. Those around him just tried to tune him out."

Mershon spent several hours with Ray Hernandez, and by the time he was finished, the detective was familiar with Mel's long history of moody behavior. Hernandez felt certain that, when angered by Anita's betrayal, Mel had found the courage to do exactly what he had threatened to do all along.

Mershon had witnessed firsthand that Mel would badger, insult, ridicule, and hurt all those around him. Mershon had watched this for several years. He claimed Mel's worst actions were directed toward his wife, Anita.

"I'd watch him interact with her, detective. I've never seen a human being treat another human being that way. He'd call her a cunt in front of her rabbi. Anita got so she couldn't respond at all. She'd just roll her eyes and stay quiet."

"Were you close with Melvin at the time?" Hernandez asked.

"Mel and I used to talk about our wives a lot. I had some problems with my ex-wife, so we'd talk. Anyway, I said, 'The way you carry on with Anita, when it comes to divorce, she's going to be able to nail you for everything, because I've never seen any human being abuse another human being as badly as you abuse Anita.' That's when he made the threats. I even asked him how he would do it—because I wanted to get him to talk about it, to see how stupid what he was saying was. He said, 'I know some people. I know some sicko bums. I'd get them to kill her.'"

Hernandez was fascinated. Melvin had actually talked with people about having his wife eighty-sixed. Not a common occurrence. Most people planning to kill someone don't talk about it. Melvin Green was a boastful man.

"Do you have any idea of how Melvin would actually hire somebody to kill his wife?" the detective asked.

"Melvin has associated with many lowlife types over the years, drug addicts and the like. Perhaps one of them would do this." Mershon added, "I don't think he'd just lay some money out and hire somebody. He'd have to know them. It would have to be someone over whom he had leverage and control. As I said, Melvin likes to control and own the people around him."

Ray Hernandez paced the floor of the small interview room excitedly. For the first time ever, it was obvious to him what had happened. Mershon's answers painted a vivid picture, and his words were hard to digest at once. Clearly Mel had known exactly how Anita would be killed. Either he planned it, or he was a damn good psychic.

When Mershon got up to leave, he told Ray he had many files and letters in his office that might assist the police department with their investigation. The detective went immediately to Gil Mershon's office, where he gathered more information for "the file," including letters, telephone numbers, possible suspects. Mershon was definitely out to get Melvin Green. He despised the man.

Reading Mershon's files, Ray Hernandez was struck by the fact that Mel had the unusual habit of profuse letter-writing about things that annoyed or irritated him. Anita was usually the topic of these letters. Ray decided to get a search warrant to go through Mel's office, where hopefully he'd find more letters that might help him.

Ray Hernandez didn't know what to make of the vast collection of letters people were beginning to bring in to him. Soon he would collect more than two hundred letters: love letters, hate letters, obsessive letters, threatening letters, years of letters Melvin Green had painstakingly labored over for many hours each day.

Feeling a little like a voyeur, Ray Hernandez began to study the letters. Oblivious at first to the extent of damage these letters would bring to Melvin Green, Ray found he was fascinated by them. Fortunately, Melvin Green remained oblivious too, and he continued to write as many as twenty letters each day, outlining his inappropriate feelings to anyone who would take the time to read his words.

Later, as Ray sat in his Jacuzzi with a stiff shot of gin in one hand, he tried to relax so he could finally get some sleep. He just couldn't get Melvin Green or his letters out of his mind. The letters incensed him. Somehow Ray knew they held the key. They were filled with inappropriate threats that he was certain would put away Green.

Perhaps it was the gin, or the lateness of the hour, or the fact that Ray hadn't had much sleep since he picked up this case, but he finally fell asleep in his Jacuzzi. He dreamed of the three things that stood out in his mind: Mel's strange actions at the crime scene, hospital, and funeral; his actual arranging of the time and place Anita was to be when she was shot; and now, Mel's own admitted intentions.

21

Fitting in the Pieces

Ray Hernandez spent the next week gathering enough information to go to the prosecutors with. A less motivated investigator might have given up. But Hernandez doggedly built his case, and he grew more confident daily. Fortunately, people were spilling their guts about his suspect.

During the long week filled with often outrageous stories about the Greens, he received one phone call that was particularly illuminating. It came from Anita's hairdresser, Gina Siguenza.

Ray went to meet with her. Even before the meeting, he sensed that her information would be crucial. After all, she was just Anita's hairdresser, and she, unlike many of the others who had come forward, had no reason to "burn" Melvin. It just so happened that Hernandez's intuition proved right.

Gina told Ray Hernandez that she had been Anita's hairdresser for three or four years and that she did her hair three times a month. One time they had even lunched together, and Anita had confided in Gina about how miserable her marriage had grown. She claimed that she was afraid to leave because of her husband's violent temper. Anita said that on two occasions Mel had beaten her.

"As time passed, Anita kept telling me that her marriage was getting worse. She finally moved out in July. I asked her if she was happy. I'll never forget how sad she looked when she answered. She told me she liked being on her own, but that

Melvin wouldn't leave her alone. He kept calling her and bothering her for the stupidest reasons."

"What kind of reasons?" Ray asked. Gina was Hispanic, and her heavy accent was difficult to understand. Hernandez wanted to speak in Spanish but refrained from doing so, because he knew that Gina's testimony would come across better in English during a trial.

"All kinds, just to bother her. In early October when I did her hair, Anita told me that she still had not received any money from Melvin. At that time, Mel called my shop, and I could tell from their conversation that Melvin promised to give her money. On the call, she begged Mel to stop arguing with her. She told him she just wanted to settle everything peacefully."

"Did she get a check?"

"Not then. Anita told me that if she didn't get money soon she would have to get a job. She was not willing to pick up a check in person for the work he already owed her money for. She was afraid."

Gina then told the detective that Anita had gone out of town with her mother to San Francisco. When she came back, on October 24, the day before she was shot, Gina did her hair. Gina described Anita as quiet and sad that day, and claimed to have questioned Anita about her mood. Anita's answer was filled with pain and despair.

" 'Everything in my life is a mess, Gina. My marriage is making me crazy. Mel won't leave me alone.'" Gina explained, "That's when he called, detective. Right after she said that." The hairdresser was drained. She was crying, and Ray could tell that she was a little frightened when she talked about Mel.

"Anita told Mel that she was too busy to pick up her check and that he had promised to mail it to her. I heard her say it." Gina was crying openly now. She wasn't ashamed, but took a few minutes to compose herself. "Anita hung up the phone and told me that Melvin demanded that if she wanted her check, she had to pick it up Thursday at 10:30 A.M. I heard her part of the conversation with Melvin, word for word."

"Are you certain?" Hernandez asked.

"I am," Gina replied. "Melvin was the one who set up the day and time she was supposed to arrive at his place of business. It was not Anita's idea."

Ray kept writing and Gina kept talking. "Anita got off the phone and looked in my eyes. She told me that she did not want to pick up her check in person because she was afraid that he might do something to her. She was terrified. She hugged me and that was the last time I saw her alive."

"Do you think Mel hired someone to kill her? Was he capable of doing something like that?"

Gina never hesitated. "In my opinion Melvin Green was a very jealous person who became very angry when Anita moved out and filed for divorce. Melvin set up the exact time and place where Anita could be found by someone. I'm certain he is responsible for what happened."

Ray Hernandez was right. Gina Siguenza would be a powerful weapon for the prosecution's case. Now, if only he had the real weapon. Ray spent the rest of the week filling in holes.

As time passed, the detective found much of the information that people brought to him was circumstantial at best. He was discouraged until Anita and Mel's close friend, Phyllis Baltin, came into the station. Phyllis's illuminating words gave the frustrated detective a much-needed shot in the arm. Phyllis and her boyfriend, Lance, confirmed Gilbert Mershon's story. It appeared that Mel really wanted to find someone to kill his wife and at the time of her death was actively soliciting someone to do the job.

After questioning Phyllis for an entire day, Ray knew he was far from finished with the Greens. He spent the next five days meeting with Mel's eldest son, Michael; his first wife, Bernyce; and with several other family members and friends. Though they supported Melvin and believed in his innocence, their interviews proved that Hernandez was on the right track.

Meanwhile, the temple members and the community were desperately groping for answers. City officials joined police and religious leaders in offering a thirty-thousand-dollar reward for help in solving the crime. When Homicide Coordinator Michael Coffey attended the press conference that announced the reward, he was besieged by questions from information-hungry reporters. The rumors had been spreading through the Valley at a rapid rate. Was the crime motivated by anti-Semitism? Did the police have any suspects? Was Melvin Green involved?

When Coffey told him about the press conference, Ray Hernandez began shaking his head. Now that a reward had been offered, there was no telling what kind of crazy leads would flow into the station to unnecessarily take up the detectives' time; leads that Mel's attorney would expect them to follow up on. This was the very thing Ray was trying to avoid.

Frustrated, Hernandez finally set off to interview the victim's mother, Riva Rice. He had waited an appropriate amount of time. This was the interview he dreaded the most. He debated with himself about letting her in on what they had so far. He didn't want to get her hopes up, nor did he want her to hear some of the things being said about her late daughter. Ray just wanted to protect her and knew he would never be able to do so.

Riva met with Ray Hernandez in her home. He found her to be gracious and kind. She was sad about her daughter, but calm. She really wanted to help, but she didn't know much. She told the detective that her daughter's friends knew more about Anita than she did.

Riva told Ray that Anita had wanted to move out for quite a while, but that she had waited until July because of tax season. In July, when she initially moved, Melvin had given her ten thousand dollars for expenses. That had lasted all summer.

On October 12, Anita and Riva traveled to San Francisco for a short trip and returned on Monday night, October 15. It was then that Anita asked to borrow money because her husband had refused to give her anymore. Riva told the detective that she had loaned Anita twenty-five thousand dollars on Tuesday evening. That was the last time she saw her daughter alive.

Ray Hernandez promised himself that he would be gentle. But it just didn't seem plausible that Anita's mother did not know anything about what was going on. She seemed to have been close to her daughter. They had even recently vacationed together.

Hernandez pressed a little harder. He was straightforward and honest. "I need your help."

"I want to give it to you." Riva seemed sincere, and Ray liked her. "I don't know if Melvin ever threatened to harm or kill Anita. She would never tell me anything like that because she would not want to worry me." Riva thought for a moment.

"I do know that Anita's marriage to Melvin was bizarre. He liked to be in control."

The interview had only lasted a half hour. Once again Ray Hernandez had heard how strange Mel was, but that was about it. For the next few weeks all he would continue to hear was how strange Mel was. It was time to take his suspicions to the prosecutor.

22

A Tough District Attorney

When Ray Hernandez learned that Deputy District Attorney Kent Cahill had been assigned to this case, he felt as though he was going in with two strikes against him. Ray knew Cahill's reputation and it bothered him. Though he had completed dozens of interviews, he still didn't have a smoking gun, a solicitation letter, or a witness who could in any concrete way tie Melvin Green to the murder. Cahill was a stickler for those things. If Cahill couldn't be convinced beyond a reasonable doubt, how could he expect anything more from a jury?

Second, though he had been assigned to this case less than a month ago, on October 25, Hernandez had a premonition that, even if he investigated Melvin Green for a hundred years, he would never be able to discern what the exact events leading up to Anita's murder were. Cahill would want those answers.

Ray knew that Kent Cahill was certain to look at the case like a defense attorney. He could say that everything the detective had gathered was merely a hodgepodge of supposition and coincidence, pasted together with the letters and ramblings of a guy who happened to be obnoxious and inappropriate. Inappropriate behavior, no matter how bizarre, is not grounds enough for a murder conviction. It figured that he and Cahill had been assigned to work together on one of the messier cases in Ray's long career, a case where the detective found himself with so many missing pieces. The physical evidence was weak, but Hernandez knew that he might not ever be able to present anything stronger. And he was convinced that Melvin Green was guilty!

Ray Hernandez stormed around the San Fernando court and fumed about his upcoming appointment with Kent Cahill. He was so worried and concerned about it that he almost tripped over one of his favorite young prosecutors, Steven Ipsen. Only months earlier, at age thirty-one, Ipsen had become the youngest district attorney in Los Angeles County to get a death-penalty conviction. Previously that record had been held for seven years by...Kent Cahill.

"What's up, Ray? I haven't seen you around for a while," Steve said.

Steven Ipsen and Ray Hernandez had worked together on several cases over the past few years and had developed a good working relationship. They trusted and respected each other. Ray lamented that he was upset about who had been assigned to the Green case and that he was worried about working with Kent Cahill. "Is he as bad as they say?"

Steven laughed and replied, "Ray, calm down. Cahill is the best around. Certainly in this office. You wouldn't want another D.A. for a case this difficult, especially if you want to win. He's my supervisor and I know he's good."

"What's he like to work with?" Ray asked.

"He's tough, because he expects the best of people and he always thinks that you will see things his way. But, if anyone feels the weight of responsibility on their shoulders, it's Kent Cahill."

Ray hoped Steve was right. He knew in his gut that Melvin Green was guilty, and he was not willing to let the guy just walk away. All Ray kept seeing over and over in his mind was Anita's swollen body at the autopsy. Ray swore if it had to be by the sheer force of his own will, Melvin Green would pay for the murder Ray was certain he had orchestrated.

What Ray Hernandez didn't know was that Kent Cahill had felt this same way about other suspects in other cases. He knew firsthand what being obsessed was all about. He could be equally obsessive and focused. That was one of the reasons that Billy Webb, the head of the San Fernando District Attorney's Office, had assigned Kent to the case.

Webb knew that the case was both difficult and political from the beginning. There was not a lot of hard evidence. There was pressure from the Jewish community, and the case was sure to get a lot of press. Webb didn't give a damn about those kinds of things. He never did. Politics rubbed him the wrong way and nobody ever pressured Billy Webb. He held the reputation for being one of the most respected prosecutors in the state, and Kent Cahill was one of his finest deputies.

Unlike many prosecutors, Webb didn't care about win/loss percentages or about the new matrix in Washington that showed how to run a D.A.'s office with 98 percent convictions. Sure, the theories said if the defendant was caught at the scene with a gun and the people are holding him down, you probably have a 99 percent chance of a conviction. Webb did not run his office that way. If Webb thought someone had committed a crime, then he was going to have his deputies give it a shot, even if conviction was estimated at 10 percent or less.

From the minute Ray Hernandez brought Webb the case, he became as convinced as the detective was about who was guilty. Ray had told Webb that he needed help and that he wanted to "get" Mel before he fled. Billy Webb agreed and asked Hernandez whom he wanted to work with, suggesting several of his top guns.

"I know it is going to be a difficult and complex case," Ray explained. Billy nodded in agreement. "I need someone who has the time to do a good job. You decide for me."

Webb thought carefully about it and chose Kent Cahill. He needed somebody who was a very good lawyer, and he needed someone with an extremely strong personality. Kent was abrasive enough to push his inventiveness through the courts and, hopefully, would be more creative than most when figuring out how to put all the little pieces together.

Ray and Kent would be perfect partners for this trial. Kent would carefully build the case. He was so straightforward that at times he came across as rude and obnoxious. Ray would take care of the people, get the witnesses, prepare them for trial, hold their hands. Neither man knew it at the time, but as a team, they would prove to be awesome.

In the beginning of November, less than two weeks after

Anita's murder, Ray Hernandez met with Kent Cahill over lunch to explain the case to him. He told Kent all that he knew, which was mostly that Melvin Green was the most obnoxious man he had ever met, and that he had mentioned to a lot of people how badly he hated his wife. Ray also told Kent about the specific threats, the affairs, Mel's fears of Anita blowing the whistle on his business, and the way Melvin had tried to steer the police investigation away from him.

Cahill was a man of substantial girth, with a neatly trimmed beard and a slightly receding hairline. He looked like he might be more comfortable cutting down trees than being in the courtroom. He had a gentle face, a rapier-like wit, and an impressive vocabulary. Kent Cahill looked a little like a big bear.

Ray eyed Kent Cahill suspiciously as he briefed him about Melvin Green. The detective sensed immediately how bright Kent was. He appeared to be smart and intense; he bent his head toward Ray as he listened, and his eyes widened and focused when he found a fact interesting or particularly illuminating. At times he raised his eyebrows when he heard something that he had difficulty believing.

"I don't like him," Ray said. "I hate that he thinks he is better than everyone else. I get the feeling that he thinks he is above the law."

"He certainly seems strange," Kent said.

Ray looked straight at Kent and answered, "You don't know the half of it. We have never seen anyone like him." He then spent another hour telling "Mel" stories.

Kent was shocked. He shook his head back and forth and said, "This guy is unbelievable." From what he had heard, Kent Cahill felt that the guy was probably guilty. But he didn't file a case just because he thought that someone did it. He had to weigh the evidence and decide whether he thought a reasonable jury could be expected to convict. It was a very personal decision, one that had been honed by more than a decade of experiences in the District Attorney's Office. Usually Kent was more likely to file a difficult case than less experienced prosecutors were. He liked the challenge.

As he listened to Hernandez, Kent Cahill thought that clearly Melvin Green was a suspect. He had actually talked about killing his wife, and now she was dead and he was still alive. But threats, no matter how obnoxious, were at this time not enough. Cahill felt that a competent investigator like Hernandez still had a lot to do to get the case ready to file, and it was still early enough after the murder to wait and see how things would turn out. He had reason to believe that if Ray kept working, he would find more. Otherwise, he later recalled, "I would have filed immediately."

The Melvin Greens of the world were just the kind of people Cahill detested the most. Even if they found the gunman in the future, or if Mel led them to him one day, in Kent's mind, hiring a shooter made Mel completely responsible for what had transpired. Melvin was the one who had knowingly caused his wife's death and it appeared that he had done it for the basest of motives: greed, jealousy, power, and control. Cahill knew already that he too wanted to get the guy, but he had to remain more objective than Hernandez.

Kent listened patiently as the detective poured out his heart to him. Ray could see him playing several scenarios through his head as he struggled to put it all together. Cahill looked at Ray. Finally he spoke, and he did not beat around the bush. Kent Cahill was not one to practice common courtesies or niceties. "I'm fairly certain that he did it, but I need more. Keep working on it."

Kent could see that Ray was disappointed. He didn't blame him. Then, out of character, he added compassionately, "I'm not willing to let a man like Melvin Green have Anita Green killed and just walk away from it either, Ray. I hate what he did."

Before saying goodbye, Cahill gave the detective his shopping list. He wanted Ray to look to see if there were any life insurance policies on Anita. He wanted Ray to talk with the rest of Green's family: his first wife, his employees, anyone else who would say anything that might shed some light on the murder. Finally, Kent told Ray to follow the money. If Mel had orchestrated all this, like they both suspected that he had, how had he paid for it?

Part V

Accused

April 1991–February 1992

23

Starting Over

Ray Hernandez spent the next six months working in a slow and methodical way with his partner, Gary Arnold, to accumulate enough evidence to arrest Melvin Green. It was the single obsession that governed all his days.

Through the late fall and winter of 1990 and into the new year, Ray found out more than he ever wanted to know about Melvin Morton Green: his bizarre sex practices, his real estate deals, his money-laundering schemes. The more Hernandez learned about the man and his unethical practices and the way he treated his fellow human beings, the deeper his hatred for Melvin grew. And the more he grew to detest him, the more convinced he became that Melvin was guilty. Yet he was still unable to actually tie Mel Green to the murder.

Much of the district attorney's shopping list turned up nothing new. Hernandez could not find out how Mel had paid for the murder. He was never able to trace any money to a gunman; nor was he able to find any insurance policies on Anita. All Ray had been able to do was take what he already had and flush it out. Yet there had to be something he was missing. Hernandez kept reading Melvin Green's extensive correspondence searching them carefully for clues.

According to the letters, Anita Green had become a menace to Melvin. She was threatening to expose him, and his fear was driving him mad. He no longer was able to act rationally around her. All he could think of was stopping her before she would do irreparable damage to his business, as she had already done to his life.

209

By early February 1991, Ray knew he was as close to arresting Melvin as he would ever be. He called a meeting of those closest to the victim in order to prepare them for the events certain to follow an arrest. Ray expected Riva, Scott, and Rabbi Jacobs to be eager to attend. The detective was shocked when the rabbi acted reluctant. "Just show up," Ray demanded.

Riva would never forget Rabbi Jacobs's reaction to Ray's announcement that Melvin would soon be arrested. "He turned as red as a beet. When the detective told us how to handle the press, and that the police would make all the statements, the rabbi went crazy. He said, 'There can't be any statements. I want to keep a low profile. This can't get out to the press. I'm a rabbi.' All he cared about was himself. He didn't want there to be an arrest or a trial if his name would come up. It made me sick. This was the man who killed my daughter and the rabbi didn't seem to care whether Mel paid for his actions or not."

Meanwhile, during Ray's investigation, Melvin Green had asked another woman to marry him just three short weeks after his wife's murder. This single act caused him to lose most of his few remaining supporters. What few people realized at this point was that Melvin was simply terrified of being alone and of confronting the demons that he now certainly found himself facing.

Melvin had met a young woman eighteen years his junior at a tax seminar in the middle of November. At the time of their meeting, Alexandra Leeds was a struggling young mother with two young girls. Jewish and intelligent, Alexandra worked in an office and was studying to become a therapist. In addition to her family, schooling, and job, Alexandra volunteered at North Hollywood Community Hospital—the hospital Anita was brought to after her shooting—where she counseled people with eating disorders. Melvin Green asked her out to lunch just three weeks after his wife's murder. With no intention other than to be a friend, the young woman readily agreed. On their first date, Melvin placed eighteen hundred dollars on the table. Alexandra would never have to struggle again. She took the offer.

Melvin Green was not used to people reaching out to him, especially in the weeks after his wife's death. After less than an hour with Alexandra Leeds, he asked, "Do you ever believe you have known someone before? I would like to meet your children. Will you marry me?"

Leeds was shocked. "He tried to get into my head," she later recalled. "He flooded me and forced me to do whatever he wanted."

By Thanksgiving, Alexandra had agreed to let Melvin come over to her apartment to meet her daughters. He walked into her home, kissed her on the forehead, got down on his knees, and immediately asked her two giggling daughters, "May I have your mother's hand in marriage?"

The two girls looked up to him and answered yes. Melvin was overjoyed. The next day, the apartment was filled with flowers. Alexandra felt cornered and trapped. Melvin began to shower her and her young daughters with presents and cash. "He became obsessed with me. It was like I replaced food, and he could not get enough of me."

Mel's generosity, combined with the terrible financial straits Alexandra had found herself in since her recent divorce, allowed her to get involved in a relationship that she had initially greeted with skepticism. Alexandra was impressed by Mel's wealth and his intellect, the same traits that had attracted Anita a decade earlier. By January, Alexandra and her daughters moved into Mel's house—the house he had shared with Anita for ten years. Almost immediately she made plans to remodel the home. The house was Anita's, and Alexandra wanted to make it her own.

A few months later, Mel and Alexandra excitedly left the Hall of Records after applying for a marriage license. Mel could not remember the last time he had been so happy. In his mind, April 10, 1991 was a day for new beginnings.

Alexandra followed him into his office, and together they called Temple Stephen S. Wise and reserved April 18 for their wedding ceremony. The number eighteen in the Jewish religion symbolizes life. Melvin and Alexandra were starting a new life together. They were told that the date was fine but that the rabbi's secretary would call back later with a time. Mel vowed that this time he would not let his need to control and dominate ruin another marriage. Mel would continue to go to counseling with Alexandra, and together he was certain that they would get it right.

Just the night before he had been feeling overwhelmed by a flood of conflicting emotions. Although he had not heard from the police in months, he was fearful of their investigation. He was annoyed that the IRS investigation he thought Anita had started still wasn't completely behind him, and yet he felt love like he had never known before. Though he didn't completely trust Alexandra's motives for loving him, he did not want to respond as he had in the past, with threats and intimidation.

He had spent a frantic half hour on the phone with his therapist and then kept Alexandra up half the night talking. Tossing and turning and sweating profusely, Melvin got through the night by dreaming of how beautiful his wedding would be and of how he would never again be alone.

Now he had only a week to wait and he could barely concentrate on his work. This morning's trip made it all real somehow. Excitedly, Alexandra kissed Mel good-bye and headed out to pick up her daughters' dresses. Lily, Irene, and the rest of the office were thankful for Mel's newfound happiness. It had been like walking on eggshells around the accounting office lately. No one had been the same since Anita's murder. Tax season only intensified everyone's uneasiness.

It was late afternoon on the same day, just six months after Anita's murder, and Mel was in the middle of a meeting with his client and dear friend, Milt Brown. During the meeting, he asked Milt to his upcoming wedding. "We would love to have you share our happiness."

Milt replied jokingly, "Can't you afford invitations?" Then Milt grabbed a business card off the desk and asked Mel what time the wedding was scheduled for so he could write it down.

"I don't know," Mel replied. "The rabbi hasn't gotten back to me yet." Mel picked up the phone and got Rabbi Isaiah Zeldin's secretary on the phone. "We are very excited about the wedding and would like to get an exact time confirmed. Has the rabbi been able to schedule us yet?" Mel asked excitedly.

Mel's joy was to be short-lived. Just then, Ray Hernandez burst into the office unannounced with seven or eight armed police officers.

"Hang up the phone, Melvin," Hernandez ordered.

"Wait a minute," Mel said, trying to regain control. "I'm on with my rabbi." Brown sat and watched the exchange in disbelief. Shit, there must be a whole squad of officers, Mel thought. They immediately surrounded Melvin and stood ready.

Hernandez had waited seven months for this moment and was not about to wait a second longer. He grabbed the phone from Mel's hand, slammed it down, and pulled out his handcuffs.

"Melvin Morton Green, you are under arrest for murder," Hernandez stated.

"What?" Mel asked, genuinely stunned. "What did you say?"

"You're under arrest for the murder of your wife, Anita Molly Green. I have a warrant here. The charge is murder in the first degree."

While Ray Hernandez arrested Mel, a uniformed officer escorted Brown out and asked, "Does he do your taxes?"

"Yes, he does."

"It's time to start looking for another accountant," the officer said.

"Stand up, Melvin!" Hernandez commanded. "Let's go."

Knowing that Mel kept a loaded gun in the top drawer of his desk, the detective pushed Mel away from the desk, steadying his other hand on his holstered gun. Then he moved Melvin to the side of the room, handcuffed him, and sat him in a chair. While Mel sat there, Ray Hernandez searched his desk.

"I don't want to find anything missing when I check my desk in the morning," Mel said.

"What morning are you referring to, Melvin? In what life?" Hernandez asked. The cops assisting him smirked. Melvin glared at them.

The two uniformed officers who led Mel out to a waiting car found that he offered no resistance. The prisoner was left alone in the backseat to fume. By now, the street was filled with gawkers, and Mel was embarrassed. It was undignified to be arrested with so many people watching.

The front and side of the building swarmed with police cars and Mel was literally surrounded. In addition to the cars, the street was crawling with officers on foot, all carrying radios and guns. For many of the detectives who had worked on the case and had witnessed Green in action, this was the moment cops live for. They parked their cars in front of Mel's office and watched as Ray Hernandez arrested the "son of a bitch."

In the office, Irene Sherwyn started to cry. She had absolute faith in Melvin's innocence. "Where are you taking him?"

Ray answered, "We're taking him to the North Hollywood station to book him and then we're taking him to jail."

"What are you booking him for?" Irene asked.

Not unkindly, the detective replied, "For the murder of his wife. You know we've been investigating him for quite awhile." He wanted to be nice to these people, so he added, "Feel free to contact his attorney and tell him he can meet me at the jail."

At the police station in North Hollywood, Mel was isolated and placed in a holding tank. Unshackled, he stormed and fumed. He paced around the cell like a caged lion. The officers kept refusing to answer his questions, and that fact alone made him wild with anger. He demanded to talk with his attorney and kept calling out for something or complaining about something else. When yelling did nothing, Mel began to whimper in a child's voice.

Ray Hernandez arrived at the station over an hour later. "How you doing, Mel?" he asked sarcastically.

The detective led Mel into a small interrogation room. Mike Coffey was present, but Ray did the talking.

Ray spelled Mel's rights out to him. Mel heard "You have the right to remain silent...." But this wasn't TV, and Mel got angrier by the minute. He refused to waive his rights and he refused to answer their questions.

Ray Hernandez put Mel in handcuffs and leg braces and took him to the Van Nuys jail for booking. He had never felt this amount of disdain for a perp before. Hopefully, a few nights in jail would set Mel straight.

On the way to the jail, Ray tried to keep Mel talking. Since Mel had refused to sign his rights waiver, Hernandez could not ask direct questions about the murder. But Mel could volunteer information that Ray could later have admitted through Miranda rights. Mel did not say much and Ray was annoyed.

At Ray's direction Melvin Green was put through the works

while Hernandez supervised the entire process, which was meant to further humiliate Mel and let him know who was in charge.

First, they removed all his clothes. Ray noticed that Mel's skin hung from him in accordion-like folds. "He looked like one of those Charpee dogs, and I always think of Mel when I see one of those dogs now. It was disgusting. He had lost so much weight and he had pounds of flesh hanging. He was humiliated and embarrassed that we saw him that way, which is just the reaction I had hoped for."

Mel was told to bend over while a full cavity search was done on him. Ray took his time. Mel asked him why such a search was necessary and Ray answered, "Because I am booking you for your wife's murder and I don't trust you."

"I'm holding you personally responsible for my treatment here, detective," Mel bellowed.

"What's going to happen, Mel?" Ray asked. "Do you think anyone will bother trying to touch you?" Some of the jailers laughed, but Ray didn't bother.

Next, they took down Mel's driver's license number and fingerprinted him. "I'm not a common criminal," he said. "I know high people in government who won't let you do this to me."

"Shut up, Melvin," Hernandez snarled.

Mel was weighed, measured, and photographed. He told the officers that their scale was inaccurate and made a big deal about letting the officer taking notes know that the weight he wrote down was three pounds higher than what Mel had weighed at home that morning. This was important because his scale had been calibrated with the doctor's scale and Mel was obsessed with his weight. Why was Mel worrying about his weight when he could be facing the gas chamber?

"I need to have a doctor with me at all times," Mel hollered. "I can't be put in this jail or I will become very ill." "Too bad," someone yelled back. "That's no longer your option." Melvin demanded to speak with his attorney.

For legal reasons, it was decided that Mel should indeed be examined by a doctor. He had been on a modified fast for close to a year. The county didn't want to be responsible if anything happened to him.

Ray Hernandez guided Mel down to the jail's dispensary.

Dr. Paul Gragerson examined him there. Throughout the entire exam, Mel complained that the jail's medical facility was obsolete and unsanitary. He needed state-of-the-art medical equipment to detect his numerous ailments. When Dr. Gragerson finished, Mel insisted that the doctor's exam was not sufficient.

"Book him," Dr. Gragerson said disgustedly.

"Are you certain?" Hernandez asked.

"I'm certain," replied the doctor. "There's nothing wrong with the old man." Then Gragerson impatiently instructed Melvin how to go back on real food. There were to be no provisions made for Mel's special diet in jail. After all, this was not the Hilton or some sort of health resort.

It was decided that Melvin would be housed at the Van Nuys station for the night, pending his arraignment Thursday morning. He was to stay there instead of at the main county jail so Dr. Gragerson could make sure that he was successfully weaned off his protein powder.

And so, Ray Hernandez left Melvin Green fuming in the county jail. Mel's attitude really pissed him off. It was obvious that Green thought there was no basis for a case against him. He even told Ray that he would certainly be out of jail by morning. As confident as Mel sounded, Hernandez noticed that when he was taken to the downtown jail he looked scared. Melvin knew his world was caving in.

24

What Do the Police Know That I Don't?

Arthur Alexander hung up his phone in disbelief. Mel had just been arrested. The lawyer hadn't the foggiest idea what the police had to base their arrest on other than his client's inappropriate comments. What had changed? Was there any new evidence to warrant filing charges?

He began the fifteen-minute drive across the Valley to the small North Hollywood jail where Green was being held on the charge of first-degree murder with special circumstances, a charge that Alexander knew all too well meant Melvin Green could face the gas chamber. Mel must be frantic by now.

When he arrived at the jail, Alexander was told that Mel was not there. "Well, where is he?" the lawyer asked, losing patience.

"He's been transferred," a clerk answered. "Why don't you try Van Nuys?"

As Alexander set off to find Mel, he contemplated the facts of the investigation and remained certain that whatever the police had was not enough to convict. Mel didn't need to prove his innocence to anyone. The prosecution needed to prove Mel's guilt. Arthur Alexander remained unaware of the existence of evidence substantial enough to do that.

As he drove, Art worried that a man like Mel, who was used to life's luxuries, would find the jail environment completely foreign. He hoped that Green would somehow be able to adapt, until he was able to get him out of there. In the back of his mind, Arthur knew that might not be possible.

Arthur Alexander met Melvin in the attorney-client section of the jail. The lawyer did his best to calm Mel down. Alexander sat on one side of the table; Mel sat shackled on the other. The attorney visiting room was small and filthy. Everything in the jail was dirty, and Mel, compulsive about hygiene, complained. The conditions in the holding cell were disgusting, but at least he was alone. He worried about being put into a cell with one of the "animals," and he referred to the jail population as the "miscreants" of the world. Mel said he did not belong with these people and he wanted Art to get him out.

Mel's face was covered with perspiration. His color was ashen, and he was moving and talking so quickly that he appeared to be on drugs.

"I just wanted to get on with my life and put this all behind me," Mel said.

"I know," Art replied. "If she loves you perhaps she will stick by you."

"She will," Mel answered confidently.

Art prepared Mel as best he could for what would take place during the next few days. He explained the legal proceedings that would follow and told Mel to keep his spirits up. "This will be a difficult case for them to win," he said, his voice filled with optimism. When the lawyer finally got up to leave, Mel panicked.

"Call my family. Tell them this is all a big mistake," Mel said in a broken voice. "When will I see you again? Can they come down to visit me? There are some things I need."

"Mel, it doesn't work like that." Art tried to be gentle with him. "I'll see you tomorrow. We'll see what can be done about setting bail and getting you out of here." Then he added, "I don't think the judge will go for it, considering the charge. It is highly unlikely that any judge would set bail. It's the law now. But I'll try."

"Make them," Mel replied. "There has to be something you can do." His voice was filled with desperation and terror.

Arthur Alexander strongly believed in Mel's innocence. In his heart, he did not think that Melvin Green had hired someone to kill Anita. He simply had not seen the evidence to prove otherwise.

At nine that evening, while the lawyer was busy working on the motion for bail, Alexandra Leeds walked into his office and introduced herself. She was frightened and had an air of self-pity about her. In seconds, however, her thoughts turned back to Melvin, and she felt guilty for having felt sorry for herself for even a moment.

Alexandra was worried about Mel. She was concerned about his diet, about his health, and about how he would fare in jail. Most of all, she was concerned about his future. Did he have a chance of winning? (And though she didn't have the courage to ask, did Alexander think that he was guilty?)

She began to pace. Why had the police talked to her? Would they be back? Was there any chance she would be arrested? She really knew nothing. She had even confronted Mel several times about the shooting, and he kept denying all involvement in Anita's murder. She believed him. That was why she had moved her two young daughters into his home.

Arthur Alexander looked compassionately at the woman sitting across from him. His heart went out to her. She had led an honest, law-abiding life, and now she found herself in the middle of a sordid murder case. It was as if a bomb had just exploded in her living room. There was really nothing he could do to put back the pieces of her life. He could be there so she would have someone to share her fears with, and he could keep her informed of all the legal procedures, but there was no way he could prepare her for what she was about to endure.

He took a deep breath and told Alexandra that what she was about to go through might prove to be the most difficult experience in her life. He hoped she could understand that she needed to remain strong and clearheaded. Finally, he wanted her to know that his door was always open to her.

The accused murderer made his first court appearance the following morning. He was visibly upset and could barely stand without the support of his attorney. It appeared jail had finally stripped away Melvin Green's pride.

He wore blue jailhouse coveralls, and his hands were cuffed behind him. His eyes were swollen from lack of sleep and there were huge circles under them. His voice was calm and emotionless as he entered his plea of "not guilty."

The small San Fernando courtroom was filled to capacity with reporters and photographers, as well as with Mel's family and supporters.

The local papers had covered his arrest and a new shock wave swept through the community. Members of Shir Chadash were dismayed to find their suspicions confirmed by an arrest, but many were certain that the police had arrested the right man. None came to support him. Whatever they would learn about their past supporter's fate would come from the newspapers or from the gossip filling the phone lines.

Sylvia Holste-Lillie, a member of the congregation and the rabbi's personal secretary, was quoted in the paper as saying that she hoped whatever action the police took "will bring a certain amount of peace to the community." Most people shared her sentiments and felt that she had expressed them tactfully.

During the short arraignment procedure Mel's attorney asked the court to release Mel on his own recognizance by setting bail. He promised that the esteemed tax-preparer would show up for the trial. Arthur Alexander argued that Melvin Green was an upstanding member of the community with "virtually no criminal record other than a minor infraction." (Mel had a misdemeanor conviction for selling stolen typewriters.) Mel had a business to support. Finally, Alexander added that Mel was on a special diet that could cause him to become violently ill if he went off it.

Los Angeles County Deputy District Attorney Kent Cahill implored the court to keep Melvin Green behind bars where he belonged. He argued that this was a capital case and for the purpose of a bail motion, the charges were presumed to be true. Mel had been charged with arranging for the murder of someone who posed a threat to him economically. "If he is released, there will be a still greater threat to those who pose a threat to his very life." Cahill knew how intimidating Mel could be, and he didn't want him bothering any of the witnesses.

The commissioner, Gerald T. Richardson, agreed. Melvin Green was denied bail, and deputies returned a somber man to his cell to await the outcome of his preliminary hearing, which was scheduled for April 23.

25

A One-Sided Affair

From the time of the arrest until the preliminary hearing two weeks later, Arthur Alexander's main job was to extract from the District Attorney's Office the things they were supposed to voluntarily give him. All he had been given so far was a tiny booklet prepared by Detective Hernandez, which was sort of like a *Reader's Digest* version of the case.

For days, Art Alexander called the District Attorney's Office and pleaded for the police material. Deputy District Attorney Kent Cahill was sympathetic because he, too, had yet to receive more than Ray's minibooklet. Finally, less than two days before the hearing, the material arrived, and it came in volumes.

Art spent the next forty-eight hours frantically preparing for the preliminary hearing. As he read through the police interviews, he was shocked. It seemed Detective Hernandez had selective recall when interviewing. He had written down only those parts of the interviews that were the most damaging to Art's client. Alexander didn't trust Ray Hernandez, and yet, due to a change in the law, the outcome of the preliminary hearing would be based solely on his testimony.

As Alexander expected, Detective Hernandez's testimony of what certain witnesses would say in a trial against Melvin Green caused Judge Paul Metzler to rule that Melvin would have to stand trial for murder.

Hernandez testified that after the killing he had collected information from acquaintances who told of threats made by Melvin Green against his wife. He told the court that Anita Green had feared for her life. "She told friends that she knew of improprieties in his business practices that would destroy him. She was afraid that he might destroy her first."

Alexander was furious. After hearing Hernandez's remarks, he was certain that what Ray said the witnesses were going to say was not reflected in his reports. He unsuccessfully sought the dismissal of the case, saying it was "ludicrous" to believe that Melvin Green would actually talk about killing his wife with several people if he intended to do so.

"I have heard no testimony that connects Mr. Green in any way to the shooting," Alexander said. "I don't care how many times this man threatened this lady's life, this does not make him the man who contracted for the murder."

Finally, Art pleaded with the judge to reconsider. "Your Honor, this procedure of presenting the statements of the witnesses through the conduit of Detective Hernandez, rather than having them here to speak for themselves, is unconstitutional." Then he added emphatically, "It denies my client his constitutional rights to confront and cross-examine the witnesses against him at a critical stage of the proceeding."

District Attorney Kent Cahill implored the judge to stick by his decision. "Your Honor, as you well know, I am not in love with Proposition 115," Cahill stated while looking at both Alexander and Green. (Proposition 115 allowed detectives to take the stand during preliminary trials, rather than the witnesses themselves.) "I understand why the defense doesn't like it because it leaves much to be desired. But the voters of California have passed this law, and the Supreme Court has upheld it as constitutional. Like it or not, it is the law of the land."

Judge Metzler stuck by his decision. "The evidence is sufficient to hold Mr. Green. I don't think it convinces me beyond a reasonable doubt, and the prosecution needs to work on the case, which is circumstantial," Metzler said. "There is no doubt about motive. The question is whether Mr. Green is the one...."

The implication was clear. Mel would probably win his trial, but he would remain in jail and would have to spend a small fortune to defend himself.

In the small hallway in front of the courtroom, Kent Cahill was busy talking with reporters. He was confident and it showed. "Someone arranged to have that man blow Anita Green's head off," Cahill exclaimed. "That's exactly what Melvin Green had been saying he would do since 1987."

Cary Green approached Cahill, with his grandfather and brother, Michael, closely following at his side. He stared at the reporters who got up to leave. He seemed relatively calm and appeared as if he wanted to talk.

Art noticed and tried to stop Cary, but Cary needed answers. "What if you are wrong?" Cary asked. "How are you going to live with yourself if you are wrong?"

Kent Cahill was quick to seize the opportunity to talk about what he felt. "I don't think I am wrong. But we'll let a jury decide that. It's the possibility we have to face in every case."

Cary pressed further. "But what if you are wrong?"

Cahill wondered if Melvin Green would ever admit the truth to his sons. Ever so gently he answered, "Cary, that would be a very difficult thing to have to live with."

"Maybe it would be impossible," Cary answered.

The district attorney nodded his head in agreement. Suddenly, Hy Green, Mel's ailing father, screamed out, "You bastard! You don't give a damn about anyone! You don't care about us. Don't make it out like you care if Mel is innocent or not!"

"Be quiet, Hy," Art said as he led the group toward the door. "You do not have to talk with him," he added. His heart went out to them. They were hurt, frightened, and angry, and most of all they were lost. The Greens wanted answers, and Art Alexander wanted to make sure that they did not hurt Mel further by looking for the whole truth.

Almost a year would pass before the start of Melvin Green's trial. At the close of their father's preliminary hearing, his two sons had decided they would support their father throughout the long year. Although she was groping for answers, Alexandra Leeds decided the same thing. She could not abandon Melvin in his time of need. But some of the things he said did not make sense. Alexandra prepared herself for the day when she might have to face the truth.

26

Preparing for Their Day in Court

Kent Cahill knew he had a monstrous job ahead of him. Perhaps more than any of the cases he had tried before, this case had not a single, solid piece of hard evidence. Kent knew there was no gun, no gunman, no witness tying Melvin Green to a gunman, no paper or money trail. As he sat in his small, windowless office with Darren Levine, another prosecutor, he focused on what he did have.

Kent would have to weave together a web of evidence tight enough to convict Melvin. That web, in Kent's mind, began with Anita and Mel's marriage.

"The marriage was not so much a matter of partnership as ownership," Kent explained to Darren. "I plan to show evidence to the court of how Mel considered Anita a prized possession." Kent elaborated that he wanted to show the jury how Mel had controlled Anita for such a long time. He had to get across how, over the course of a decade, the marriage had turned very, very dark.

Planning to use Mel and Anita's personal correspondence as evidence, Kent spent many nights rereading Mel's long-winded letters. He knew Mel's own words would paint a picture to the jury of an obsessive and an abusive man—a man capable of murder.

Kent would introduce the Greens' strange premarital and marital contracts and with them the possibility that such bizarre documents could only have been signed under duress, and therefore could be contested during a divorce. Such an action would have then cost Mel millions of dollars that he had sought to keep for himself. Cahill felt certain that a reasonable jury would see Mel's motives represented in the documents.

Although *jealous rage* is typically used by a prosecutor in a case where the husband actually pulled the trigger, in this case, Kent Cahill culled the letters and interviews and was able to piece together a picture of *jealous rage* as a motive here too. The police interviews, the community members who came forward, and even his own employees would all be able to testify to Mel's fits, his loud threats, and his incessant jealousy. Mel had complained to many that his wife was a "cunt" who slept around. He hated that she was having an affair with their temple's rabbi, even while he was still guaranteeing the temple loan. Mel thought about the rabbi and Anita constantly and wrote letters about them to whoever would read them. With these letters, Kent would show the jury that Melvin's jealousy made him unable to deal with Anita in any way short of murder. This would be the easiest part for Kent to substantiate.

But to get a conviction, Kent Cahill had to remove any shadow of doubt from twelve people's minds. To do this, he would have to bolster the jealousy motive with a stronger one.

Sitting at his desk, Kent spent considerable time running Mel's numerous motives through his head. After many hours, he decided that perhaps Melvin feared exposure more than anything else. He simply would die before being publicly made a fool of. The D.A. knew that Melvin really believed that his wife, Anita Green, would attempt to blackmail him into submitting to her financial requirements in the divorce. She knew his diplomas were fakes. In fact, she knew everything that went on in the office and where all his skeletons were buried. Furthermore, Kent could call an IRS investigator to the stand who would elaborate on the extent of Mel's business problems; problems Anita could have used to her advantage.

One afternoon, Cahill sat in the San Fernando Court's cafeteria and brainstormed with a group of his colleagues. The trial attorneys listened as Kent explained why the IRS information was so crucial. "Mel had great anxiety over his belief that Anita was dealing with the Internal Revenue Service and that it would hurt both his clients and his business."

Passionately and vividly, Kent elaborated to his friends

about how Mel's business was his life. He had worked hard for it and would not tolerate Anita's destruction of it. "That, my friends, is the reason that he had to set her up."

"Did it look like a setup?" one young D.A. asked.

"From the beginning, Ray and I were certain that the shooting was a planned, execution-style hit. I have to show the jury that Mel alone planned where Anita would be shot and that he lured her to the office at the appointed hour with the promise of a check. He was taking advantage of her financial situation at the time."

In theory, this should not have been too difficult to show. But Steven Ipsen reminded Kent that he had to give considerable thought to the fact that Mel had chosen the office.

Cahill had already thought about what Steve was saying. He always tried to see each part of a case the way a defense attorney might view it. In this case, he was almost certain that the defense would argue that Mel would never have had her killed at his place of work. But the more he thought about it, the more Kent believed that just the opposite was true. Mel had to have Anita murdered at the office so he would have an ironclad alibi. "We'll talk about it some more after the game. I can't think about this anymore right now; it is making me crazy." The men left the cafeteria for the basketball courts with Cahill leading the pack.

A tradition of survival at the San Fernando Courthouse is a three-times-a-week, no-holds-barred, pickup basketball game. Faced with a stress level unmatched by most professions, the D.A.'s, young and old, fight mercilessly on the court—the only court where the D.A.'s make all the rules and are truly invincible. Kent's basketball T-shirt read THE PHANTOM because no matter how slow his extra weight made him, he still managed to sneak up on the best of them to score his points. Kent always seemed to win, not by his athletic ability or polished skill, but by brute will—the will to win at everything he did. Unlike the other D.A.'s for whom the asphalt court was a stress-release, for Kent it was just another battlefield. Over basketball, Kent finished his earlier discussion with his fellow district attorney teammates. His tone was filled with the bitter gallows humor that typically just comes with the job. "Fuck him. He probably wanted to watch what he had paid for go down. At the office he would not miss the action and, better yet, he would have an ironclad alibi."

Above all, Cahill was certain that in a circumstantial case, the defense team would bring up reasonable doubt. He would have to craft his statements so carefully that a jury would grasp his beliefs.

As Kent sat up late with his yellow legal pad and his pile of blue and red markers, he began to carefully script his case that, beyond a shadow of a doubt, Melvin Green was the only human being on the face of the planet with a motive to order the professional-style execution of Anita Green.

To back him up that Anita's murder was indeed such a hit, Kent wrote a note to himself to call and consult with an FBI expert in assassin-style killings in the morning.

Meanwhile, as Kent was meticulously plotting how to keep Melvin Green locked up, Melvin sat fuming in jail. While he believed wholeheartedly in himself, he was not as convinced that the system would work to proclaim him innocent. His murdered wife had been an esteemed member of the community and Mel was certain that Hernandez's and Cahill's jobs were on the line to find someone to nail with a conviction.

With that in mind, he retained the best defense money could buy and hired not only Arthur Alexander, but the esteemed Gerry Chaleff as well. Chaleff was the lead defense attorney in Los Angeles's famous *People* v. *Angelo Buono* case, more commonly known as the Hillside Strangler case. Chaleff's reputation was impeccable, and he was known to be one of the top two or three defense attorneys in the state.

Gerry Chaleff was senior partner in the prestigious law firm of Chaleff, English, and Catalano. He ran his office out of a refurbished multimillion-dollar home located on Ocean Avenue in one of the few beach-view office areas on the coast. The house had been remodeled and turned into suites of law offices. There was a picture-perfect ocean view in the front and an even lovelier garden view in back. Chaleff's large and airy office looked out onto the pool and gardens. It did not seem a likely setting from which to plan the defenses of some of the state's most notorious criminals.

Gerry Chaleff was a wisp of a man, with dark hair and a neatly trimmed beard. Despite his grueling schedule, he looked years younger than his fifty years. His intensity was apparent. When he listened to people, he was so attentive that often he could finish their sentences before they did. One got the feeling that nothing, not the color of a lock of hair nor the hanging threads on a piece of fabric, escaped Gerry's intense stare.

Chaleff specialized in both criminal and juvenile law. He had a business degree from the University of California and was a Harvard Law School honors graduate. Besides handling a full load of cases, he held coveted positions on many of the Los Angeles County Bar Association's most influential committees. He cochaired the city's Homeless Committee and was vice chairperson of the Judicial Evaluations Committee. Chaleff had recently been appointed to the mayor's special task force to investigate the police department's actions in the famous Rodney King case. Some referred to the attorney as Los Angeles's "rebel with a cause."

Since his twelfth birthday, Gerry Chaleff had been consumed with a single purpose—to become a trial attorney. It was around that time that he had first read Clarence Darrow's book on trial law and was so inspired by it that he decided that defending people was the only thing he wanted to do. He worked hard, but he worked smart, and it seemed to many that things came easily to him.

In legal circles, it was common knowledge that Chaleff was one of the brightest defense attorneys on the West Coast. His reputation and his record were nearly perfect. He was polite but aggressive in court, and judges looked forward to working with him. Chaleff did his homework and never entered their courts with an attitude. Many a prosecutor cringed in his presence. Tough and fiercely competitive, some called him "the barracuda."

Melvin Green was awed. Gerry Chaleff was major league. Melvin had never met a man as powerful or as bright. At last Mel had an attorney who would be clever enough to understand what he was talking about. Mel appreciated Gerry's thoughtful and intense assessment of his predicament. He told others that with Chaleff on board, his guilt or innocence was not the issue, but rather the facts of the case, which would now speak for themselves. Mel was certain they were simply not enough to convict him.

Melvin also liked Gerry's quick sense of humor. The man could see the light side of every situation, no matter how tragic. Gerry Chaleff had the ability to make Melvin laugh, and few people could still do that. More than any other lawyer with whom he had met, Gerry had, at first, treated Mel with the respect and dignity that Melvin thought he deserved.

Perhaps more important and impressive to Melvin than humor, power, or even integrity, were Gerry's price tag and his Harvard Law degree. To a man as showy as Melvin Green, Gerry Chaleff was a mark of status. Mel could now boast confidently to his friends that he literally had the best and most expensive lawyer on his team.

Of all the famous criminal attorneys in the state, Gerry Chaleff remained one of the few both respected and trusted by the police department because of his cool professionalism and his personal integrity. He would not lie on behalf of his clients. He let the facts of the case speak for themselves and he always argued his cases honestly.

As a team, Gerry Chaleff and Arthur Alexander would work well together. There was no question who was lead attorney. Chaleff was the heavyweight. But Alexander had the patience to work with Mel and keep him in line, and Mel liked the feeling of continuity that Arthur brought to the case. Mel was certain that Arthur Alexander believed in his innocence, and that reassured him.

From the first day Chaleff was hired, he and Alexander agreed on a strategy for Melvin's case. Basically, their client had been sold out. Melvin was simply the easiest person for the police to accuse. Both lawyers felt the prosecution had possibly jumped the gun by going to trial with so little evidence, evidence that never tied Mel directly in any way to the murder.

The defense team saw that there were other theories that worked. Mel was not the only person who knew where Anita was going that day. Besides, not only did he know where she was going, he was very open about it. Chaleff could not accept the idea that if Mel was really planning to murder his wife, he would be as vocal about it or that he would have it done at his office.

One of the team's biggest problems was the question, if not Mel, then who killed Anita Green? They knew jurors would be groping for answers. If this was a hit (which, unlike the prosecution, they were not certain that it was), someone must have ordered it. Using that logic, and troubled by their client's strange behavior, Chaleff and Alexander hired an investigator to follow not only Mel's leads but those the police detectives were finding as well.

The man they chose was Theodore Woolsey, an appealing, quick-thinking and tough investigator with a reputation for being brutal at times. Woolsey could frighten witnesses into silence without ever threatening them.

The lawyers decided that the first thing Woolsey ought to do was take a closer look at Melvin and his strange family. They did not want any surprises. They also wanted Ted to look at the witnesses the prosecution planned on calling. There were an awful lot of people who had crossed swords with Melvin Green and who had reasons to want to see him locked up. As time passed, they were finding out more and more that their client was a man who evoked strong emotions in people. Many of those emotions were negative, and quite possibly for a lot of the witnesses, this was payback time.

As they sat in Gerry's Santa Monica office during yet another of their half-day planning sessions, the three men with the only chance of keeping Melvin Green from prison felt confident that they would be able to do just that. But their task would not be easy, simply because Mel was such an easy answer. The estranged and scorned husband was always an easy answer. And in this case, perhaps more than in any other they had ever worked on, it was an especially easy answer because of the nature of Mel's inappropriate and often horrible behavior, and because no one seemed to know the specifics of what had actually happened.

It was frustrating for both the lawyers. Gerry Chaleff was not one of those defense attorneys who followed the theory that, in order to provide the best defense for a client, it was best not to know everything about the crime, particularly if the client was guilty. He liked knowing the specifics. For Gerry, guilt or innocence did not determine whether he took a case; it merely determined his strategy. He believed that everyone had the right to a fair trial and that it was the job of the district attorney to demonstrate guilt.

Although Mel consistently denied any involvement in Anita's murder, Gerry and Art knew there were problems with his case. There were five things that the defense had to accomplish in order to win, and they spent the rest of the year working tirelessly toward that goal.

And as the clock ticked away, they still had Melvin to contend with. Melvin could be very time consuming and extremely demanding, especially since he was paying the bill. The lawyers had a difficult time trying to get him to focus on his plight. He remained arrogant and cocky, unlike a normal person who was possibly facing the death penalty or the possibility of being locked away for the rest of his life.

In their countless meetings with him at county jail, Melvin complained incessantly. He needed more phone calls; he wanted them to send him his accounting papers via legal mail; he wanted to be allowed more visitors; he wanted an extra mattress; and, if need be, he wanted a court order to have his own personal doctor examine him.

What Melvin Green actually told his attorneys about Anita's shooting remains unknown because of attorney-client privilege, but jail insiders say he flatly denied every claim that was made against him. According to Mel, there was no problem with the IRS, his diplomas were valid and he had never cheated on anything. He insisted that all of the defense witnesses had an axe to grind with him and were lying to get even. Melvin Green asserted that he alone was telling the truth. The police, he explained, were angry because he was obviously smarter than they were. They also despised that he had money and was Jewish. Mel believed most cops were anti-Semitic. Furthermore, Melvin Green believed that the police were changing the facts around and pushing people into saying things that never really happened. Art and Gerry could not have agreed more with that fact. In their opinion, it was not unreasonable for their client to feel that the police were against him and, in a sense, were breaking the rules. The police investigation was sloppy and at times inaccurate.

Still, the biggest obstacle standing in the defense team's way was not the police but rather Mel himself. Mel wanted to take the stand, and with the courtroom as his stage, be vindicated before the world. The lawyers' fear was that if he did that he stood a good chance of being convicted, notwithstanding the absence of any really strong evidence, because of his personality.

They had to keep Green off the stand and away from the jury, even if that meant that the jury might be suspicious of what they were hiding. Despite the fact that a judge would instruct the jury of a person's right to avoid taking the stand, juries usually are suspicious of defendants who avoid speaking out on their own behalf.

Arthur Alexander knew that most people did not know how to deal with a bizarre personality. If everybody goes along and plays according to the rules, everybody gets along okay. But Melvin Green was strikingly different and never followed society's rules. He said a lot of things to shock people, and Arthur knew some of those things were the dumbest things anyone could possibly say. The lawyer was certain Melvin's words would be hard to battle.

On his defense team's advice, Mel consented to hours of psychiatric and IQ tests and then bragged to visitors about how he had passed them all with flying colors. He told a friend that he had asked his attorneys if they thought he was obsessive or crazy and that they replied that he was the most sane and loving man they had ever met. Mel claimed the tests proved his IQ was far beyond genius.

But there was a rumor among those closest to Melvin Green that the tests revealed exactly the opposite. Melvin was ruled by his compulsions, and the tests did nothing to help his case. Furthermore, while his IQ test was well above normal, it was not nearly as high as he claimed it to be.

Mel's fiancée had begged Arthur and Gerry to seek a defense of insanity so at least Melvin could get the help he needed. She felt that a hospital would be less oppressive than a prison. Mel's lawyers decided against her wishes, citing the fact that insanity pleas are hard to win since the judicial backlash of the famous Hinckley case. They also knew full well that despite the fact that Alexandra Leeds insisted that Mel would do anything to avoid prison, their client would cringe at the thought of being portrayed as less than perfect mentally.

During this time, one of Mel's clients who visited him at the jail said that Mel would not do anything to help his lawyers if he thought what they wanted to do made him look bad. The client shook his head in disbelief. "He will not listen to anyone. He is certain he is innocent. If you are to be allowed the privilege of visiting him a second time in jail, then you have to be equally certain. But his story is not always plausible, even about the little things. He makes up whatever he wants. He must be making his lawyers' jobs very difficult."

Arthur Alexander and Gerry Chaleff responded to their difficult client in a way that later angered Melvin immensely. They stopped seeking his input and did what they had to do on their own.

Because the shooter was an unknown and because, in their minds, the people's evidence was so weak, Arthur and Gerry were resigned to shadowboxing. Their weekly meetings continued, and the same five problems were addressed over and over again.

It was a given that there was no way that Mel had actually shot Anita, but it was harder to prove that there was no link between him and the motorcyclist who had, even though there was no concrete evidence.

Mel's behavior was still their biggest obstacle to overcome. The jury could see from his letters (which the defense team hoped a judge would not allow to be entered as evidence) that there was nothing typical about him. But the lawyers had to convince a jury that you do not convict a man for murder based on his obnoxious letters and ramblings.

The defense would have to minimize Mel's problems with the IRS, but both lawyers felt the problems really were minimal. Mel was aware that he was being investigated, and penalties were already being discussed with the IRS.

Although bolstered by the flaws and weaknesses in the state's case, as well as by the fact that it did not look like the state was progressing further in finding more conclusive evidence against their client, Chaleff and Alexander were all too cognizant of the hurdles they still had to overcome to win. As the appointed date for the trial drew nearer, the lawyers became more obsessive about how they would tackle those concerns.

Of all the issues to contend with, jealousy might prove to be the most plausible. Melvin's letters showed he was obsessed by the fact that the rabbi was sleeping with Anita. Once the rabbi was called to the stand, there was the possibility that Mel might explode in front of the jury. Even though the judge would instruct the jurors to disregard any outbursts by Mel, the emotional impact of seeing him act like a raving madman could convict him. The lawyers' job was to paint a very different picture, a picture of a loving husband who had simply had enough of his marriage; a husband who wanted the divorce as much as Anita did.

As the trial date approached, Melvin's lawyers grew increasingly more aware that the most challenging hurdle of the Green case would be to convey to the jury the difficult and often abstract concept of reasonable doubt. In the attorneys' minds, the state simply did not have the evidence to show beyond a shadow of a doubt that Melvin Green had hired someone to kill his wife. But as any good trial lawyer knows, anything can happen in a jury trial.

Part VI

The Trial

February–March 1992

27

On the Eve of the Trial

There was a story circulating around the Valley that the reason Rabbi Jacobs had married so quickly after Anita's murder was because he needed a "beard". Miriam Jacobs was the perfect disguise. Her beauty and charm would quickly dispel any doubts as to the rabbi's fidelity and quiet the rumors that were continuing to circulate. It appeared that Jacobs had to be married by the time of Melvin Green's trial.

Miriam Jacobs was a blonde bombshell. A native of Texas, she looked like a Dallas Cowboys cheerleader. She and the rabbi had met through mutual friends just four short months after Anita's murder and a short time after Miriam's conversion to Judaism. Steven Jacobs fell in love instantly, and after a whirlwind three-week courtship, proposed to her.

"He asked me three times before I finally said yes. I was so in love with him, but I never understood why he was in such a rush. It just did not seem right somehow."

Later, Steven told a friend that marrying Miriam was the biggest mistake of his life, but that he could not resist the power of her body and her beauty. Miriam was Steven's trophy, and at the time he seemed to need her.

The rabbi's marriage was originally scheduled for November, but he kept pressuring Miriam to move up the date. "He told me that he wanted to get married right away, that he loved me and that it did not look good for him to sleep at my place because he was a rabbi and in the public's eye. So we moved the ceremony up to August and my parents changed their plans again."

But even August was not soon enough for Steven Jacobs.

After Melvin's arrest in April, the story once again appeared in the newspapers, and the rabbi's strategic silence could no longer be maintained. Desperate for a quick solution, Jacobs drove to the spa in Ojai, California, where his future bride was vacationing. He arrived flushed and agitated, ranting about an article that had just appeared in the *Los Angeles Times*. Miriam recalled, "He did not tell me what the article said, but he was upset about it. Then he pushed the date up again, and we were married two weeks later on May 14, 1991."

Mel's murder trial promised to be a sensational event, filled with the potential for scandal and gossip. For a community and a leader so consumed with appearances, Miriam Jacobs appeared to be the answer to their prayers.

By the time of the trial in February 1992, Melvin Green's incarceration and Anita Green's death illustrated to many in the San Fernando Valley the possible repercussions of adultery. *Fatal Attraction* was available on videocassette, but the real version was about to play live in a Los Angeles courtroom.

So graphic were the media's depictions of Mel's life in jail, along with pathetic photos running in the newspapers, that many in the Jewish community found themselves extremely uncomfortable. The fact that middle-class, middle-aged Jewish men do not commonly commit murder illustrated that anything could happen. There were no rules and no one was safe. Anita's murder showed many how fragile and vulnerable we all are.

By now, Jews around town had heard the rumors about Anita and Rabbi Jacobs's torrid affair. The debate that raged in beauty shops and cafes in the Valley posed this question: Who is more culpable—the man who murders or the man who some think might have to bear a degree of responsibility for the murder? What kind of rabbi slept with his temple president, and a married one at that? Wasn't the rabbi married to a pretty young blonde? When did he meet her? Certainly this kind of behavior did not sound very rabbinical.

Despite the monetary rewards—a reward had been offered by the city council and the temple for information leading to an arrest of Anita's killer—and the fanfare of publicity surrounding the investigation, the Jewish community of Los Angeles had moved on. Most people were not eagerly awaiting the opening of Melvin Green's trial on February 3, 1992. Though some wanted answers, most shied away from the trial.

The vast majority of Shir Chadash members felt this way. The temple was in deep financial difficulty, and it seemed that building in the near future was highly unlikely. Membership was up, and the school was full, but the building fund had been depleted through necessary but unexpected expenses. By the new year, the temple was nearly ninety thousand dollars in arrears on land payments. Members were personally called upon to attend February's annual dinner dance. "Now more than ever we need your assistance" was the plea. The temple's new president, Paul Glaser, wrote a letter to the congregation saying that the temple's very survival depended on each member's support of the dance.

Riva Rice was angry that Anita's temple family had not planned on attending the trial. She was not really surprised because she knew they did not want to embarrass their leader by listening to his testimony. But still, she saw their choice as one more way the rabbi was insulting her daughter's memory. To Riva, the rabbi, charismatic though he may have been, merely viewed his relationship with her daughter as a career mistake. Riva doubted he would have ever married Anita. Even after her death, he wanted to keep their relationship a secret, especially since it could be viewed as a precipitating factor in her death. The rabbi had even told others that he just wished the trial would go away. His words made it back to Riva and she became even angrier. If he had loved Anita, surely he wouldn't feel this way.

The night before the start of the trial, Riva spoke on the phone to her daughter, Linda Borsen, in Philadelphia. "It's as if to these people she never lived. Their lives go on unchanged."

"Do you want me to come out to Los Angeles to be with you?" Linda asked.

"No, stay with the kids, darling. I will be fine. It is not you I am angry with. Besides, what can you do here?" Riva answered.

And so, Riva Rice found herself facing the trial alone. As a witness, she was barred from the courtroom, and once again she would not find the answers she was searching for. Riva wondered who would come through for Anita. Who would be brave enough to tell the truth? Would anyone admit knowledge of the rabbi and Anita's liaison, which obviously had gone on long enough to send Mel over the edge? Riva doubted anyone would go against Steven Jacobs by standing up for Anita. She also had her doubts about whether the rabbi was brave enough to tell the whole truth.

Rabbi Jacobs seemed, on the surface, to have rebounded quite nicely by the time of the trial. He had given up his rental house, and the two newlyweds were living together in Miriam's Westside condo while waiting for their new home in Woodland Hills to be remodeled. Ironically, the home Anita had pushed for in Rabbi Jacobs's contract would be occupied by another woman.

Throughout the months of December and January, the rabbi's counsel, Leonard Levine, a respected Century City criminal attorney, attempted to reach prosecutor Kent Cahill about the nature of the rabbi's testimony. It was clear that the rabbi was, at best, a reluctant witness. Obviously he was frightened by what his affair could do to his career.

Rabbi Jacobs desperately needed to act like a rabbi. He married quickly, joined all types of prestigious committees, and he was granted an Honorary Doctor of Divinity from Hebrew Union College. The rabbi became even more involved in social action than usual. But still, Jacobs appeared to be running scared. The rabbi had his lawyer draft a letter to the District Attorney's Office. It read:

Dear Mr. Cahill,

Rabbi Steven Jacobs has asked me to contact you concerning a subpoena he recently received from your office in the above-mentioned case. As a rabbi, he is somewhat concerned with the prospect of testifying in this case, and what the subject matter of his testimony might be.

I informed him that the subpoena only required that he be on call, and is no guarantee that his testimony will be needed. However, I informed him that I would contact you and try to determine what the subject matter of his testimony might be if called, and what the prospects are of his testimony being necessary for the prosecution. He has not been interviewed yet by anyone from your office.

When you have the time, could you please give me a call so that we can discuss this matter further. Until then, you can assume by way of this response that Rabbi Jacobs is agreeable to being on call, and will be available to testify if necessary.

Sincerely,

Leonard B. Levine

The district attorney found the whole incident rather pathetic and called the rabbi at the temple. He talked with the rabbi's personal secretary.

"The subpoena doesn't have RSVP written on it. Attendance is mandatory," Mr. Cahill explained. "Can I expect the rabbi here?" he asked the secretary.

"He's a busy man and has a hectic schedule," she answered protectively.

"He'll be here, or I'll send an officer out there to escort him here," the district attorney answered. Cahill loathed people who thought they were above the law or that they deserved preferential treatment because of who they were.

The district attorney's orders meant Rabbi Jacobs and his pretty young wife, Miriam, still weren't free to get on with their new life together. The trial and the publicity surrounding it was putting considerable strain on their relationship.

Back at Melvin Green's house in Encino, Mel's fiancée, Alexandra Leeds, felt the same way. Faced with the likelihood of Mel's being convicted, she was unsure of what to do or how to act. Just visiting Mel in jail each Sunday depressed her for a week. It was difficult, if not impossible, to bond with someone who was behind bars.

Alexandra loved parts of Melvin Green very much: his intelligence, his spirituality, his compassion toward her two young daughters. She had remained tolerant of his obsessions because she knew he was under extreme pressure. She could not abandon him now, on the eve of his trial, just when he needed her the most. Still, she did not know what to do about a situation that made her extremely uncomfortable. Alexandra had met Melvin after the murder, and he swore to her many times that he did not know how his wife had been killed. But the more she questioned Melvin, the more his answers sounded peculiar and the more his moods would swing.

As the trial date moved closer, Alexandra found herself more and more unsure about her future with Melvin. She knew she could not spend the rest of her life with a man who was in prison. She also knew that she wanted to give Mel some hope for the future, so she did not abandon him. Still, in the year that had passed since Mel's arrest, Alexandra had grown aloof from him, despite the fact that she and her daughters were living in his house, supported by his money.

Though Alexandra Leeds may have loved Melvin Green very much, at the time of the trial she was not, by any means, convinced of his innocence. By now, he had said far too many things that did not make sense. One thing was certain; Alexandra knew she had to do something to keep Melvin from opening his mouth during the trial. On the evening before his first court appearance, Alexandra waited for Mel's call.

"Sweetheart, pretend like you're kissing me when you want to yell out something. You can't talk when you're kissing someone," Alexandra suggested seriously.

Melvin agreed. He knew his mouth continued to be his greatest enemy.

On the eve of the trial, Melvin Green's sons found themselves on opposite sides, as they had been throughout their young lives. They rarely spoke to one another other than to argue about their father's guilt or innocence.

Cary was back in college, at California State University, Northridge, studying business administration and accounting. He would graduate in the summer after completing one more semester and summer school. Cary continued to be Mel's Golden Boy, doing whatever his father asked of him. He was in the driver's seat at Melvin Green, Incorporated, where he held down the fort for his old man. He remained convinced his father would beat the system.

Throughout the trial, Cary and one of Mel's friends, Robert Hall, worked closely with the defense lawyers and their investigator to dig up information to help his father's case. He remained Mel's greatest ally and closest confidant. But Cary admitted to a friend that his father scared him and exerted considerable control over him from his jail cell.

Cary was tired, anxious, and very moody. Oblivious at first to the extent of Mel's control over his hours, he continued to try and fulfill his father's incessant requests for things. Cary suffered from stress brought on by the strain of school, work, and administering to his father's demands from jail. He was very difficult to get along with, and many family members just stayed away from him rather than face his wrath.

What upset Cary the most was that many people had already tried and judged his father. "People are so quick to form an opinion," Cary said to a friend. "My dad has done so many good things for so many people, especially for people at the temple. Now everyone has forgotten. Only a few friends have stuck by him, and they will stick by him till the end of time. I just don't understand people."

Michael Green was equally confused, but for different reasons. He viewed the same facts with an entirely different set of eyes from his brother, Cary. Michael told his cousin that he did not know what to think.

Michael stopped visiting his father in jail, though he continued to write to him. Mel and Michael's relationship was always strained, so it was difficult to say if the incarceration and trial had anything to do with their recent difficulties.

Michael lived with his ailing grandfather, Hy Green. He didn't work regularly, and continued to live on the same small allowance his father had given him for years. He had grown into a pathetic and angry young man.

In jail, Mel admitted to visitors that he and Michael were not speaking. "I can't control him; he has his own mind. I will always love him, but he is of no use to me right now. I am in a desperate and precarious position for the time being. I cannot afford to let anyone bring me down. I need everyone to adhere to my plan. People need to do things my way right now."

So Mel's two sons found themselves completely alone emotionally at the time of the trial, as they had been for their entire lives. They would only continue to have a father if they continued to do whatever he wanted and to take care of whatever he needed.

Anita's son, Scott Arnow, wanted the whole sordid mess to finish. He hoped with all his might they would get the son of a bitch, but he was embarrassed by the things the trial might reveal about his mother. He did not know what he would do if Mel got off.

Mel's father remained in complete denial. In his mind, the Greens were always right. If Mel said he was innocent, then Hy believed it. "They don't have anything on him," Hy told his sister the day before the trial opened. "He'll beat those bastards."

Melvin Green was optimistic about the outcome. He told reporters, "I am innocent. I remain confident that a jury of my peers will look at the evidence and see that there is absolutely nothing to tie me to the murder." Mel told friends that he knew Cahill's case was pitifully inadequate. He assured them that soon he would once again be home.

While he waited, Mel kept insisting to his lawyers, to his supporters, and to anyone else who would listen that the entire case was a frame-up. He said the police, especially Ray Hernandez, were jealous of his money. They were also being pressured by the city council, the same council offering a reward, to find someone to pin this high-profile murder on. Hernandez's job was on the line and the prosecutor was merely an agent of the police. Besides, Mel said, Cahill was a known anti-Semite. Mel had no explanation for the fact that Kent Cahill's wife was Jewish. By the time of his trial, Melvin Green was down to 218 pounds and was literally less than half the man he had once been.

28

A City of Angels

About a week before it was slated to begin, *People* v. *Melvin Green* was moved from the small San Fernando court, where the prosecutor came from, to the huge criminal court in Los Angeles. The old, decaying granite building was located in the heart of the busy downtown civic center, adjacent to the hall of records, the law library, and city hall. It was bordered by the hustle and bustle of Chinatown, Union Station, the Hispanic Olvera Street, and the Music Center theatre complex.

An institutional gray monolith emerging from the Los Angeles sky, the criminal courts building looks like a fortress. February's dark gray skies and the unusual crashing rain made it look even more foreboding. In a town famous for Hollywood melodrama, even the most heavy-handed and clichéd director would not have had the nerve to make the heavens pour forth so much water on the opening day of this courtroom drama.

Unprepared for the sudden downpour of rain, the long line of people waiting to pass through security's metal detectors and into the large building's many courtrooms were drenched by the heavy storm. A few dozen of Los Angeles's homeless huddled under the building's large awning. Two or three of the daring held out cups to beg a spare change from those waiting to be cleared into the building.

Just past the homeless was another man, curiously trudging through the muddy plants and ivy just to the side of the courthouse. This uniformed guard's job was to retrieve the knives and other metal weapons tossed there by what he referred to as the "testiliars" (gang members and other riffraff) going to testify for their friends and caught off-guard by the metal detector. Every day, the guard's challenge was to collect the contraband before their owners could retrieve them. This lone private security guard was, in his mind, waging his own war against the violence that was destroying Los Angeles. He was not about to let Los Angeles's worst storm in twenty years stop him.

Mel's future would be decided in Criminal Division 104, where the case was assigned to Judge George Trammel. Serious and open-minded, Trammel had sat twenty years on the bench, the past two in Division 104.

Judge Trammel held a rare and coveted position in Los Angeles's criminal court system hierarchy, most of the cases he heard were exciting, the types other judges waited years for. His assignment was long-term criminal cases, mostly murder trials, the backlog of death-penalty cases plaguing Los Angeles courts and other multimonth trials. His court was designed to handle these complex matters as he did not need to adhere to a regular court calendar.

Deputy District Attorney Kent Cahill was not happy about the move to downtown Los Angeles. He worried about what kind of jury he would get there. While San Fernando jurors are known to be hard on crime, Central Los Angeles jurors did not have the same reputation. Kent worried about the judge. In his mind, Trammel was an unknown. Kent had worked with all the judges in San Fernando and he did not like the idea of having an unfamiliar judge on this important case. Kent was also angry about the long commute he had in the pouring rain. By the time he entered the huge building, he felt as though he had lost his first battle.

The defense was delighted with the decision to move the trial downtown. Since Trammel did not have a court calendar to contend with, the actual trial portion would move quickly. They would have long days and get a lot accomplished.

Second, Trammel's court was a high-security court. The spectators were sealed off from the trial by locked glass doors. The witnesses and their client would be more secure in it. A high-security courtroom would also make their client feel important. Things like that made a difference to Melvin Green.

Though sealed off by glass, Trammel's courtroom did not fit the drama that was about to unfold. It was neither the traditional courtroom one usually sees on television nor the fancy courtroom seen in many eastern cities. Trammel's court was a thoroughly modern government courtroom, stark and institutional. The paneled walls were made of fake wood, a low-budget government attempt at giving the room a parliamentary feeling. There were brightly colored swivel chairs set before the counsel tables, and the jury sat in similar chairs a few steps above and to the side.

The judge sat above them all and presided over the small room, which was separated from the three short rows of spectator benches by glass panels and locking doors. There were rows of computers on the counsel table, as well as before the judge and the other officers of the court. Trammel was one of the first judges in the state to try out a new computerized system, in which everything, including exhibits, could be called up and reviewed instantly by all the courtroom participants. Everyone sat before his own screen except Melvin.

On the first day of the actual trial, the hour commute from the San Fernando Valley to downtown Los Angeles took closer to three hours. Both jurors and witnesses struggled to arrive on time and were frustrated by the delays.

While most fought the storm and the freeways, Melvin Green sat in his holding cell and fumed. He, too, was frustrated this morning, and his frustration was deeper than any he had ever known before. The list of indignities he kept being forced to suffer grew longer each day. He was being treated like a second-class citizen, and he had not been convicted of anything yet.

Mel had been awakened at four in the morning to begin the lengthy process of getting ready. He had been through all this before. For almost two weeks now during jury selection, he had gotten up before dawn, taken a "birdbath" in the sink, shaved without a mirror, eaten a cold breakfast, picked up his lunch, and awaited his transportation to the courts. The process could take hours, though the courthouse was only a mile away from the jail.

All through jury selection and pretrial motions, Mel had endured these indignities, but his patience was wearing thin. Mel detested the thought of going into trial without proper attire. He was forbidden to wear a belt, a tie clip, or cuff links.

The rules annoyed him. What did they think he would do with these objects? Still, he had managed to look distinguished in the new camel jacket, conservative dark slacks, beige shirt, and tie that his fiancée had carefully picked out for him.

Mel had assigned a friend and, in a sense, a personal assistant, the important job of bringing him a fresh shirt, underwear, and change of clothes each day. He was also to be responsible for taking care of Mel's dirty laundry. Melvin would never appear before the court looking like the scumbags with whom he now spent his days.

At 8:30 A.M., Arthur Alexander and Gerry Chaleff came in to see him. Mel was angered by their delay. It was difficult for him to talk in this setting, and he complained about their lack of privacy.

Gerry patiently did his best at calming Mel. Before returning to the counsel table, he instructed the bailiff, Deputy Sheriff Steven Piel, to remove all handcuffs from his client before Melvin entered the courtroom. Chaleff insisted that for the remainder of the trial, Melvin was to never be bound or shackled in any way before the jury and the press.

A few minutes before nine, the side door to the courtroom was opened. The spectators and jury grew silent as Melvin Green was escorted in. Melvin tried to ignore the stares. He looked straight into the cameras that were taking his picture for the following day's articles. He carried his legal files and notepads, and looked as if he were going off to an important business meeting. His hair was cut and neatly combed back. He held his head high and seemed self-assured and determined. Before sitting down, he looked through the glass, searched the crowd, and smiled at his family and supporters, most of whom occupied the first row of seats behind the glass.

Mel sat next to his two attorneys, Arthur Alexander and Gerry Chaleff. At the other end of the counsel table sat Kent Cahill flanked by Detective Ray Hernandez, who would serve as his assistant for many of the witnesses.

When the time came for prosecutor Kent Cahill to make his opening statement, he looked like he was about to explode. A year of hard work had gone into this trial, and he had spent several months preparing what he was about to say. A trial attorney lived for these moments and none more than Cahill, especially when he believed as strongly as he did in the guilt of the defendant.

The prosecutor took his position. He looked at the jury and smiled. He knew that juries liked to feel that a lawyer believed in his case, and Kent Cahill hoped the jury would see the outrage in his eyes and hear it in his words. He had planned his words carefully. The jurors seemed intelligent, and he was careful not to talk down to them.

Kent Cahill's opening statement brought few surprises. But what did surprise many, especially those on Melvin's side, was the force and intensity with which he delivered it. No one knew that he had been a champion debater throughout school and that his two strengths were his public speaking skills and his flair for words. The jury appeared to be mesmerized by his words. In just minutes, it was obvious why Kent Cahill had been chosen for this case.

Cahill instructed the jury to consider his opening statement a road map to guide them. He spent the next few minutes explaining the details of Anita Green's shooting and then the more intricate and shocking aspects of a marriage that had basically deteriorated into living hell.

Cahill made it clear that the murder was a planned, execution-style hit and that Mel Green had set the time and place for the meeting Anita was coming to when she was killed. He explained passionately and succinctly that over the years Mel had lost his ability to control his wife.

"He lured her to that time and that place, October 25, 1990, between 10:20 and 10:30 in the morning. She had an appointment to meet with Melvin Green at that location. You will hear the appointment existed. You'll hear the reasons why she kept that appointment, the way in which he enticed her to be at that time and place, where she was summarily executed for spite, for jealousy, for greed, some of the oldest motivations I know of. That is what I believe the evidence is going to show."

The jury listened attentively. Cahill's words made an impact on them, and they were impressed by his sincerity. They watched Mel's face for reaction. The defendant just stared at his yellow legal pad and kept taking notes. He seemed relieved when it was his counsel's turn.

Arthur Alexander quickly attacked everything Kent Cahill

had said. "There is not one shred of evidence that is going to be presented that will connect my client, Melvin Green, with that motorcyclist."

About the only thing that both Alexander and Cahill agreed on was that Melvin Green was not the shooter. Alexander said that Detective Hernandez and the Los Angeles Police Department focused solely on Melvin Green from the very day of the shooting, as soon as they learned that he was in the process of divorcing his wife.

Looking directly at the jury, Alexander explained that there was nothing typical about Melvin and his behavior. "Just about every witness who is going to testify as to some life contact, some observation, some hearing, some conversation is going to testify that in some respects Mr. Green never, almost never, at any rate, acts in a typical manner."

If Cahill was brief and to the point, Alexander was long-winded and confusing. He spent a half hour downplaying the motives as circumstantial. He said that the police concentrated their investigation on Green because he was the easiest suspect. Alexander rambled on to try and discredit the IRS problems, to explain Mel's habit of letter writing, to downplay the theme of jealousy because both parties wanted a divorce, and to explain that Mel was not afraid of losing his fortune as a result of the divorce, because his personal property before the marriage exceeded the value of any community property he would have had to divide with Anita.

With these words, the defense hoped to diminish the impact of the anticipated prosecution testimony before it could even be presented. Perhaps it was not his intention, but Alexander seemed to want to confuse the jury so that by the time he was finished, they would think that the prosecution was grasping at straws. He inundated them with facts, and at this point it was impossible to know the significance of the facts to which he was referring.

Still, though confusing, on two points the attorney was crystal clear: If Anita had really been afraid of her husband. she would have set up restraining orders to keep him from her; and Mel greatly suffered financially by Anita's death.

Alexander continued to focus on Anita, not as an innocent victim, but as a woman who was worth more to Melvin Green alive than dead. "If for nothing else, under the laws of California, the death of a spouse negates the prenuptial agreement. It would have been to Mel's advantage to have the divorce proceedings continue."

From the onset, the defense wanted to plant seeds in the jurors' minds as to why Melvin Green was on trial. Certainly the police department had gone with the easiest scenario—the estranged husband. But the defense realized that this had not just been pulled out of thin air.

"Melvin has a big mouth," Alexander began, in a carefully crafted attempt to prepare the jury to accept Mel's often-shocking conduct. "Melvin is one of those people who likes to shock people with the things he says and the things he does. He is fully capable of making an inappropriate comment at the most inappropriate time. This is payback time for a lot of people," he said. "These witnesses are paying him back by testifying against him." As he listened, Melvin Green leaned back in his chair and sighed.

29

Taking My Mother Away

During the next two days, Kent Cahill called up a series of people's witnesses to testify on the simple surface facts of Anita Green's murder.

Detective Michael Coffey went through the crime scene particulars. Mixed in with his time, date, body positioning, and number of people present, was one statement that perked up the ears of the jurors.

"I directed Mr. Green to the north of the driveway and identified myself. He told me his name, and I asked him, 'What is going on here? What is this about?' At which time, Mr. Green told me, 'Why don't you check into the guys that she's screwing?' And I said, 'Who would that be?' and he told me the three individuals: Rabbi Jacobs, Mr. Lebowitz, and Mr. Mitchell."

The jurors appeared shocked. Gerry Chaleff stood up to cross-examine the detective. He strode confidently over to the podium. Everything about Chaleff was cool and calm. His suit was stylish and expensive, his glasses were of the latest design and he looked like he just walked off the set of "LA Law." Following the defense attorney's maxim, Gerry's suit was light colored, to subtly suggest to the jury that he was the "good guy." He had an intensity about him, and his intelligence came instantly to bear.

This was the first time that the jurors had a chance to see him in action. Chaleff could not challenge Coffey on the details in the crime report. Instead, he focused on those items in his testimony that had not appeared in the original crime-scene account. In particular, Chaleff focused on why Coffey now recalled such an inflammatory statement in such detail, yet never wrote it down in his original notes. Following Alexander's lead, Chaleff again sowed seeds of doubt as he implied that there were problems with the accuracy or recollection of the police detectives' investigation.

Coffey's testimony was followed by that of the pathologist who confirmed the cause of death; the roofer who had heard the shot and caught a glimpse of the assailant before he sped away; and by the trucker who saw the motorcyclist without his helmet. The roofer's testimony set the stage. He told the court where Anita was parked, how her body slumped over her steering wheel, and how the motorcyclist had sped away. All of this was necessary testimony, but none of it tied Melvin Green to the murder.

Skillfully, Kent Cahill chose to close his first day in court on an emotional note. He knew that calling the victim's only child would tug at the jurors' hearts.

So, at a little after 3:00 P.M., a very nervous and soft-spoken Scott Arnow walked slowly up to the witness stand. Scott, who had just celebrated his twenty-fourth birthday, looked even younger. He wore a pair of simple dark slacks and a heavy sweater. Scott spent most of the few minutes that he was on the stand staring at his hands or nervously glancing toward Melvin, the man that he was certain from day one was responsible for his mother's murder. Scott fit the part; he was a victim who would never recover from his tragic loss.

Scott described living in the house with Melvin and Anita over the course of their ten-year marriage. He claimed that in the beginning things were fine, but that about five years into the union the marriage began to deteriorate as Melvin began to lose control of Anita. Scott painted a vivid portrait of a marriage gone bad.

Scott explained, "It would start out as screaming, and then eventually he would go up to his room, lock her out of the room, tell her to be quiet or he would smack her, these types of things. It was usually him talking and her listening. He thought that he was the king of the house."

Scott went on to elaborate that Mel often called his mother horrible names. Mel would listen in on her phone calls and hang up the phone if he did not approve of whom she was talking to.

Scott's graphic testimony showed how Mel's outbursts had

grown more frequent because he was upset by the amount of time Anita spent working on temple functions. "He stated that he was not getting any time. She was spending all her time at the temple."

Before he finished, Scott Arnow left the jury with a vivid picture. "He would dump out the contents of her purse. Everything that was in the purse he would dump on the floor. He would go through the items and examine the contents."

"Did he ever indicate to you exactly what he was looking for?" Cahill asked.

"Cigarettes. He objected to her smoking cigarettes."

Chaleff wanted to discredit Scott's testimony by establishing that Scott had an ulterior motive for testifying against his stepfather. Chaleff knew that Scott stood to collect a great deal of money if Mel was convicted. The defense attorney strode confidently over to the microphone to begin his attack. Looking directly at Scott, Chaleff asked, "Is there not a lawsuit pending in which you were trying to obtain some of Mr. Green's assets?"

Scott was shocked. "A lawsuit pending?" It took him a minute to comprehend what the lawyer was getting at.

"Yes," Gerry Chalett answered.

"From me?" Scott asked incredulously.

"Yes."

Scott answered truthfully, "Not that I am aware of." His voice was racked with emotion.

Chaleff struggled to make his point. "Don't you have a lawyer at Loeb and Loeb named Andrew Garb?"

"To use to obtain my mother's assets. I don't care about his money," Scott answered, his voice rising in answer.

Chaleff was not about to let go. "Has anybody told you that if Mr. Green gets convicted, you are going to get more money?"

Scott stared at him. He was really trying hard to hold back both his anger and his tears. "No. I could care less about his money."

It took Chaleff awhile, but he finally realized his questions had backfired. "I have nothing further."

"I do," Cahill asserted angrily. This was just the type of thing he hated. Why was Chaleff trying to make Scott look greedy when the opposite was true?

"You just testified to the fact that some sort of legal action is being taken relative to Mr. Green in which you are a party to some sort of proceedings, is that right?"

"Yes."

"You also testified that you don't care about his money?"

"Right," Scott answered, and then explained, "My grandmother has a lawyer investigating what money was my mother's. Personally, I would rather not go ahead with that." He looked at Mel bitterly and added, "I don't want anything to do with the person or with the money."

Seizing the first sparks in the day's testimony, Cahill fired back with a direct question. "Do you hate Mr. Green?"

"Yes."

The prosecutor pressed further. "But not over money?"

"No."

Playing to the jury, Cahill took his questioning to its final step. "What is it over?"

"Losing my mother," Scott answered with a deep sigh, his voice racked with emotion. "Taking my mother away from me."

30

Mel's Secret Fears

Both of Los Angeles's papers and the wire services covered the trial's opening day. As opposed to the depressing photographs the papers printed the previous April showing Mel at his arrest, Mel now looked great. His hair was perfectly groomed, his weight was under control, and he was dressed handsomely. He carried a pile of papers, and he looked more like a lawyer than a man who had been accused of having his wife murdered for his own financial gain. Most agreed that Mel Green appeared to be thriving in jail.

The articles and pictures renewed interest in the Valley, and once again gossip quickly filled the phone lines. What would happen today? How could the state possibly expect to convict with so little evidence? When was the rabbi scheduled to take the stand?

Meanwhile, the drama continued downtown, and the cast of characters had just begun to get interesting. One courtroom observer remarked, "I feel like I'm at a play. I don't want to miss even a single minute of the action."

The second morning opened with Barbara Wolpow taking the stand. It was Barbara who had brought Anita to work at Melvin's office and who had worked there herself for almost eight years. Dressed in a long skirt, an expensive blouse, boots, and carrying a large umbrella, and a full raincoat, Barbara was not about to be messed with. Self-assured and poised, she answered everything with confidence.

She told the court that when she worked for Melvin Green, he abused everyone, but that he singled out Anita more than others and would often come storming into the office to start yelling at her about something. In Barbara's opinion, Mel liked to control Anita.

Cahill never missed a beat. He wanted to bring the control factor up again before the jury. He knew control was a very important component of Melvin's life, so important that it was crucial for the jury to understand it if he expected them to bring back a conviction. "Did you ever see Mr. Green take physical control of Anita's activities?"

"Well, if she was doing something that he didn't want her to do, he would sometimes come over to her desk, take it away from her and say 'GO HOME!' Or he would help her out of her chair and say: 'I want you to leave now, and don't come back!'"

"He didn't like her to use the phone for her personal reasons," Barbara said. "He would see her on the phone, come by and take the phone out of her hand, and just hang up."

Barbara stared at Mel as she continued. She carefully outlined Mel's dirty business practices, including his habit of having his clients sign blank pieces of paper, his boxes of receipts to use on audits, and his improper tax-return filings.

Barbara's testimony set the tone for the rest of the day as the prosecutor paraded out still more witnesses who painted a less than flattering picture of Melvin Green.

Janis McDonald, Anita's divorce attorney, followed Barbara Wolpow on the stand. Her accusations about the conduct and personality of the defendant were more specific than Wolpow's. McDonald told the court about some of Anita's fears that she had expressed to her.

"Among the things that Anita said was, 'There are guns. He keeps guns at the office and guns at home, and he waves the guns at me and threatens me with them and I'm afraid. I don't want to be around them.' She was terrified when she told me this."

To substantiate her claims, McDonald read her notes from a September meeting with Anita to the court.

" 'I'm afraid. We have a long history of physical violence in our relationship. He's been very physically violent with me in the past.'" McDonald read on. " 'He has hit me enumerable times, thrown me on the bed.... He waves his guns at me. He screams and yells at me. I don't want to take that abuse any longer.'" The jury stared at Melvin as they listened to the attorney's statements. He continued to show no emotion.

To provide a more balanced perspective of how Mel was viewed by others, Cahill called forward one of Mel's most faithful employees, Lily Lopez. A small Hispanic woman who was dressed simply in dark slacks and a white blouse, Lily was loyal to Melvin not just because he was her employer, but because he had lent her husband fifteen thousand dollars to start a new business. Before taking the stand, Lily was overheard talking to another person in the hall. "I do not think that Mel could have ever done anything like this. He is being picked on because he has a Dr. Jekyll and Mr. Hyde-type personality, but right now I remain convinced of his innocence."

Whether convinced or beholden, Lily answered everything asked of her simply and honestly. Occasionally she would glance over at Melvin and smile as he nodded encouragingly. Some jurors took notes. Judge Trammel stared at Mel throughout Lily's testimony.

Lily admitted that her employer and Anita had quarreled often, mostly due to Anita's lack of attention toward the business and the amount of time she spent at the temple.

Taking a large appointment book labeled PEOPLE'S EXHIBIT 11, Cahill asked about the scheduled appointment on October 25, 1990, between Anita and Melvin, "Is there an appointment indicated for 10:30?"

"Yes."

"And who is that appointment with?"

"Anita."

With the appointment confirmed, Cahill now concentrated on the body of outrageous letters that Mel had Lily type during the course of her employment and the specific comments she had heard while she worked there.

Lily, clearly uncomfortable, answered as quickly as possible, usually with one-word statements that she did not elaborate on.

"Did Mr. Green accuse Mrs. Green of lacking fidelity in their marriage and of having affairs?"

"Yes."

"Did he represent that as far as the divorce was concerned,

he did not intend to give her one more penny than she was entitled to?"

"Yes." Mel's loyal employee glanced nervously at him as she spoke. She wished Cahill would stop. Why was he asking her these things? What did they have to do with Anita's murder? She wanted to tell the truth. But some of her answers sounded bad, and Melvin still paid her salary.

"Did he state that Anita Green was trying to damage his business and destroy him and malign his clients?"

"Yes."

"Did he indicate that he believed she was shooting her mouth off to people and accusing him of unethical business practices relative to the IRS?"

Chaleff was on his feet. "Objection. The questions do not delineate whether she got that from dictation or things he was actually saying in the office."

Judge Trammel looked at the two lawyers. "I assumed that all of the questions dealt with the comments she heard the defendant make rather than the subject matter of the letters."

Cahill confirmed that fact and resumed questioning. "Did he express around the office that she was shooting her mouth off, accusing him of unethical practices and threatening him relative to the IRS?

"Yes."

Lily was questioned about a particular incident that had really upset Melvin. "On August 14, do you recall an incident where Mr. Green returned from visiting the IRS particularly angry about something he had observed at the building?"

"Yes."

"What was that?"

"He saw Anita's car in the parking lot."

"Did he express that he believed she was there to malign him to the IRS?"

"Yes."

"Did he go into great detail about searching the building, looking for her car while she was there?"

"Objection," Chaleff called out. "The questions are leading."

Even with the objection, Cahill had achieved his goal. He had shown that even Mel's most loyal supporters knew that he was an obsessive man, driven by fears and paranoia, who would go to unreasonable lengths to have his way. And despite the picture the defense was trying to paint, Mel was indeed frightened by the IRS.

Cahill glanced over his shoulder to gauge the reaction of the courtroom groupies and saw by their nods of approval that he had indeed scored points. The prosecutor smiled and winked at a young reporter before calling up his next witness. Clearly, Kent Cahill enjoyed being onstage.

Corroborating Lopez's testimony was Janet Frangy. Frangy, a middle-aged woman dressed properly in her dark-blue lawyer suit, was previously Mel and Anita's attorney and a social acquaintance of Anita and Rabbi Jacobs's. She testified in a strong voice filled with conviction. Anita had told her that she had information that could hurt Mel seriously with the IRS.

Mel was obviously upset by Frangy's presence and kept shaking his head in disbelief. Then he turned around to his family and smiled calmly. He needed them to see that he was self-assured and confident, even if her testimony made him ill at ease. There was simply no case against him, and he was certain that his side would take care of things.

Chaleff needed to show that Janet Frangy, like a lot of other witnesses, had her own agenda for today and that she most certainly was not impartial.

"Was the statement you are referring to about the damage she could do to Melvin made before or after Anita and Mel filed for divorce?"

"It was after she decided to divorce Mr. Green."

"You know Janis McDonald and in fact you brought Anita to her?"

"Yes."

"Did Mrs. Green make this statement to you with other people present or just yourself?"

"Just myself."

"You did do things with Ms. Green socially?"

For the first time ever. this self-assured and eager woman seemed hesitant. "That's hard to answer. Can I explain?"

Chaleff stared at her. "Let me ask a different way so we don't get into uncharted waters. Did you, for example, go to a baseball game with her and Rabbi Jacobs and whoever else you were with?"

"Yes."

"When was that?"

"Before September of 1990."

"Was she living by herself then?"

"Yes," Janet answered, and then added, "We also all had dinner before too."

"I have nothing further."

Before dismissing the jurors for the remainder of the week, Judge Trammel sternly warned them to avoid the press. The trial was beginning to be covered extensively, and he did not want their opinions manipulated by the media.

While Judge Trammel was able to control his jurors, he could not stop the tide of gossip that would quickly engulf the Valley.

31

An Eye for an Eye

Monday morning dawned cold and crisp, but at least the sun had finally returned to the Los Angeles skies. After a week's recess both the defense and prosecution teams were prepared for a long day of testimony. By day's end, the jurors would have listened to ten witnesses for the prosecution and one for the defense.

So far, the prosecution had established that Melvin Green had the personality and disposition to commit murder and that he may even have had motives to commit murder, but Cahill still had not established any links that tied Mel to the shooting.

The state called Mel and Anita's personal friend and client of over eighteen years, Robert Keith. Keith, like the others, confirmed Anita's threats about the IRS. He said Anita knew a lot and could cause some serious damage to Melvin. This further refuted the defense's position that the IRS situation was nothing to worry about. During Keith's testimony, Melvin appeared to slink lower into his chair as he scowled angrily at his old friend.

Moments later, Cahill called Berta Solis with the intention of showing further what life with Melvin Green was really like. Berta had worked in the Greens' home for several years as a housekeeper. She vividly reinforced Scott's testimony. Mel's household was a place of screaming, yelling, and constant arguments.

The terrified woman glanced timidly at Melvin as she described years of abuse. She had spent months working up the courage to speak today and had only done so because of her deep love for Anita.

A few minutes later, another of Melvin's old friends, Gilbert Mershon, took the stand for the prosecution. Cahill believed that Mershon would be the first person to actually tie Melvin to the murder. Mershon was angry and arrogant. He spoke in a fast, loud, sharp tone, and it seemed that he was actually leering at Melvin.

"He said, 'I'd just hire somebody, and someday she will be getting out of her car and somebody will just walk up and blow her brains out.'"

The jurors gasped. Mershon's testimony sent a stir through the courtroom. These details, if accurate, matched the way in which Anita was actually executed. The facts could not have been culled from newspaper articles, because the jurors had already learned that the police had intentionally told the papers that Anita had been shot in the torso.

Cahill smiled. He knew Mershon's remarks would only get better. "Did he indicate to you that he knew some people that he could contact for this purpose?"

Merson nodded. "I asked him. I said, 'Where are you going to get somebody to do that? Have you ever really thought about this? Have you thought about it from the standpoint of reality?' He said, 'It's easy. There are people that you can hire.'"

"Did you discuss with him some specific individuals that he had in mind?"

"No."

"At some later conversation, did he tell you that he knew some people, that he knew some people specifically that he could go to for something like this?"

"I recall him saying that you just go out to the desert and you hire a biker, or you get some lowlife and they will do it."

Beads of perspiration formed on Mel's neck. He tried to get Mershon to look at him while he spoke, but the witness avoided Mel's stare. When Mel couldn't get Gilbert to look at him, he began to fidget. He wadded up balls of paper in his hands. He started to frantically take notes. The jurors stared at him.

Cahill pushed ahead. "Now, you indicated on one occasion that he said she would be getting out of her car and somebody would walk up and blow her head off. Was he that specific every time, or was it just that one time?"

"That was just that one time."

"Did you warn Anita Green about what Mr. Green had told you?"

"Yes," Mershon said. "I did."

Cahill had made his point. Mershon's testimony was the most damaging yet. Now it would be up to Chaleff to try and discredit the validity of Mershon's recollections. Chaleff hammered away at Mershon. Why had Mershon not given such a vivid description of Mel's threats before? Why did Mershon's sworn statement to Hernandez not mention a gunman walking up behind Anita and blowing her brains out?

"Did you ever tell Detective Hernandez while you were in that interview room in North Hollywood that Mr. Green made that statement, 'Some day she's going to get out of her car and she's going to get blown away'?"

"No," Mershon answered. "I recalled it the next day when I was going back over the facts and going back over all my memories and recalling the things that were important about it, those specific words."

Now Mershon, too, was sweating. He glanced nervously at Cahill. The spectators began to whisper. Chaleff had tried to discredit the accuracy of Mershon's words, but Cahill was prepared.

Rosemarie Mershon, Gilbert's mother, immediately followed her son on the stand. A nervous woman in a large overcoat, she confirmed that her son had relayed the strange conversation to her long before Anita's death. Her testimony made her son's seem more plausible.

Keeping up the pace, Cahill called Angela Ramos to the stand. The stepsister of Berta Solis, she had been the Greens' maid from 1982 until 1987, when she left the house because of Mel's growing temper. Appearing on the stand in a miniskirt and T-shirt, the housekeeper again reiterated that the house was in constant turmoil with Mel's nonstop yelling and screaming at Anita.

But Cahill had taken the court's time to call her to the stand because she had something new to add. He read to the court from her police deposition. "He said that she could run away but that she would not live to spend his money?"

"Yes."

Judge Trammel peered over his glasses and stared at Melvin Green as the housekeeper whispered her last answer. Watching, Cahill smiled. He strode back to his chair and winked at the reporters. The morning had obviously gone his way and Cahill was feeling cocky.

In the afternoon, an IRS agent testified with a federal attorney standing by. Amanda Truett was pretty, blond, and definitely nervous. Given the nature of her job, this woman was used to adversarial relationships in her daily work, but Melvin Green was one man whom she would never forget. He had harassed her; he had abused her verbally in a sexual way, and all this over an audit. She had had nightmares about the man for months and finally sought counseling to deal with her pain.

More than her words, the way that she testified made it clear that Amanda Truett was afraid of Melvin. She refused to look at him the entire time she was on the stand. Building on earlier testimony, Truett established concretely to the jury that Mel had just cause to fear the IRS. Additionally, Melvin had made threatening statements about Anita to her.

"He went into a discussion about how Anita had better be careful, about every time she picked up a glass of wine she had to be careful. Every time she walked under a chandelier, she better be careful."

Amanda Truett explained how Mel had boasted to her that he was an expert in pharmaceuticals and that he knew how toxins worked. She was certain that Mel considered poisoning his wife. She ended her testimony by saying that she did not feel he was saying these things in a joking manner. Chaleff made sure her opinion was struck from the record.

Melvin looked worried during Amanda Truett's testimony, but when the next witness came forward, he appeared terrified. Phyllis Baltin had waited months for her time on the stand. Barred from the courtroom and forbidden to hear the specifics of what had already transpired there, she was eager to let her version of the truth be known.

Phyllis's makeup was carefully applied. She wore a black skirt and a matching short black jacket. She had an ankle brace on her left ankle and walked with a slight limp. She held her head high and avoided Mel's stares.

Phyllis's testimony was the most damning yet. After recounting her twenty-year relationship with Anita and Mel, she focused in on one phone call that had changed her life.

Phyllis recalled being in her kitchen with her married boyfriend, Lance Shoemaker, the day Melvin called. Although Melvin hardly knew Lance, he asked to speak with him. Because Phyllis had installed a hearing-impaired amplified telephone, she was able to hear both sides of the conversation.

"Mel asked if it was possible that Lance would eventually be leaving his wife. Then Mel asked Lance if he would be interested in having his wife knocked off in return for Anita."

The prosecution's bombshell had been dropped. Cahill knew Phyllis Baltin was a strong weapon, and he watched for the jurors' reactions. They appeared to be shocked. "Now, before he talked about this trade, did he discuss a money arrangement?"

"Yes, he did," Phyllis replied. "He asked Lance how much it would cost to do this, to have Anita taken care of, and Lance said five million dollars." Phyllis rambled on, but her words made an unforgettable impact on the jury. They kept glancing back and forth from Phyllis to Mel, studying their faces.

Lance Shoemaker, who had been kept from hearing Phyllis's testimony, was immediately called into the courtroom. A simple, working-class man, Shoemaker's skin was tanned and weathered from his years of climbing utility poles. He looked ill at ease in his blue pin-striped suit. Forced to testify against his will, not being sure of his rights and how he could protect himself, and being terrified that his wife might find out about his affair with Phyllis made his answers short and direct. A man of few words, Lance corroborated Phyllis's more detailed description of the phone call.

In what had clearly been the prosecution's day, it was the defense team's turn to call a witness. Chaleff knew that everyone had their own agenda. As unlikely as he might appear at first as a defense witness, Chaleff called to the stand the man who had worked the longest to get Melvin Green, Detective Ray Hernandez.

Chaleff appeared to be not so much interested in discrediting Hernandez, but rather in showing the jury how shoddy and selective the detective's investigation had been. To some in the courtroom, the often bitter line of questioning made it appear as if Chaleff was grasping at straws. The best evidence that he could bring forward from his lengthy badgering was that Hernandez's comments about Melvin's inappropriate statements were nowhere to be found in the original crime-scene report.

Later, both defense attorneys would again stress that the police investigation of this case was shoddy and biased from the beginning. It was a theme that the defense kept trying to impress on the jury, a jury made up of Los Angeles citizens who were already growing distrustful of their police department since the media blitz surrounding the beating of Rodney King and subsequent cover-up.

At the close of the day, it was clear the prosecution was still on a roll. Mel appeared to be a man with a lot of motives for getting rid of his wife. Mel's lawyers reminded his family to remain optimistic. The state had not proved anything yet.

32

The Ninth Commandment

The Wednesday, February 19, morning papers ran headlines reiterating Melvin Green's threats to his wife. Unlike the testimony, which portrayed a strong and angry man, the newspaper photos showed a man whose confidence had waned.

On the way to the courthouse for their second day of testimony, Phyllis and Lance picked up Riva Rice, who was also supposed to take the stand. As Phyllis maneuvered her small Saab through the busy freeway and the pouring rain, she fretted about what they could put her through today. Hell, they already told the jury she was sleeping with a married man, and Lance's testimony was on the front page of the newspapers. What else would they bring up?

Phyllis, Lance, and Riva entered the courthouse at a little before 9:00 A.M. In the hallway outside of Division 104, the cast of characters was beginning to assemble. Rabbi Jacobs and his pretty new wife, Miriam, were in the hall. He, too, was in the hot seat today, Phyllis thought. How she wished she could hear his testimony. The rabbi and Miriam approached and greeted Phyllis, Lance, and Riva. Before retreating to the opposite end of the hall to cuddle, the rabbi spoke to Lance. "I read about your testimony in the paper today. I can't believe how courageous you were to tell the truth."

Phyllis was shocked by the rabbi's words as well as by his appearance. He was flushed and nervous and looked like he would rather be anywhere other than where he was. Phyllis sighed. She had already heard from the district attorney how reluctant the rabbi was to testify. The fact that there were three reporters, an author, and a movie producer sitting in the spectator area did little to calm him. Phyllis found the rabbi's terror the only laughable moment of the day.

Mel's family members filed by and entered the courtroom one by one. They stared at Phyllis Baltin as if she were a traitor. They did not even bother to look at Riva Rice. Phyllis shuddered and lit up another cigarette. Would she ever be rid of the Greens? They followed her everywhere. She dreamed about them nightly as she tried desperately to sleep. She was awakened often by their phone calls. Phyllis had received dozens of such calls in the months since she had gone to the police, and she held Melvin responsible for all of them.

Phyllis wondered what was going on in the courtroom. She was told that Mel's employee, Kimberly Wheeler, was the first person to take the stand.

Kimberly was short, with blond hair. The young girl had only held Anita's former job at Melvin Green, Incorporated since five days before Mr. Green's arrest. Currently she was responsible for payroll checks and other company expenditures. Cahill's questioning forced Kimberly, who was obviously a hostile witness, to tell the court that no payroll checks, or any other checks for that matter, had gone out to Anita Green after August 1990.

The district attorney intended to show that Anita needed money and that Mel had really pushed her into poverty. That was why Anita needed to keep her appointment with Mel, the appointment that Mel had lured her to with the promise of a check. Mel had known all too well the extent of her financial problems.

Chaleff was on his feet immediately. Obviously concerned by what the defense had shown the jury, he wanted to get across the idea that Cahill's premise was not valid. By the time Chaleff was finished with her, most jurors were uncertain as to just why Kimberly was on the stand in the first place. Score one for the defense.

As she left the stand, Kimberly touched Mel lightly on the cheek, defying the rule that physical contact with a prisoner was not permitted. She then sauntered out of the courtroom with a smirk on her face. Melvin Green appeared to be elated.

Sympathy may not have been Kent Cahill's chief motivation

for calling his next witness, Anita's mother, Riva Rice, to the stand, but by the time he was finished with her, there was not a juror present who was not moved by her brief testimony. Riva confirmed that Anita was really penniless at the time of her death, no matter what Gerry Chaleff said.

"She told me she wanted to borrow money from me because she had no money to exist."

"Did you loan her money at that time for her to get by on?"

"Yes. Twenty-five thousand dollars."

Riva's testimony alone meant nothing, but her presence did. Brave and determined, she refused to even glance at the man who had once been her son-in-law. Instead, she stared straight ahead at the jury.

Her obvious hatred caught Mel off-guard. He squirmed in his chair and looked both uncomfortable and sad.

Riva set the tone for the next witness, the one person who had no axe to grind against Melvin Green and whose emotional testimony would prove to be the prosecution's most lethal weapon. If true, her words would confirm, beyond a shadow of a doubt, that Melvin Green had indeed forced his wife into making an appointment she never wanted to keep.

Why would any jury doubt the small, chubby, sweet-dispositioned Hispanic woman who walked into the courtroom? Anita's hairdresser, Gina Siguneza, was determined to do the right thing.

Though she told the court she was nervous, Siguneza coolly and calmly explained what she had overheard shortly before Anita's death, on October 3, 1990. That was the day that Anita received not one, but two calls from her irate husband, Melvin Green, at the tiny beauty shop where Siguneza worked.

"Anita, she says to Mel, 'You can mail my check. You can mail my check because I don't have time to pick it up at the office,'" Gina told the jury, as they strained to make out her heavily accented words. "She got upset."

"Excuse me. Nonresponsive. I object," Chaleff said.

"Did you hear any more words in that particular conversation?"

"Yes. She says she was busy and she don't want to go to the office to pick up the check. Then she repeated again, 'Please mail the check, mail my check to my house.'"

Gina elaborated that a few weeks later, on October 24, Anita once again came to have her hair done, and Melvin once again called the beauty shop several times demanding to speak with his wife.

"The first time, she says, 'Mel, I cannot go to the office because I have business to attend to tomorrow early in the morning over the hill.' He again requested, 'You want your money, you want your check, you can come over and pick it up.'"

Chief defense counsel Gerry Chaleff piped in, "Excuse me, Your Honor. I will object to that. She was testifying to what Mr. Green said. Unless she could hear it—"

Before he finished, Judge Trammel sustained his objection.

Cahill turned to Gina. "I just want you to focus on what you heard."

Assertively and insistently Gina answered, "She says, 'I cannot go pick up the check tomorrow because I have to be over the hill.' Then she hung up the phone."

Gina Siguenza seemed to be holding the attention of the jury. If anything, her heavy accent made her appear more sympathetic and somehow more credible. Cahill asked, "After she hung up the phone, did she tell you about the conversation she had just had?"

Gina sighed deeply. She had felt okay so far, but making herself understood was difficult, and now she had to tell all these people about her tragic final conversation with her customer and friend, Anita Green. She began to sweat, and she had difficulty finding the right words in English. "She told me that she really could not go because she had another appointment over the hills in the morning." Then Gina added the clincher. "And she told me that she was afraid to go pick up the check."

The spectators and the jurors stared at this little woman. Everyone in Los Angeles knew the term "over the hills" referred to the city of Los Angeles proper. The slang was used by Valley residents to refer to any region not part of the Valley, which like all valleys is surrounded by mountains and hills. Gina's words upset Melvin, who kept writing down notes for his attorneys. Mel was sweating, and Kent Cahill was not even finished yet.

"Did she tell you what Mr. Green had said to her on the phone?"

"Yes. He said, 'If you want your check, you have to come pick it up at the office tomorrow morning at 10:30.'"

The whispers filled the spectators' box. The fatal appointment had been confirmed by this innocent little hairdresser who had nothing to gain from ruining Melvin. Even the defense attorneys seemed worried about what she had said. Arthur Alexander looked at Mel. Gerry Chaleff stared straight ahead, totally absorbed in what was unraveling before him. How was he going to cast doubt on this witness?

Cahill pressed on. "What else did Mr. Green say to her?"

"Mel insists that she go to the office the next day at 10:30 in the morning to pick up the check. And she told me she was afraid."

"Objection. I think this is hearsay," Chaleff stated strongly. "May we approach the bench, Your Honor?"

"You may," the judge said wearily.

After a short conference, Judge Trammel ruled, over Chaleff's strong protests, that fear was indeed admissible because, with respect to Gina, it was necessary for state of mind and state of conduct.

Gina concluded her illuminating testimony by saying that Anita had told her that Mel was losing his temper a lot more often lately and that she had grown afraid. But Mel had left Anita with little choice, and she told Gina she was so broke that she needed to go to the office for the money or she would have to start looking for another job to support herself. Finally, Gina added that Anita had said her marriage was a mess and she was very afraid. As she concluded, her eyes filled with tears. "I told her, 'Don't go.'"

Gina Siguenza's testimony sent a stir through the courtroom. Chaleff tried to destroy what she had said on redirect and to create the impression that Gina had been confused and that Anita really was not desperate for funds. "When she told you she needed money, did she tell you that she had gotten some money from her mother?"

"No."

"Did she tell you Mr. Green had given her about four thousand dollars since she had moved out?"

"No, she never told me that."

As they watched the proud hairdresser leave the stand, spectators and reporters agreed that Gina's testimony was the most damaging yet to Mel's case. It was the most conclusive piece of evidence they had heard because it confirmed that Melvin had lured Anita to the office at a specific time. Many went to discuss the hairdresser's revelations over coffee during the twenty-minute break in the proceedings.

Meanwhile, out in the hall, Phyllis Baltin was a mess. She was going to testify again, and her entire dress had fallen apart. She had split both her zipper and the back of her skirt. She began to panic. What should she do? Not unkindly, the rabbi's new wife came over and offered her assistance. "I have some safety pins in my shoulder pads. Let's go into the ladies' room and pin you together," Miriam said.

Phyllis was grateful. She looked at Miriam and noticed that she really was one of the most exquisite women she had ever seen. Miriam was dressed in a black suede skirt, a finely tailored blouse, and a beautiful red blazer. Her graceful hands had long, delicate fingers with perfectly manicured nails. Her skin was like porcelain. Phyllis kept staring at her. She could not take her eyes off of Miriam, and she wondered what Miriam saw in the rabbi. As the two women walked into the bathroom, Miriam said, "He wanted me to come today. I was sick, but he said he needed my support. He is very frightened. I keep asking him why he is so afraid, but he won't answer me. He's up next." Then she turned to Phyllis and pleaded, "What is going on?" Phyllis shrugged and kept walking.

Once they entered the rest room and Miriam began to fix her dress, Phyllis stared at her and asked, "You really don't know what's going on, do you?"

Miriam was dumbfounded. She shook her head and asked, "What kind of person was Anita? What kind of person was Mel? Do you really think he did this?" She kept asking questions, and she seemed sincerely puzzled.

Phyllis was taken off-guard and momentarily speechless. "She was wonderful and kind and generous and totally committed to building that temple." And then she added one more point. Ever so softly she whispered, "Yes, I really think Mel did this."

Miriam shuddered. "Why would he want to do something so horrible?" Then she added, "The rabbi says that Anita was wonderful too, very devoted, and they were very close friends."

Phyllis stared at her and then began to laugh. "You call your husband 'the rabbi'? Don't you call him honey or Steve?"

Miriam stared at her. "Oh no," she said incredulously. "He always wants me to call him 'the rabbi' in public."

Phyllis stared at her and said, "Oh honey, some marriage." As she watched Miriam leave the rest room and walk down the hall toward her husband, Phyllis was struck by her innocence. Miriam really knew nothing about what had happened and Phyllis felt sorry for her. Just wait until she heard her new husband's testimony. As Phyllis watched Miriam greet Steven, she overheard her say, "Rabbi, we need to talk." It was just then that Kent Cahill came out to announce that it was time for Rabbi Jacobs to take the stand.

From her bench in the hallway, Riva Rice stared at Rabbi Jacobs and turned to one observer, a young woman journalist who was a member of the rabbi's congregation. "Go. I want you to hear what your rabbi has to say."

The woman entered reluctantly and sat next to the rabbi's new wife, Miriam. A hush came over the courtroom as Steven Jacobs, the rabbi, was sworn in.

"Would you raise your right hand? Do you solemnly swear the testimony you may now give in the cause now pending before this court shall be the truth, the whole truth, and nothing but the truth, so help you God?"

"Yes, sir."

A very nervous, ruddy-skinned man in a beautifully tailored black-and-white pin-striped suit sat down and stared at the lawyers. His beautiful wife smiled reassuringly at him and gave him the thumbs-up sign.

Mel did not notice, but he glowered anyway. His nemesis was once again before him, and it took all Mel's will to control himself. The rabbi glanced at Mel and then turned quickly away. Rabbi Jacobs confirmed that he too knew Anita had a 10:30 appointment with Melvin at the office on the day of her murder.

As discreetly as possible, Cahill asked where Anita had slept the night before she was murdered.

"She stayed, I mean, I presumed she stayed at my house." The rabbi's voice was filled with contempt, "She came back after a temple meeting to my home. She was very nervous and came back. She was not there in the morning."

"She left before you got up?"

"Correct."

Then Kent Cahill asked one simple question that seemed irrelevant. He asked the rabbi how to get from his house to Mel's office. Rabbi Jacobs answered, "You can take the 405 Freeway to the Burbank exit and go east, or you can take the Hollywood freeway and get off on Oxnard."

Cahill had carefully scripted his next question. "Either way, do you end up on Oxnard Street before you reach the office?"

"Yes."

Only Melvin Green and Ray Hernandez knew the significance of Cahill's questioning, and both were excited by it, but for different reasons. It would be a little while until this seemingly insignificant fact would come into play.

When Chaleff cross-examined the rabbi, he honed in on one, irrefutable fact—that Anita had slept at the rabbi's house the night before she was killed. Because he was questioning a rabbi, he decided to be somewhat more subtle in his questioning than he might have liked to be. Still, he implied to the jury that the rabbi had his own reasons for doing what he was doing.

"Weren't you having an intimate relationship with her?"

Rabbi Jacobs looked miserable, like he wanted to get up and run from the courtroom. "I was dating her. I was single at the time."

"I am not asking you to justify it. I am asking if you had an intimate relationship with her," Gerry Chaleff quipped.

Rabbi Jacobs was firm. "I was dating her."

Chaleff, a little impatient, was now getting angry. This was a man of the cloth on the stand and he had sworn to tell the truth. Chaleff expected him to do so. "Do you recall telling Detective Hernandez that you and she were having an intimate relationship?"

"Um, I don't recall," the rabbi said, and then added, "At the moment, I probably could have said that. It would not be unusual." Rabbi Jacobs slumped down in his chair. If he could have crawled out of the courtroom, he most certainly would have.

"That would have been the truth, right?"

"Correct."

By having the rabbi admit that he was having an affair with Anita, no matter how reluctantly he admitted it, Chaleff had tried to show the jury two things: first, that Mel's accusations were based in truth, and second, that Rabbi Jacobs had a motive for trying to hurt Mel with his testimony. Obviously, public confession of the affair and its relationship to the murder could possibly be the end of Rabbi Jacobs's career. The rabbi's face grew redder by the minute, and he kept looking over at his wife for reassurance.

Chaleff was not finished making him squirm. He had the rabbi elaborate on many things: his relationship with Anita, whom they socialized with, whether or not Mel still did his taxes. The thrust of his focus, however, was on whether Anita had told the rabbi her reasons for going to the office that morning. If she had been going to pick up a check, that would coincide with Cahill's theory that she had been lured to her death with money. If, however, she had just been going to pick up work, then her visit was arguably more routine and of less significance.

Chaleff pursued this line of questioning with confidence because he knew that the rabbi's statement to the police had made no mention of the mysterious check. Chaleff was therefore understandably upset when out of the clear blue sky, after more than a year of not recalling a check, the rabbi stunned counsel and onlookers alike with his sudden and vivid recollection that Anita had indeed mentioned a check as the reason for her visit with Mel.

Chaleff was so taken aback that he took several moments to recover. He began pacing. Then, speaking ever so slowly, with just a slight smile, the defense attorney dropped his bombshell. He wanted Rabbi Jacobs to return the next morning.

The rabbi appeared furious. He looked to be on the verge of losing control. He restrained himself as he walked out of the courtroom. Now he would have twenty-four hours to read about the trial in the papers; to face his new wife, who would surely have many questions; and to fume about what might still be uncovered the following day.

The afternoon passed quickly and was far less dramatic. Lily Lopez was recalled to confirm a few physical details about the layout of Mel's office building and parking lot. With the layout of the alley and the parking lot firmly established, Cahill called his last big gun, Mel's roommate at the time of the murder, Joseph Corrado.

A tall, lanky, olive-skinned man wearing dark slacks and a comfortable sweater ambled toward the witness stand. He stared at Mel. Once he was on the stand, he kept slinking further and further into his seat as he tried to focus on his testimony.

Cahill was direct and to the point. "On Monday, October 29, four days after Anita Green had been shot, did you have a conversation with Mr. Green in his kitchen about the incident?"

"Yes," Corrado answered. "We discussed the fact that she had been shot, and Melvin was telling me that she probably cut this guy off on the freeway, and she was coming west, westbound on Oxnard, and made a right turn on Wilkinson.

"And so I mentioned to him that I once lived in Sherman Oaks and I usually come down Oxnard and I'm usually going eastbound on Oxnard and make a left turn on Wilkinson. Then he explained to me that she definitely made a right turn, and so we got into a discussion about right turn and left turn."

"Did this discussion become an argument?" Cahill inquired.

"Yeah, I would say so. He was kind of trying to pretty forcefully to convince me she was coming from the freeway," Corrado explained. "Melvin has a way of banging on the table and being demonstrative. I was just curious how he was so positive she was coming from the freeway, or westbound, and he mentioned that there was a roofer across the street who told him she was coming westbound and made a right turn on to Wilkinson."

Cahill and Corrado went on and on describing the bizarre argument just days after Anita's death. The district attorney wanted to use this testimony to show two things. First, that Melvin had no patience for people who didn't see the world as he did, and second, that Melvin had constructed what he thought was a perfect story of what had happened and was frustrated when he couldn't get his story to fly with his friend, let alone the roofer or the police detective.

Cahill shook his head back and forth in disbelief. Looking at the jury, he said, "The defendant was vehement, said that's the way it happened. I think when the defendant set this up with the phone call from the beauty shop, he already had his scenario or story all planned out. He decided he was going to blame this on someone following her off the freeway, and that's what he was going to go with, and he didn't like it when someone didn't accept that story. He got angry about it. It wasn't selling well."

Corrado's testimony was quite lucid. Chaleff would spend hours trying to discredit it by implying that Corrado was not a credible witness because he too had changed his police report. It was the theme of selective recollection that Chaleff kept bringing up in his objections, a theme he wanted to hammer into the jurors' minds.

By late afternoon, an exhausted Phyllis Baltin returned to the stand in her dress that was barely holding together, with the feeling that she was not doing much better.

Cahill asked, "Ms. Baltin, directing your attention back to October 25, 1990, when did you first learn that Anita had been shot?"

Phyllis answered, "At about four o'clock in the afternoon."

"What was the source of that information?"

"There was a message left on my machine from Melvin Green."

Phyllis produced the tape for the district attorney, and Cahill submitted it to the judge and asked to be allowed to play it for the jury.

The jurors strained forward in their seats to hear. Phyllis confirmed the voice on the tape was that of Melvin Morton Green. "Phyllis, this is Melvin. I'm sorry to have to tell you this, but Anita has been shot. Detective Coffey may contact you. I told them about Jacobs, Lebowitz, and Mitchell. Feel free to tell them anything. Thank you. Thank you, dear."

Phyllis told the court that when Melvin later questioned her about what she had told the police, she said, "The truth."

Cahill explained that this tape proved that Melvin was trying to orchestrate the police investigation of the murder so that ultimately he could steer the police away from himself.

A revealing and exhausting day of testimony was now coming to an end. Traditionally, the state calls its strongest witness to the stand last, with the hope of leaving the jury with the impression that the prosecution knew what it was talking about. In this case, Cahill lacked a single witness who had definitive evidence linking Melvin to the murder. But Cahill knew that the defense kept attacking the police investigation, and with that in mind he called Detective Ray Hernandez to testify.

Looking straight at Cahill, Ray Hernandez walked calmly and confidently to the witness stand. He was dressed in a brown suit for the occasion. Ray began to outline for the court how he had conducted his police investigation. By the time he finished, Cahill had successfully tied together most of the loose ends and had shown the jury that the police were not messing up the investigation by changing around or omitting facts. The detectives were simply doing their job as best they knew how.

The consensus among onlookers was that the district attorney had skillfully shown that Melvin Green was a bizarre and controlling person who had become frightened by his wife's threats to expose him. To his credit, Cahill had also done some pretty amazing lawyering to weave together intricate bits of information and the testimony of many different witnesses to form a revealing picture of what might have been. Now it was up to the defense to prove, not that Mel was innocent, but, rather, that the inferences Cahill wanted the jury to adopt were simply not valid.

33

Beyond a Shadow of a Doubt

The defense of Melvin Green was not really a defense, but rather an attack on the alleged failings of the prosecution and an attempt to show the jury that Kent Cahill's inferences about the case were, quite simply, not valid. The defense strived to do this by relentlessly attacking the people's witnesses. Every step of the way the defense team shouted warnings to the jury which all came down to one credo, "Don't be misled by innuendo."

It seemed to many courtroom insiders that the defense legend, Gerry Chaleff, had underestimated the strength of the prosecution and the intensity of Kent Cahill's commitment. There was the feeling that Chaleff and Alexander had entered the courtroom prepared for the battle, but only in the sense that they did not see there was any way the prosecution could win. Their confidence came from the fact that they had not yet been persuaded that the state's case against Melvin Green rested on a firm foundation. They approached the trial with the attitude that once the state put forth its evidence, they would quickly be able to show the jury why the evidence did not show that Melvin Green had hired someone to shoot his wife, at least not beyond a reasonable doubt and to a moral certainty. When the state's attorney came across so strongly convinced of Melvin's guilt, Gerry Chaleff seemed to be momentarily caught off guard.

From day one Chaleff and Alexander's strategy had been that since they had neither answers nor an affirmative defense, the burden of proof was on the prosecution to show beyond a reasonable doubt that Melvin Green had hired someone to kill his wife. And, in their minds, there was an element of doubt about almost every fact the witnesses were telling the jury. Melvin could not have shouted "Ask the men she's screwing" in the parking lot, or Mike Coffey would have written it down in his original report. Melvin could not have been obsessive, like the man in *Sleeping With the Enemy*, because Anita *had* gotten away from him; they were getting a divorce. His letters may have rambled on and sounded inappropriate, but they did not show a man who wanted to murder; instead, they showed a person who wanted to do what was right.

With each passing day of the trial, it became more evident how good the prosecutor was. Chaleff and Alexander, however, were aware of the serious flaws in the state's case. They felt strongly that it was impossible to prove that Mel had done anything on the basis of several witnesses' uncorroborated testimony.

One of the biggest problems they would have to face for the remainder of the trial was that Judge Trammel had allowed many of their client's obsessive letters to be admitted as evidence, letters that presented an extremely negative view of Melvin, and which, in their minds, even if accurate, had nothing to do with the case at hand. They had argued strongly against introducing the correspondence, but in the end Judge Trammel admitted it on the grounds that the nature of the relationship between the Greens was a revelation before the jury.

But the judge had also ruled in their favor on many instances. In a particularly unusual ruling, Trammel had prevented Mel's statement, "I'm innocent because I would have drowned her in the pool months ago. . . ." from being allowed into the trial.

Judge Trammel's reaction to the statement was, "Oh my God, I'm shocked by that statement. I can just imagine what the jurors would think." With that in mind, he said that it was more inflammatory than necessary. It appealed to the jurors' emotions rather than to their intellect. Judge Trammel felt that the jury would be so appalled by the statement that they would not be fair to Mr. Green.

Judge Trammel had similarly ruled that the prosecution would not be allowed to prove to the jury that the diploma the defendant displayed on his wall, which purported to confer a degree in taxation, had in fact been purchased from a mail-order diploma mill.

So with these decisions already made, it was their turn to chip away at the evidence, piece by piece, that Kent Cahill had laboriously put before the jury. Gerry Chaleff was to speak first for the defense team. He rose and walked confidently over to call his first witness. He wanted the jury to focus on the weak parts of the state's case, and he chose witnesses whom he thought would force the jurors into some hard thinking, thinking that would show them that, in this case, none of the facts had been carved in stone and nothing was certain beyond a shadow of a doubt. So certain was Chaleff in this belief, that only minutes before, while the jury was still in the jury room, he had tried passionately to get the judge to have the court drop the charges against his client. First, he tried to get the "special circumstance" clause removed, a qualification that meant if Mel was convicted he would never be eligible for parole.

Chaleff argued many cases to the judge, all trying to convince him that for the financial-gain part of the clause to hold, the murder would have had to have been committed for that motive alone, and that surely was not the case. Clearly, if Melvin had Anita murdered because he was jealous of her affair with the rabbi, that could not sustain a conviction of murder for financial gain. Besides, it appeared that money didn't mean a thing to Melvin Green. He only used it for leverage over people.

Chaleff also argued to drop the murder charges because the prosecution had not presented any hard evidence that connected Mr. Green to the murder. There was not even a scintilla of real evidence and no *nexus*, or connection, between the circumstantial evidence that had so far been presented.

The patient judge listened attentively to Chaleff's pleas. He removed his glasses and answered, "My feelings are, that there is sufficient evidence that, should there be a conviction, should there be a binding proof of those special-circumstance allegations, that both of those verdicts would be upheld on appeal."

The defense team's theory of doubt would have to be

reinforced by the witnesses, because clearly the judge himself was not convinced. He thought that the case and those issues, financial gain especially, could be decided by the jury.

After the judge's decisions, Mel's family and supporters made their way into the courtroom. They sat behind the glass, in the spectators' section, and waited patiently for Gerry Chaleff to begin. The jurors stared at the Greens, searching their faces for some sign of emotion. But the Greens looked straight ahead, never smiling at anyone, only occasionally nodding their heads at Melvin.

Cary Green sat with the others from Melvin's office, wearing a finely tailored business suit befitting his new position as the temporary president of Melvin Green, Incorporated. His older brother, Michael, wore jeans and a T-shirt. Michael remained next to his grandfather, Hy Green, who sat in the front row and repeatedly adjusted his hearing aid. Although she was officially barred from hearing the other witnesses' testimony, on this day, Lily Lopez went against the judge's ruling and sat in the courtroom as well.

Melvin's family and supporters looked tired and forlorn. For a week now, they had watched witness after witness tear apart their Melvin. The man who had always been in control now sat as a prisoner, and in their opinion, the state had offered nothing to prove that he had done anything. They saw Kent Cahill as an arrogant, cocky, self-assured son of a bitch. And he was sarcastic, too. The Greens hated sarcasm. Well, finally their side would have its turn. They looked at Gerry Chaleff hopefully.

Chaleff recalled a visibly shaken Steven Jacobs as his first witness. The last twenty-four hours had been particularly unnerving for the rabbi, and his discomfort showed. After spending a long night avoiding Miriam's questions, the rabbi was not as successful at avoiding the papers', which once again linked him directly to Anita and indirectly to the husband who was accused of murdering her. During his testimony, the rabbi was somewhat testier than he had been the day before. Perhaps that was why many on the jury decided that they did not trust him.

Later, after the trial, several jurors told an interviewer that they had spent over a day debating the rabbi's involvement. Was it possible he had played a bigger role in Anita's death? They were certain that his testimony was not right somehow.

Chaleff questioned Steven Jacobs on whether he cashed checks for Anita. "Is this Anita's check?" he asked.

"Yes," the rabbi replied.

"Is that your signature on the back?"

"Yes."

Through this testimony, Chaleff was trying to counteract Cahill's claims that, using Anita's poverty, Melvin had forced her to the office that fateful morning. It was one of the subtler seeds he was trying to plant.

Once finished, in calm, cool, and calculated moves, Chaleff showed the court that the temple building project had not progressed much since Anita's death. Since Melvin Green still guaranteed the temple loan, he had reason to want Anita to remain alive even if she was no longer his wife. Why would he kill his wife when he would be released of his pressing financial obligations to the congregation only if and when the temple was built?

"As part of the process to begin being able to build a synagogue, did certain individuals guarantee loans to a bank?" Chaleff asked.

"Yes."

"Was one of those persons who guaranteed a loan Mr. Green, Mr. Melvin Green?"

"Yes."

"How much was the total loan?"

"The original loan was 1.5 million dollars and then it was increased later on up to three million dollars."

The answer caused quite a stir among the spectators. So it was true; Anita had slept with the rabbi while her husband's money helped build her lover's edifice.

Mel's family and employees began to shake their heads back and forth and whisper among themselves. Some rolled their eyes, and on one of the few such occasions during the trial, Judge Trammel harshly asked one woman to stop talking.

Chaleff pressed on. "How much of that was guaranteed by Mr. Green?"

The rabbi's expression changed, and his brows furrowed as

he answered. "I'm not sure. I think it was fifty thousand dollars, but I'm not sure." His voice seemed cold and indifferent.

"Were there different instruments that Mr. and Mrs. Green signed to help in the process of building this synagogue?"

"Yes."

"What other kinds of documents or instruments?"

"A pledge."

"And was the total of Mr. and Mrs. Green's obligation $372,000?"

After several objections by the district attorney and several false starts by Chaleff, the rabbi's testimony finally revealed what the defense attorney wanted. "It was the intention of the congregation when you bought the land to use part for the temple, and you were going to try and sell or lease the rest of the land to pay back the money you were going to use to build the temple, is that correct?"

"Correct."

"Because of the delays that happened, you were not able to accomplish that in the time frame that you wanted, is that correct?"

"Yes."

"And the fact is that if you weren't able to do this with the other twelve acres, you might not be able to pay the bank back?"

"Yes."

"If you couldn't pay back the bank, the guarantees could become due?"

"Yes."

"Thank you. Now, in 1990, was Anita Green the president of the temple?"

"Yes."

"And at that point was Anita the person who was most involved with trying to get the temple built, to get this land, the other part of the land, either leased or sold? Was she the person most involved in that?"

"Yes."

"Is it fair to say, um, was she the driving force?"

"Yes."

It wasn't what Chaleff said, but rather what he didn't say, in this line of questioning that caused damage to the prosecution. Chaleff showed the jury that Mel was a generous man, not likely to kill over money, and that Mel had every incentive to keep his wife alive because only she could get the temple built and only then could he be released from his obligations.

On cross-examination Cahill made sure that the rabbi explained that the temple had a new leader and that the building project had not been abandoned with Anita's death. But still, he was not able to repair the damage that the rabbi's testimony had already done.

Rabbi Jacobs was not the only nervous person to testify that day. Ray Hernandez was fretting about his turn on the stand. Chaleff was tough, and Ray knew that he was going to really work him over. Chaleff had to get the jury to look at the cops with suspicion, and that fact didn't make Ray feel any better, nor did his knowledge that Melvin would enjoy watching him squirm.

Before putting Ray Hernandez on the stand, Chaleff recalled Mel's receptionist and loyal secretary, Lily Lopez. He needed to set the stage for Ray's testimony that would take place a little later in the day, testimony that was intended to reveal that the police were a bunch of idiots intent on ensnaring their quarry.

Lily confirmed the cops' numerous mistakes. They had mistakenly thought a simple light in the office parking lot was a security camera. They had taken a Polaroid snapshot from Mel's bulletin board. The snapshot was of a toilet bowl with a piece of paper in it, bearing the words, *It's over* written on it. The police assumed that the words had something to do with the murder. Lily confirmed that the photo had been in the office long before Anita was shot and that it referred to Melvin's massive weight loss. The police wanted to pin this murder on Melvin Green so badly that they imagined things that never existed and turned other things that did exist into things that they were not.

Chaleff skillfully questioned everything. The district attorney had painted a picture of Melvin Green with his questioning, and Chaleff's work was a deliberate wash-off of the colors on Cahill's canvas. Rather than show the jury that Melvin could not have committed such a crime, he showed them that the prosecution's evidence was not strong enough to prove that he had committed such a crime.

As good as Gerry Chaleff was, the defense had a major problem. They could not risk calling a character witness, for then the prosecutor would be allowed to call whomever he wanted to refute what their witness would say. Perhaps they knew that, considering their client, character testimony had to be avoided because too many people could say how awful Melvin's character could be. So, in the end, not a single character witness was called to speak on Mel's behalf.

Keeping the problem of Mel's character in mind, the defense called Mel's first wife, Bernyce, to the stand with the stipulation that she was not to talk about Mel's personality during their thirteen-year marriage nor about their divorce settlement. This decision by Judge Trammel was an obvious blow, because the defense had hoped to show that Mel had been more than generous in his divorce settlement with Bernyce.

After having waited patiently for his turn, Arthur Alexander's questioning was severely curtailed by the Judge's decision. Now the scope of Bernyce's testimony would not be as detailed as Alexander had hoped. Frustrated, he nevertheless questioned Bernyce to establish for certain that Melvin and Anita's property was indeed separate and not community property.

Cahill seethed. He did not like what they were attempting to do and he didn't trust Bernyce. Besides, for days he had listened to the defense shout over and over again to the jurors that all his witnesses had an axe to grind against Melvin. Certainly this one had one to grind against Anita.

On cross-examination Cahill asked, "At the time of the breakup of your marriage, did you harbor feelings of extreme bitterness toward Anita Green?"

"No."

"I'm going to read you a passage of something you wrote. I'm going to ask if you wrote this, if this is your signature."

Perhaps sensing that what Cahill was about to do would do more harm than good for his side, and also aware that Mel's two sons were in the courtroom and that they had already been hurt so badly, Arthur Alexander took a major risk. "May we approach the bench, Your Honor?" he asked.

"You may." At sidebar, out of the hearing of the jury, defendant, spectators, and press, Alexander asked, "Hasn't this family been through enough?"

Although unmoved with the plight of the family, Judge Trammel ruled that the letter in question amounted to impermissible character evidence.

Bernyce's testimony unintentionally inflicted more damage to the defense team and Chaleff looked frustrated. He glanced at the spectators. Mel's sons and his father stared at him expectedly for reassurance.

Gerry Chaleff glanced at the clock. The day was quickly coming to an end. Throughout the trial, the defense had been claiming that the police had made mistakes. Now he had to show the courtroom just how biased and sloppy this police work really had been. Chaleff looked like he could barely wait for Detective Ray Hernandez to take the stand and answer his questions.

Carefully, the defense attorney grilled the detective on his interviewing techniques, making sure that the jury understood that in Chaleff's mind it was apparent that there were problems with these techniques.

"Why do you have people sign their police statements?"

"I want them to read the statement that I wrote and see if that is what they have said. If it is, they sign it."

"Okay. So prior to them signing it, you ask them to read it?"

"Yes." The detective did not see what he was getting into, and when he figured it out, he practically fell out of his seat.

"Do you tell them anything else? Like...if there's something incorrect in here we can change it?"

"Yes." Ray was getting angry. "If they have any additional information they should call me, because usually people don't recall everything the initial time." The jurors looked at Ray and smiled. He came across as just a cop doing his job. Still, the defense attorney would not let up.

Chaleff showed the jury exhibits that he felt showed that often the detective added information to people's statements. The attorney questioned Hernandez more specifically about Corrado's, Mershon's, and, finally, the rabbi's statements. He hammered on the single fact that Hernandez did not always write things down, things that, if he had really heard them, were important enough to write down.

"So what happens is you come in and you sit in the interview room, and then you have some conversation, and then you turn on the tape? You finish the interview, and what usually happens is, after the interview is over, the witness wants to add something else that doesn't get on tape. Is that what happens?"

Ray Hernandez fidgeted. The lawyer was trying to put words into his mouth, thoughts into his head. "No. That's not true, Mr. Chaleff." He tried not to sound defensive, but he did. Some jurors looked annoyed. They glanced back at Chaleff, but he had already backed off. The damage had already been done.

The detective felt that he had to do something to explain. He sat rigidly in his seat, looked first at Cahill, then at the jury, and finally directly into Gerry Chaleff's eyes. "When I left Mr. Mershon on our first interview he was very nervous. He was excited. He was also very afraid that he was going to be next. We sat down; I talked with him, and I left him with the thought, if you have anything additional, call me."

The volleying between the defense attorney and the detective continued for well over an hour. The jurors seemed bored by it. When Chaleff was finished, the impression of the police he left the jurors with appeared far less questionable than the negative impression the defense team had hoped for. Ray's note-taking was simply the way he did his job. During an interview the detective concentrated on what was being said and on who was saying it. His interrogation skills were used on both suspects and witnesses, and his tough personality may have scared people into telling him the truth, but he never *made* them tell him something, nor did he force them into getting carried away with their recollections. Still, once again, Gerry Chaleff had planted a seed of doubt, no matter how small, that the police had something against Melvin Green.

Until this time, the defense team's tactics had made sense. They questioned the police, they questioned the prosecution's witnesses' motives for testifying, and they argued reasonable doubt over and over again to the jurors. But their next action appeared to be a desperate attempt at showing another scenario of what *could* have happened.

While the jurors were still at lunch, in a bench motion before the judge and the district attorney, Chaleff tried to introduce the testimony of a woman named Sharon Iverson. It was his hope that her testimony would show the court that indeed Anita's murder was not a setup, but rather a random act of Los Angeles violence.

Iverson was sworn in before Judge Trammel, and he patiently listened to what she had to say. Sometime between October 16 and October 22, a motorcyclist had followed her for quite a while on the Hollywood freeway. Ms. Iverson claimed the driver had made a pass at her, and when she turned him down, he continued to follow her in a menacing way. When Chaleff showed her the composite picture of Anita's shooter, Iverson noticed significant similarities.

"I was so concerned about it. When my husband heard through the media about the murder, he said, 'You know, a lady was followed off the freeway and killed. I think you ought to call the police.' He encouraged me to call the police and so I did."

Judge Trammell looked at Chaleff and Cahill and smiled. He turned to the prosecutor and shook his head. "Counselor?"

Cahill replied, "This was a different motorcycle, a different person, a different day. Things happen on the California freeways, but this is too farfetched."

The judge agreed. There was no connection, and Chaleff knew it. "I see absolutely no relevancy. If anything, it's on the zero side or the minus side of zero."

Sheepishly, Chaleff answered, "We only had two motorcycles. We needed a third one."

"Good try," Judge Trammel added, and smiled.

"Thank you," Chaleff said, and then tried to back himself out of a hole as he explained, "The reason I subpoenaed her was the original stuff she told me was a little different. I thought it happened on the same day, at about the same time."

Judge Trammel looked at Gerry Chaleff and once again smiled. "I'll take your word for it."

When the jurors came back into the courtroom, all Chaleff had left to do was try to show them once again that there were other scenarios that could have happened. The strategy remained the same: Refute Cahill's witnesses. It was time to put Mel's divorce attorney, Marian Stanton, on the stand to do just that.

Stanton, a prominent Encino divorce lawyer, was the picture of respectability. Tall and attractive, she smiled at Mel from the witness stand. Marian Stanton was one of the first witnesses to look at Melvin like a human being, and that fact was not lost on the jury. The other witnesses had stared at Melvin with contempt, disdain, and hatred, or had avoided his eyes altogether. Stanton didn't, and the compassion in her eyes showed that she indeed seemed to feel badly about the plight her client now found himself in. Or she was a damn good actress.

Stanton wore a dark blue suit and carried a briefcase. Her testimony attempted to refute everything that Janis McDonald's testimony had said. It was her word against Anita's lawyer's words. She was questioned by Arthur Alexander, the attorney to whom she had sent Mel after learning of his wife's shooting and with whom she also happened to share office suites.

Stanton said that she had been retained by Mel in May of 1990 to handle his divorce from Anita Green. She confirmed that a four-way meeting had taken place in Anita's attorney's office in early September. At that meeting, Anita had not yet decided whether she intended to challenge the nuptial and prenuptial contracts. Her attorney planned to notify Marian Stanton of Anita's decision after Stanton returned from a two-week vacation. When she arrived home, she had more than ten letters from Anita and her attorney, but none that mentioned the contracts. She had even called Janis McDonald and asked her to read the contracts again and then to get back to her.

"Mrs. McDonald testified that in that conversation she expressly rejected the validity of the contract. Did she do so in the conversation with you?"

"Absolutely not."

Stanton then added that September's four-way meeting had focused on how to find a way to get Anita back into the business so Anita could complete what needed to be done. The problem was that Anita was not receptive to any solutions. "She said that she couldn't work in the office anymore because her husband kept harassing her. She said he would come into the office every five minutes. He would check the lines she was on and listen in on her conversations. He was constantly needing to see what she was doing and whether she was having outside conversations other than business."

"Was there any mention of there being guns on or about the premises?"

"Sure, someone mentioned that there were guns in the safe or in the gun locker."

"Was that the extent of the comment?"

"That's correct."

Marian Stanton said that it was clear that Anita did not want to work in the same building with Mel and that she wanted to find an alternative, so they began exploring the possibility of Anita picking up work and bringing it back. At that point, Mel had gotten a little upset because he was concerned about logistics, and about how he would pay Anita and about all the particulars, but he had soon quieted down.

Mel's attorney said her client had more than generously given Anita two separate checks that summer for ten thousand dollars each, and Anita had acknowledged receipt of them in writing, so she had plenty of money on which to live. What she did with that money was not certain, but certainly it was implied that twenty thousand dollars was more than ample money for someone from June to October, even with the expenses associated with moving and setting up a new apartment. And furthermore, the jury knew that Anita had borrowed money from her mother and from another person for almost a total of twenty-nine thousand dollars. What was she doing with all this money? What was she spending it on?

Marian Stanton's testimony cast doubt for the first time on whether Anita really needed more money, money that the district attorney claimed she desperately had to have. Money the state said she had been lured to the office for and then shot.

On another level, ever so subtly, the testimony suggested that Anita was not only unfaithful but greedy as well. Another seed had been planted. Was she really just an innocent victim?

Throughout the long trial—due to the rain and the February presidential holidays, six days of trial had spread out over two weeks—people had looked at Melvin. Everyone present in the courtroom had heard the whispers, "When is Green taking the stand?" Some stared at him excitedly. They could not wait to see this guy in action. Were all the bizarre things people were saying about him true? The buzz filled the hallways, the small snack bars, the cafeteria, and the elevators. They had listened to Cahill's taunts as he cross-examined witnesses. The prosecutor could not mask his keen desire to question Melvin. It would certainly be an interesting exchange.

Mel Green's lawyers had made the decision long ago. Melvin Morton Green would not take the stand to testify in his own defense. Everyone present was upset by their decision, but few doubted that Melvin's lawyers had made the right choice.

There was no way the defense team could have put Melvin on the stand and gotten anything positive from him, especially not a tense Melvin Green. California law says that if a defendant takes the stand and swears to tell the truth, the prosecutor can ask anything he wants on the facts of the case or the credibility of the witness. It was clear that Cahill would tear him apart. And Melvin's own writings proved that he never did well under pressure; that's when he became his most obnoxious and bullying.

Now was not the time to take chances. Melvin was, for the most part, uncontrollable. If he insisted on taking the stand, he could very well seal his own fate.

The problem with this decision is that the jury usually uses a defendant's constitutional right not to testify against him or her. Although Judge Trammel passionately instructed them not to do so, Mel's avoidance of the stand did not look right to some of the jurors.

Later, one young man who had been on the jury said, "I listened to the judge, and I did not let Green's refusal to be questioned play a part in my decision. But, in the back of my mind, there was always the nagging thought that the guy never stood up to tell us exactly what had happened. He couldn't. That, plus the fact that he never cried, not when the coroner took the stand, not when Anita's son took the stand. Maybe, once in the beginning, he shed a fake tear or two. But the man was so unemotional, and I thought he might have something to do with it. That's how I felt when we got ready to hear the closing arguments."

It was up to Melvin's counsel to do his work for him. That's what they were being paid for. Since Melvin remained silent, they had the difficult job of convincing the ten men and two women of various races that the state's case against Melvin Morton Green had simply not been proved beyond a reasonable doubt and to a moral certainty. And they knew that single concept, the concept of reasonable doubt, was a difficult one to get across to jurors. Jurors want answers. They want to know who did it.

The night before the closing arguments Melvin called Alexandra Leeds from jail. "They've put up no evidence that shows I did it. I'll be home soon, sweetheart."

"How can you be so certain, Melvin? Cahill may be mean, but he's good, and the jury likes him." Then, realizing that she alone could keep up his hope, she added, "You're right, Melvin. I heard Gerry was wonderful today."

"Gerry wouldn't let me speak on my own behalf. Can you believe it? He thinks he knows more than I do."

"I don't mean to upset you, Mellie," Alexandra said lovingly, "but Gerry does know more about these things. Listen to him."

Mel changed the subject. "I hate it here," he stated. "These are animals living with me. The miscreants of the world. I don't belong here."

Melvin was nervous, irritable, and mean. Alexandra tried to calm him. "I know, sweetheart."

"I don't belong here, and I don't intend to stay."

"I'm sure you'll be out soon. I have faith in you."

"Honey, innocence is on my side. The system will work, I promise." Then Mel added softly, "Alexandra, if I didn't shoot her, which even Cahill says I didn't, then there is no connection. Therefore, there is way more than reasonable doubt."

Alexandra thought about his words. Did Mel have a different definition for murder than she did? Was he implying that sure he had benefited from it, and sure he had suggested that somebody do it, maybe he even paid them, but since he absolutely had not pulled the trigger, then he could not be guilty of murder? Until now, he had always said he had nothing to do with Anita's murder. He still insisted he was innocent. But was this his way of saying that he *had* something to do with it, but cloaked within his own personal definition of innocence? Alexandra shuddered. She did not know what to think. She was grateful that she had been barred from the courtroom because Cahill thought he might call her to the stand. She cried herself to sleep that long, lonely night.

34

Weaving the Tapestry

The date was Friday, February 24, and Melvin Green's trial was almost two weeks old. More than a year had passed since Anita's brutal murder, and people were still waiting for answers. As if on cue, the sunlight finally peeked out from the layers of clouds that had filled the sky for so many weeks. The rain stopped falling, and the city set the stage. In the case of *People* v. *Green*, the high drama was about to begin.

For the first time since the trial started, the spectator section in Judge Trammel's courthouse was filled to capacity. This was like an E-ticket ride at Disneyland. Many were so excited to hear how this prosecutor thought he had enough evidence to convict Melvin Green that they waited around for seats. Even a few temple members forgot about discretion and, against their better judgment, decided to attend.

Melvin's family, friends, and staff members filled the first row of the spectators' box. The one friend who had faithfully brought him a clean set of clothes each day gave Mel the okay sign, a smile, and a nod of approval.

Four newspaper reporters sat huddled together in the second row of the spectator section and whispered. This case had been far more exciting than the other routine trials they frequently covered, and they were looking forward to the prosecutor's opening statement. Kent Cahill gave them his usual wink and smiled. His colleagues from the downtown D.A.'s office had flocked to hear his closing remarks. They looked at him encouragingly. Cahill's adrenaline would not let up. He strutted into position.

Kent Cahill believed he would win. He felt that he had skillfully cross-examined the few witnesses Chaleff and Alexander had paraded before the jury. The closing argument was to be his grand finale. He knew that it carried more weight then the entire script he had written so far. It was show time, and Cahill wanted his presentation and his words to be unforgettable.

For the performance of his career, Kent wore a black suit. He looked handsome, which was a word that was rarely used to describe him. He had paid more attention than usual to dressing today, but it wasn't that. It was his confidence and self-assuredness, the way he carried himself. There was something different about Kent Cahill this day and everyone saw it. There was a power about him, an aura. The one place in the world where Kent felt most sure of himself was in the courtroom, and never more so than when he was arguing before a jury. He was the star of the show and he knew it. He had even winked at a few of the women in the spectators' box who had become his groupies, as well as at all the female reporters.

"Ladies and gentlemen of the jury," Cahill began, "listen to my argument. Then sit back and look at all the evidence as a whole. When you look at the totality of evidence, and then you step back and look at the whole picture, is there more than one reasonable interpretation that appeals to your common sense and judgment?"

Cahill spent a half hour replaying the basic facts of the case and then another half hour illustrating why those facts indicated that Melvin Green had hired someone to kill his wife. By the time he was finished attacking Melvin's character and vividly describing his motives, the defendant looked like it was all over. Melvin had slumped lower and lower into his seat. At one point, he could even be seen wiping away a few tears, but never once did he look at Cahill or the jury. At times, Mel would shake his head vigorously back and forth as he listened to things that Cahill said about him. He couldn't believe that his life was being destroyed this way. Didn't the jury see that all the witnesses' testimony had been rehearsed? It didn't mean anything at all because it was merely a script.

By the time of Cahill's argument, Mel knew what demons the prosecutor would talk about. What he did not know was that Cahill's argument was carefully scripted to hone in on five points.

"First, this was a planned hit," the lawyer explained. "The

motorcycle is a perfect assassination vehicle, and the rider's face was covered. The witnesses said the guy was in a hurry. When you commit a crime, you know that if a witness saw you he would call the police and an all-points bulletin would go out. If you are a professional, you want to change your appearance as soon as possible. The shooter gets off his bike, goes over to the victim, and puts one shot at point-blank range into the base of her skull. That's neat, that's clean, that's professional."

The jurors sat up and listened attentively. Bernyce Herzberg sighed loudly in the spectators' box. Irene Sherwyn, Mel's loyal secretary, shook her head back and forth just as Melvin did. In the front row, Mel's sons sat on opposite ends of the bench and glared furiously at Cahill. Michael kept lifting his head and looking over at Melvin as if he was trying to read Mel's face for some clue.

"An execution-style murder requires a motive," Kent Cahill explained. "It wasn't a robbery or sexual assault. This is somebody who knew his victim or was hired by somebody who knew his victim. Statements were made soliciting the death of Anita Green, and, finally, Anita Green was murdered at a time and place where she was specifically scheduled to be."

Kent Cahill walked toward Melvin. He began to shake his head back and forth dramatically as he looked at him. "Executions don't just happen. They are arranged for at a specific time and place so that the shooter can plan out his approach and map out his escape. You set up a time and place, and then you've got an ironclad alibi. Mel knows a spouse is a logical suspect, so he does it while he is in his office."

Cahill paused. He was a man who believed passionately in what he was saying. The jurors knew from his words and the intensity with which he uttered them that Mr. Cahill really believed that Melvin Green had hired someone to kill his wife. He must know more than he was allowed to put into evidence , or he would never be able to sound this sure.

Each time Cahill glanced at Melvin, the fury in his eyes could not be hidden. Mel was the most pretentious, egomaniacal man he had ever encountered. And Kent Cahill knew with all his heart that Melvin's ego would never allow him to admit to anything, ever. One single fact, that Melvin thought he could control the entire world, drove Cahill crazy.

The prosecutor took a keep breath to calm himself. He walked even closer to Melvin and stared coldly. "Anita Green defied the defendant's need to control her. We have all heard of the kind of men who regard their wives not as partners but as possessions. They own them, own them like objects. I think you can see from the testimony of her son, Scott, and from Barbara Wolpow, Mershon, and others, Melvin Green is such a man."

Cahill pointed at Melvin, his voice rising with sarcasm. "Certain things you have to respect about this man. He is a self-made millionaire. He's accustomed to having things his own way. In our society, wealth equals power. Sometimes power corrupts. A wealthy man can do anything. He is above the law. He made believe that he could own, that he could buy, anyone or anything, and, if necessary, he could even buy justice."

Cahill paused. The courtroom was completely silent. Melvin Green smiled smugly, and he actually appeared proud of himself. Cahill walked ever so slowly away from Melvin and toward the jurors. "I want to tell you that the best witness of all as to his need to control Anita is Melvin himself. That's something you haven't seen yet, the words of Melvin Green, because His Honor correctly ruled that they speak for themselves. I can't go through them all. You will be able to do that, to read them all. They are important because to really understand what this murder is about, you need to read these documents and see how this thing evolved."

"At this time, I'm going to read you a few examples...a few sentences here and there." The room remained silent. Kent Cahill strode over toward the jury. "This is a poem that Melvin Green wrote to Anita Green before they got married. I think it characterizes the way in which Melvin Green viewed Anita Green, his feelings about the nature of the marriage.

> To Anita Molly and, of
> Course, her son, Scott
> continue in your warm ways
> And make sure that Scott is taught

continue to surprise me
and make me happy,
And give me no more shit
And I promise, if we go out for a martini,
I'll give you more than the pit.
do your job without opening your mouth
Except nice things to say
And I assure you that for the rest of your life
you'll only have to say oy vay.
For if you continue with the pace you are
at this place,
You won't have more than a few years to
survive in this human race.

"Now, this is a love poem. It sets out his understanding of this relationship. You do as your are told; you keep your mouth shut except the things I want to hear, and I'll give you the world. I'll buy you everything in the world if you keep your mouth shut. Don't give me any shit or you will have 'a few years to survive in this human race.'" Then Kent Cahill added for emphasis, "I think that captures the essence of the man's feelings about what he expected out of this relationship."

Cahill kept reading. Melvin looked like he had been hit in the head. As he listened to his own letters, he grew as white as a ghost. By the time Cahill finished, it was apparent that Melvin was an extremely controlling individual. "Barbara Wolpow draws conclusions about the defendant being controlling of Anita, but nothing speaks like the defendant's own words. I think these letters show that the defendant, when it came to Anita Green, was a control freak, that he was obsessive."

The poem might have been enough, but Cahill read on and on. When the jury looked uncomfortable, the prosecutor seemed pleased with himself. And with every document that Cahill read, Melvin Green seemed to lose more of his calm exterior. Finally Cahill said, "Enough." Melvin seemed relived, but only momentarily. For Cahill added, "Please take your time with them, read them all. They are necessary to understand the nature of his obsessions."

After the trial was over, Cahill said it was the letters that really got to him and made him angry. "They were so horrible, and look, he continues to write them. He doesn't care what he puts down on paper to people. It's almost like he feels better about himself after he says these things. I don't know; it's like people who can only feel good about themselves when someone else is hurting."

Earlier, during the trial, Cahill had referred to Mel's letter writing. "Finally, we have the defendant's even more candid words in his conversations with Gil Mershon. Words that he couldn't put into a letter. But behind closed doors, he says, 'If she tries to get anything more than those contracts, if she goes after my money, I will have her killed.'"

People in the courtroom gasped. All eyes turned toward Melvin as Cahill kept on. "He says it on nine or ten different occasions. He says, 'Someday she will be getting out of her car and someone will ride up and blow her head off.'"

As if for effect, Cahill stared at Melvin for a moment and then turned back to the jury. "A clearer statement of intent and purpose, I don't think you are ever going to get."

Cahill continued for another half hour. He talked about all of Melvin's specific threats toward Anita, threats that he had verbalized to Amanda Truett, to Phyllis Baltin, to almost anyone with whom he came in contact.

"Finally, we have Phyllis and Lance. They receive a phone call. 'What would you charge me to kill Anita?' Not particularly ambiguous. Then he offers to get rid of Lance's wife. That makes sense to a man like Melvin. He knows that Lance is having an affair with Phyllis. In his way of thinking, if he's willing to have Anita taken care of, why would Lance be any different? You see the world the way you feel about it—if you are willing to get rid of an inconvenient spouse, why should Lance be any different?"

Cahill talked about Mel's conduct in very specific ways. "Number one, the defendant either created or took advantage of the victim's lack of income."

The prosecuting attorney reminded the jury of all the ways Mel had done that, and then explained, "She's waiting for a check. The defendant refuses to mail her a check. He insists that she come to the business to pick it up, at a specific time."

"Now, what is so urgent that the defendant is insisting it's got to be tomorrow? Why does it have to be a specific appointment? What is so important that this can't wait? Why? What's so urgent in the defendant's mind? I think the answer to that is absolutely transparent."

"Next, the defendant's conduct on the day of the event." The prosecutor pointed toward Mel. "The defendant was right up at the door when the woman came in to tell them that a shooting had gone down, but he hadn't been there very long. He had only been there a minute or two. Where was he before that? He was down the hall somewhere in the direction of his own office."

"This," he emphasized slowly, "is very important. His office has a window that looks down Oxnard Street. He can watch for the approach of Anita Green."

Cahill stared at the jurors. "Why would he want to do that?" he asked.

He cried out his answer. "When you know what's about to happen. You know a murder is about to go down, your adrenaline is pumping, you are nervous, you are scared. You've got to know, is it going down the way it's supposed to?"

Through this speech, Melvin sat silently. He kept shaking his head back and forth. Then Cahill said, "We know he was watching because he knew what direction she was coming from and because he lied about it. He tells Mr. Corrado that the roofer told him, only the roofer couldn't have told him because the roofer didn't even know then."

Cahill very calmly talked about Mel's actions at the crime scene. "The guy is not sobbing, not crying, angry, or hysterical. What does he say? 'Why don't you check on the guys who were screwing her?' Doesn't seem to be particularly overcome with remorse."

Cahill's voice was filled with emotion. "His wife is still alive. I know they were going through a divorce, but even so, he had spent ten years with this woman, and she'd been shot in the head."

Cahill looked disgusted. "He gives the cops fall guys and then calls Phyllis Baltin. You heard the tape. He doesn't say anything like he's concerned and what hospital she is at. He's concerned about the police investigation." Slowly, Cahill walked over to Mel and once more looked at him before adding, "That's what his attention is focused on."

"Then we have the defendant's discussion with Joseph Corrado. That's where he really slips up." Kent went over Corrado's testimony point by point, explaining why Melvin had to get Joe to believe his scenario of how Anita had traveled to the office. When he was finished, he added, "A worried and guilty man needs to be believed. You participate in a murder, you are afraid of getting caught. I don't care how calm you are, you are worried about it and you need reassurance. Melvin needed Joseph Corrado to believe him if he ever expected the cops to buy his story later."

Cahill walked right over to the jurors and talked directly to them. "Ladies and gentlemen, the evidence shows this was not a random act. This was set up. The defendant had reasons. He had motives up the wazoo."

Cahill pointed at Melvin again and added thoughtfully, "He stated his intentions, that he was going to kill her if she went after his money. She'd be riding up and someone would blow her head off. He set it up. The killing has to be arranged. You have got to know the escape route. Executions have to be prearranged. They have to be set up, and there's no mystery who set the time and place where this woman was assassinated.

"To understand what you are looking at, you have got to put the pieces together, and you have to look at them all at once. Then you see what the picture is. I think when you look at the totality of the evidence, there is only one interpretation that makes all the pieces fit.

"This had been building for a long time. She wanted divorce money. He didn't want to give it to her. She's going to wreck his business, steal his clients, cost him money. That was the straw that broke the camel's back.

"His counsel says that there is no evidence. I have got to wonder, did they expect to find a diary that read, 'Dear diary, today I hired John Smith to kill Anita. He only charged me ten thousand dollars, what a deal!'" The jurors laughed, but just for a moment. Kent Cahill jumped right in, not wanting his remark to break their concentration.

"I want to talk to you about reasonable doubt. . . . It's not the judge's job or any one jury to set the line of reasonable doubt. For all cases, you are either over the line or not. The purpose of this jury is to look at the totality of evidence in this case. Do not ask the question, where is the line, but, which side of the line is Mr. Green on? I don't think you'll have a problem because wherever you place this line of reasonable doubt, this man has crossed over, crossed over convincingly.

"We've heard the expression, getting away with murder? That is literally what someone is trying to do in this case." Kent Cahill walked away and added, "It is literally up to you to decide whether or not he's going to be able to."

For several moments, the entire courtroom was silent. Melvin Green no longer appeared to be the confident and self-assured man who had entered the courtroom just two weeks ago. Cahill's words had carved lines into his face, and he looked like he had already been sentenced to life in prison.

Mel's family didn't move, except for his older son, Michael, who walked out of the proceedings. When Melvin finally recovered enough to turn around and search their faces, they tried to smile at him. But it was an uncertain smile that he had not seen from some of them before.

Later in the afternoon of the same day, Gerry Chaleff began his closing statements. Chaleff had confided to Melvin's family before the trial that the biggest problem would be convincing the jurors that a man as obnoxious and inappropriate as Melvin, a man who obviously was in the throws of a bitter divorce and had written horrible letters for years, had nothing to do with this murder. It was not going to be easy. Chaleff had to get across that in Melvin's case, he may have been obnoxious, but as far as murder, everyone was jumping to conclusions.

A confident Gerry Chaleff addressed the jury. For his closing argument, he wore a finely tailored, light khaki suit with a beige shirt and a subtle tie in muted colors. Defense attorneys usually do not wear dark-colored suits when they are in trial. The light colors suggest they are the good guys, and Gerry Chaleff wasn't taking any chances. He did not play to the spectators as Kent Cahill had, but rather concentrated on the twelve people sitting before him in the jury box—twelve people whom he seemed to sense despised his client, Melvin Green.

Chaleff smiled at the jurors before beginning. In a calm voice, laced with a touch of disbelief, he addressed the evidence the prosecution had presented, evidence that he thought proved nothing. "Mr. Cahill, the prosecutor, has to prove to you the charges beyond a reasonable doubt and to a moral certainty. The word moral was not used without a lot of thought. It means something that's seriously convincing.

"This case is replete of people jumping to conclusions, deciding things had to be a certain way, or trying to look back and say that Mr. Green, the husband who was going through a divorce, must have killed his wife. So, in 1979, when he wrote a poem, when he was probably talking about smoking or working too hard—'if you keep it up, in this case, you are not going to be around much longer,'—he must have been talking about the fact he was going to kill her." Chaleff peered at the jury intently. "That's preposterous!"

What Gerry Chaleff was known for was his sincerity. He really believed there were problems with the prosecution's case. He argued that passionately in his closing remarks. "Mr. Cahill's rendition of the facts is not square with what I think the facts were." Gerry Chaleff then spent the next hour or so talking about all the facts that he saw differently. Chaleff said that the shot was not shot at point-blank range, that the light in the parking lot was not a camera, and that the rabbi's sudden recall of the check was the most unbelievable of all.

"I asked the rabbi, 'Did she ever tell you she was going to pick up a check?' He answers, 'Well, she may have,' and then waffles around some more. It was not like all of a sudden God came down and spoke to the rabbi, although that would have been a nice vision because he is a rabbi."

Again the jurors laughed, but their laughter was even more cautious this time. Gerry Chaleff continued, "The prosecution is trying to make you believe that Mr. Green lured his wife to the office on that day at that time. What did they have to prove that with? Gina Siguenza? What else did they have? Nothing. There was no check waiting at the office. Is there any check of any size that could get her there if she was so afraid? No. You are the judges of evidence. You are the judges of facts."

Gerry Chaleff stared intently at the jurors again. He wanted them to really think about how absurd some of the things brought out in the trial were. "Let me say my most favorite parts of this case were about the things that somebody thought they were and that turned out not to be, especially the toilet bowl. I've tried lots of cases, and I always kidded about having the kitchen sink thrown in, but now I have a toilet bowl." The jury giggled nervously. Cahill and Melvin Green smiled. Judge Trammel stared directly at Melvin while Chaleff continued addressing the jurors, more seriously now. "There's a whole bunch of exhibits like this, the toilet bowl, the TV camera, the poem...people jumping to conclusions."

Gerry Chaleff was both engaging and charming. He did not use any big words as he tried to make the jurors understand how important their task was. He tried to show the jury that Kent Cahill's arguments were based on conjecture. He even tried to tackle the letters. "One of those letters Mr. Cahill didn't read says, 'I want what I think is fair or what the courts will say, whichever is greater. And that's the end of it. I'll leave it in your hands.' If you read through those letters, he keeps telling that to his lawyer. 'I want to give her whatever is fair.'"

Gerry Chaleff spent the remainder of the afternoon attacking every prosecution witness. Much of the time he talked about reasonable doubt and the burden of proof.

Finally, he dealt with Melvin's strange ramblings. "You don't convict someone for murder because he's inappropriate. You don't convict him for murder because the prosecution didn't present enough evidence to prove he did it." Gerry Chaleff's eloquent words were delivered in a strong and forceful manner, but he was far less convincing then Kent Cahill.

Then Chaleff once again addressed his client's most difficult hurdle to overcome—the letters. "'If you do read all the letters, I guess I can go to Hawaii for a week," he started. "Look through them and see the consistency and that there is no escalation. There is no volcano building up that explodes."

Melvin Green then looked over at the jury and smiled. It was the first time during the trial that he had done that.

"You see if you can determine that the only reasonable inference you can draw from the facts in this case is that Mr. Green planned, arranged, and ordered the death of his wife. There is no evidence to support that. The evidence to support that is reversed. It is supposition. It is, he *must* have done it. The evidence in this case is not the quality and quantity of evidence to convince you beyond a reasonable doubt and to a moral certainty that Mr. Green is guilty of the charge. Thank you."

Melvin looked like he was the only person in the entire room who was not exhausted and drained. His face beamed brightly. He knew all eyes were on him, and he sat up proudly in his chair. He did not realize that his fate had already been sealed.

35

The Longest Day of the Year

By the afternoon of the fourth day of jury deliberations, prosecutor Kent Cahill was going crazy. More than anything, he worried that the case of his career would end in a hung jury.

Ordered by Judge Trammel to remain in the building and to be available for possible testimony readbacks to the jury, Cahill stormed around the criminal courthouse's long corridors and wondered what was delaying a verdict. He was certain that perhaps one or maybe two lone jurors could not make up their minds. Over and over Cahill tortured himself trying to figure out if one of the jurors he had approved was the culprit. Should he have rejected the middle-aged black woman? What about the young man in the front who kept smirking?

Only at the noon hour could Kent escape and walk downtown in the rain. He visited the Los Angeles central library, the *Los Angeles Times* building, Chinatown, and Olvera Street. He walked and walked before returning to his "prison" again. But Kent Cahill actually never escaped, because even as he walked his mind worried about what might be. Thank God it was Friday! As Kent thumbed through the *Los Angeles Times* calendar section in his borrowed downtown cubbyhole office, he was grateful that several new movies had opened over the weekend. Anything to keep his mind off the case.

Melvin Morton Green was worried too. No longer cocky and self-assured, he by now had resigned himself to his fate. This many days of deliberations didn't look good, and his lawyers were preparing him for what might happen next. He refused to lose. He would take his case to the highest court in the land if need be, and he would never admit to anything because he was innocent. He spent the weekend in the county jail calling all his friends who had sat in on the trial to get their opinions on his chances.

Back in the Valley, life went on as usual. Riva Rice, always a realist and usually negative as well, was certain Mel would get off. He always beat the system. Her only solace was knowing that he had suffered. "Well, at least he spent a year in jail. I have to look at it that way. I don't expect too much."

Phyllis Baltin and Lance Shoemaker were terrified. There had not been much hard evidence entered against Mel, yet they knew only Mel could have had Anita killed. If Melvin got off, they were certain he would come after them. They spent the entire weekend huddled in bed with the shades drawn.

The Shir Chadash annual dinner dance and gala at the Woodland Hills Marriott took place on Saturday night. It was the temple's most successful fundraiser ever and almost one hundred thousand dollars were raised to balance the temple's budget. The rabbi's new wife, Miriam, looked gorgeous in her revealing black-sequined cocktail dress. But something was different between them. People whispered about the trial, but only when the rabbi was not around.

Monday morning brought the first real sunshine to the City of Angels in over a month. The rain had cleaned away the smog and Los Angeles glistened.

After just two short hours of deliberations, the jury sent a note to the court requesting guidance. The jury foreman told Judge Trammel that the vote was eleven to one, and it had been deadlocked that way for several days. But he did not tell the judge which way they were leaning.

Judge Trammel had thought all weekend that he might have a hung jury. He had been requested to read the arguments back to them by the foreman last week and he had refused. Now the foreman told him that unless he did, there was no way they could reach a decision. Judge Trammel had to decide what to do as soon as possible.

Kent Cahill told the judge that the jury needed to work a little longer, and he implored Trammel to let them do so. Arthur Alexander and Gerry Chaleff argued twice as hard that there was no choice but to declare a mistrial. And, for the record, both objected to the rereading of the arguments.

Kent Cahill knew in his heart what Gerry and Art felt. The

jury was deadlocked at eleven to one, and his side was winning. "They asked for reread of arguments. The foreman expressed that it might make a difference. *People* v. *Gordon* very specifically approves of doing so. I'd like us to give it a shot," Cahill pleaded.

Judge Trammel knew that he had a good jury. They were working hard and seemed to be getting along well. "My gut reaction is to do it. I've never done it before, but I think I am going to allow a reread of the arguments." Looking at the defense, he added, "I'm going to put this off until two. So if you want to come up with some authority to convince me not to, feel free to do so."

The defense team spent several hours scrambling for cases. In the afternoon, Chaleff argued long and hard to stop the reading, but to no avail. It was set up for the next morning.

But anything can happen in a jury trial. On Tuesday, the lawyers spent the morning arguing over how the arguments would be reread, and frustrated, tired, and annoyed, Judge Trammel changed his mind again. He turned to the jury. "I'm going to ask the twelve of you to go back in. Hopefully, with the passage of time, maybe any or all of you will have different perspectives."

Surprisingly, after just two more hours in the jury room, putting the total deliberation time at six days, the lone stand-out joined the others.

It took a few minutes for everyone to gather for the verdict. By now, most of Mel's family were no longer waiting downtown for a decision. The reading of the jury's verdict was not like those you see on television or in the movies. It wasn't "Columbo" or "Matlock," where the families sit and cry or scream when the verdict is read. They would have had to wait days for this verdict. There were a few reporters, some courtroom groupies, and a photographer in the spectators' box. The court was quiet and somber. By this time, even the diehards had no energy left for fanfare. Not a sound could be heard as the jury foreman read the verdict.

"We, the jury, find the defendant, Melvin Morton Green, guilty of the crime of first-degree murder. We further find the allegation that the murder of Anita Green was carried out by the defendant for financial gain."

Melvin showed no emotion, nothing whatsoever. He

lowered his head for a moment and then conferred with his counsel.

"Mr. Green, you have the right to be sentenced not more than twenty-eight days from today. Are you willing to waive that right and set the matter for further proceedings, your motion for a retrial or appeal, until April 20?"

"Yes, I do, Your Honor," he whispered. His voice was barely audible.

With the verdict read, one phase of Mel's life was over. His arrogance was, for the moment, gone. He knew his lawyers would return to their homes and families all the richer from his sufferings. He struggled to remain composed. No one would see him cry. He would hold them all personally responsible for the travesty that had just come to pass. He would remember his trial forever as a mockery of justice, a carnival, and a sham. And never would he forget the people, the witnesses, all the ingrates and hypocrites who had brought him to this day.

On the night of the verdict, Rabbi Jacobs called Anita's only son, Scott, to meet him at his new house. It appeared the rabbi wanted to rid himself of the whole sordid affair. He was moving into his newly remodeled home with his new wife, Miriam, and he wanted Scott to pick up the last of Anita's belongings.

Phyllis and Lance met Scott with Lance's truck. They expected to find more possessions than Scott could fit into his car, so they drove out to the rabbi's house together. When they arrived, Rabbi Jacobs expressed anger that they were late. He sat waiting for them amidst the boxes that contained the few remaining possessions of Anita Green. There were some pictures, linens, family heirlooms, and a chair. It appeared that the rabbi intended to keep most of the furniture that Anita had purchased for her new apartment.

Later in the week, Riva called to ask the rabbi about Anita's beautiful dining-room set, her new comforter and linens, and several other items she wanted Scott to have. Riva said Jacobs became very embarrassed. He claimed that Anita had written a note leaving all her personal belongings to him if anything were to ever happen to her. The rabbi never bothered to produce that note for Anita's family.

While they were loading the truck, Phyllis asked Jacobs his

opinion of the verdict. "It's a very sad day," he replied. Phyllis never understood why he answered that way.

Legal maneuvering continued for Melvin Green after the jury delivered their guilty verdict on Wednesday, March 4, 1992. A motion for a new trial was filed in part because Melvin's attorneys thought that the additional days the jury deliberated might have pressured the lone holdout juror to vote for a guilty verdict, and because of Melvin's horrendous letters, which the defense team felt had been improperly admitted into evidence. The motion was denied.

"The motions should have been granted," said Gerry Chaleff, who had argued continually throughout the trial that the letters were confidential communications.

But Kent Cahill felt the judge was correct in his decision about the letters. "Green had made similar statements to other people about his wife. He liked to talk this way. He never considered the information to be confidential."

Apparently, Judge Trammel felt the same way. At Melvin's sentencing, the day the judge denied his motion for a new trial, the grandfatherly man looked sternly down at Melvin and the attorneys, including Melvin's new appellate attorney, Robert Gerstein, and said, "I am in my twenty-second year as a criminal judge. I sincerely doubt that there has ever been a case where I feel I know more about the inner workings of a defendant before me."

Judge Trammel glanced at Melvin Green and then at his defenders. "Your client is his own worst enemy. He has a big mouth. He doesn't know when to keep quiet. He's a man who apparently has no control over his innermost thoughts, and he imparts them to whomever will listen."

It was on this day, after all these months of silence, after listening to the judge's thoughts on him, that Melvin could no longer contain himself. He looked out at the spectators' box, at his family and friends. He needed them to hear he was still an innocent man.

The small glass room was overflowing. In addition to his family and friends, there were reporters and photographers, an author, and a television-movie producer. This was his moment to shine. Despite his jail-issue clothing, Melvin held his head up high and asked to address the court before sentencing.

"I'm innocent," Melvin proclaimed loudly. In a voice that was sure and confident. With more than a touch of anger, he looked up at Judge Trammel and said, "I did not kill my wife. Regardless of the presentation. I am absolutely innocent of this crime and all its capacities."

Melvin's fiancée, Alexandra Leeds, began to sob softly, as did a few of the ladies from his office. His elder son, Michael, wearing a T-shirt with the devil on it, angrily attempted to block a photographer who was taking a picture of his father. "Don't you care about anything but your damn pictures?" he snarled. "We're trying to listen to my father and the judge."

Melvin continued, "Items from my safe were taken by my deceased wife and given to her attorney. They were privileged. Pictures were painted, pictures that were never refuted by character witnesses. Hundreds could have said things."

Before he finished, Melvin looked straight at Judge Trammel. "I don't think the trial was equitable and fair. I really don't think the judge was appropriate. I am innocent!" He screamed, "I swear by almighty God!"

Now George Trammel looked directly at Melvin Green. "The defendant is sentenced to state prison for the remainder of his natural life. That sentence is to be served without the possibility of parole."

VII

The Aftermath

36

Unanswered Questions

I began meeting regularly with Melvin Green just a few days after his sentencing and spent the next few months talking with him about everything he had been through. When we began our visits, Melvin insisted on these ground rules: We were never to talk about Anita; he did not want to tell me anything that might ruin his chances on appeal; and he wanted me to show the completed book to his appellate lawyer, Robert Gerstein. I promised him I would follow those rules, but I stressed that neither Mr. Gerstein nor he would have approval over anything that I was to write.

Melvin agreed to be interviewed because he hoped my words would help others understand what he had been through. He said he wanted my book to help vindicate him before the world. "If I am guilty, then the punishment was not just. There were mitigating circumstances that never came out in the trial. Things Anita was doing while we were still married. I should have gotten seven years at the most. If I am innocent, then this is all insane. Help me show the world how to stop this miscarriage of justice. If I did not shoot her, then there's no connection, so there is more than one way to reasonable doubt. My innocence will come when you show the world what was really going on. How come the rabbi's life has not changed significantly and mine has been completely destroyed?" Melvin Green appeared to have a different view of justice than most people.

Through June, we met daily in the small upstairs visiting room of Los Angeles County jail as Melvin awaited his imminent transport to an unknown prison. The room was small and dank. I interviewed him through a glass partition as we talked on telephones. He looked like a sad basset hound as he stared at me through the glass. He had huge gray circles under his eyes, and the skin of his cheeks sagged.

Melvin enjoyed my visits. They were a break from the boring monotony of jail life. I, on the other hand, was exhausted and drained by the hours we spent together. Interviewing Melvin Green was the greatest challenge of my professional life. He tried to control not only our interviews but my thinking as well. Though Melvin Green spoke incessantly about the importance of honesty, he always talked circles around the truth. Often it took me an entire day to get him to answer just one question. When he finally did, I was never certain about the veracity of his words.

As soon as Melvin left for prison, I was denied access to him until his prison reception period was over. I found then there was so much more I needed to understand. Though our visits in jail had brought me closer to the truth, I knew that I wasn't there yet. And as surprising as it seemed, I really missed meeting with the man, no matter how difficult our visits had been.

Melvin Green was convicted without a gun, a bullet, or evidence of payment to a killer. Few could believe this could happen, but then they had not heard Kent Cahill's case. I had gone into Melvin's trial convinced that he was innocent, came out convinced of his guilt, and, after visiting with him, decided that I was unsure.

There were problems with the way things turned out, and missing pieces. I had to find out as many answers as possible if I was ever to know the full story of Anita's death and whether justice had been served.

The week Melvin was transferred to prison, I spent several days closeted in the evidence room of the North Hollywood police station, where I read all the letters and documents the officers had seized from Melvin's residence and business. There were hundreds that the district attorney did not use in the trial, and hundreds more the police had never paid all that much attention to. I realized that Anita's and Melvin's lives were so complicated that the police had not discovered the true meaning of many things.

One thing struck me as odd: Before Anita's murder, Melvin kept accusing her of stealing some of his prized gold coins, as well as some of the gold they had recently purchased at a temple fund-raising event. Melvin had dramatically accused Anita publicly of this theft several times; he wrote letters about it to his attorney, and he talked about it openly, claiming that Anita was the only one who knew the combination to his safe. These accusations began in early September 1990, about a month before Anita's tragic death, and about four months after Anita and Melvin purchased some of the gold at the fund-raising auction. I did not think it was likely Anita had taken the gold. It was no secret that Melvin had claimed to have had the combination to his safe changed in July, after Anita filed for divorce.

So concerned was Melvin about the coins that he had obsessed about them. Three people—Irene Sherwyn, Phyllis Baltin, and one of his sons—mentioned the coins and the possible theft in their police interviews after Anita's shooting. I wondered if it was possible that the coins had not been stolen and that possibly Melvin could have sold them. Had he hired an assassin for Anita's murder with the money that he quite possibly received for them?

I began to visit coin dealers. Now, there are not all that many coin dealers in the Valley, and at first I tried the two closest to Melvin's office. I had some idea of what I was looking for because I knew the types of coins and gold Melvin and Anita liked to collect. Melvin and Anita always bought temple gold coins, and at the last temple function they had attended together, they had purchased a large collection. Melvin had even made an inventory of his purchases and kept all the receipts, which were also on file at the temple. In fact, I soon learned that Melvin had actually crossed off on his inventory the specific coins that were missing, coins that I was now looking for. Sure enough, the second coin dealer I went to had records of buying coins from a Melvin Green in early October 1990. The dealer claimed Melvin had been paid about $30,000.

One might assume that Melvin needed to publicly accuse Anita of stealing the coins so no one would question where the money he got for them went. Especially if he intended to use that money to pay for a murder.

Once I was back in the police evidence room, I found some correspondence of Melvin's that seemed particularly illuminating. These letters had not appeared in Melvin's murder trial. However, I surmised they somehow alluded to Anita's murder.

In the letters, Melvin talked about possibly buying someone a house. Now I already knew from my interviews that Melvin liked to help people buy houses. But the timing seemed off to me. The letters were dated November 12, 1990, just two weeks after Anita's tragic death. Why would a man who was supposedly still mourning his wife take the time out to buy a friend, or anyone else for that matter, a house? It struck me as just a little too odd, even for Melvin. I wanted to know more about the purchase.

One of the letters read, "It's my way of saying thank you and of making life a little better. If others get caught up in the positive aspect of the afterglow, that's certainly alright with me." The letter sounded a bit strange to me. What "afterglow" was Melvin referring to? Was he celebrating his wife's murder? Perhaps I'd just read one too many detective novels.

Armed with the letters, I went to jail the next day to talk to Melvin about them. By coincidence, the man for whom Mel had offered to buy the house was visiting him. He sneered at me when Melvin introduced us to one another. We had previously spoken together on several occasions.

In any event, though in the past I had sometimes arrived when Melvin was with a visitor, this was the first time he asked me to leave and to wait downstairs. Now I was very curious. What was Melvin hiding from me? As the metal elevator doors slammed shut, my mind began working overtime. What, if anything, did it all mean?

Once downstairs, I realized that Melvin's male visitor could easily fit the police composite drawing of the shooter, only he had a beard and his hair was shorter. My heart raced. If I was right, this was too easy. But I didn't want to get too excited. A lot of people can look like a police composite drawing. I needed to find out more about this fellow.

I went to the parking lot and hid in my car, locking my doors. I knew the man would only be able to visit Melvin for a half hour. (Those were the rules at the county jail.) In just a few moments, I saw him exit. To my surprise, he sped away on a motorcycle, coincidentally the same color as the motorcycle the man who had shot Anita rode away on during his getaway.

Melvin was expecting me back upstairs. Nervously, I went upstairs to calm myself. Trying to keep my voice level, I asked Mel about his friend. He told me his name and that this was the one friend who had continued to visit him at least twice a week since his imprisonment.

I felt sick. Could this be the man who had shot Anita? The mere thought made my head spin. Still, I kept smiling and taking notes. As soon as I could excuse myself, I left. I drove as quickly as possible to the San Fernando District Attorney's Office to tell Kent Cahill what I had uncovered.

As I spoke, Cahill sat staring. Kent and I had grown close during the trial. We had often discussed theories about who the gunman was. With this case, it seemed everyone had a theory. But never before had Kent looked at me this way. After I had finished, he said, "Michele, I think you might be right. I want you to go to the police."

The police thought I was crazy. As far as they were concerned, this was a closed murder case. But they let me back into the property room. They knew that the guys over at the D.A.'s office were my buddies. Maybe with a little luck I was on to something.

I sat in the property room and kept reading. I soon found out that Melvin always used the Fallbrook Mortgage Company when he bought houses and that usually his ex-wife, Bernyce, a realtor, closed the deals for him. Could a house have been purchased and possibly paid for with the money Melvin Green had received from secretly selling his gold coins? It seemed plausible to me, but I had no idea how to go about finding out whether a house had been purchased after the murder.

The information I already had excited me though I wasn't certain if it meant anything at all. That's when I got stupid. I went to see Melvin on June 16. Unbeknownst to me at the time, it was to be our last visit for a while. He was transferred to prison the next morning. At our meeting, I told Melvin that I thought perhaps one of his friends had tired of hearing how much he hated Anita. "Maybe one of them got rid of her for you?" I suggested. "You didn't even know anything. They were merely helping a friend get rid of a problem."

"Like who?" he asked. Melvin stared at me and smiled. My heart beat faster in my chest. What should I do? I forced the words out of my mouth. Not wanting to upset him, I mentioned two names.

Melvin Green freaked out. This was the Melvin Green whom Kent Cahill had talked about at the trial. It was the first time I had actually seen Melvin in this condition and it frightened me. Quickly, I changed the subject, but not before agreeing with Melvin that my theory was stupid.

Before I left, Mel told me that the man I had seen at jail Tuesday, the man who rode a motorcycle, and who might match the police description of Anita's shooter, was a homeowner because of him. After he confided in me, I told him about the coins. Mel jokingly said, "Well, if you're dead after I make a phone call, you'll know who did it." I laughed nervously.

Whether I was right or not was not the issue. That was the same week my life changed. I began to get threatening letters and phone calls. Our home was vandalized, and notes were left on our property that told me to stop writing this book. Someone drove through our electric gate, and my nose was broken by an unknown attacker, twice. I did not know who was responsible, but I thought it might have something to do with my amateur sleuthing.

And I also knew there was a chance that I was right, that I had somehow stumbled upon the truth. Or at least part of the truth. For a myriad of reasons, including the coins, I now believe with all my heart that Melvin Green really did hire someone to kill his wife. I am convinced that I may know who that man is, and I am relatively certain I know how he was paid. This knowledge doesn't make me sleep any easier at night.

My new friends in law enforcement were amazed at what I had found, but it seems my timing was wrong. Los Angeles has been besieged with murder and mayhem. *People* v. *Green* closed the murder book in the eyes of the police. Though they promised me that they will not stop looking for answers, they may never have enough to file charges. The police may eventually make an arrest, but only when they are certain that an arrest will stick. Detective Coffey explained that for my safety the arrest would have to be "prosecutable." If any suspect was arrested and then released, I would be in real trouble. Besides, Mike reminded me there was always the chance that someone else was responsible for the threats. Certainly I have angered many people by writing this book.

Was I in danger? Michael Coffey told me to hire a private detective for a little while, at least until things calmed down. I explained that I could not live my life that way. But I knew that I had to do something.

The only way I could be certain of my theory was by confronting Melvin with it, no matter how difficult that confrontation might be. It was finally time to visit him in his new home, the state penitentiary in Calipatria, California. I needed Melvin to confirm my suspicions, and I hoped he was finally ready to do so.

I made the first of many long journeys to the Calipatria State Prison in October 1992 with Mel's fiancée, Alexandra Leeds. It was nearly two years after Anita's tragic shooting. Alexandra had remained loyal to Melvin because she and her children were still living rent-free in his house while she finished school. Though incarcerated, Melvin Green continued to pay all her bills. By this time, Alexandra was as convinced as I was that Melvin had something to do with Anita's murder. She was mad that he had lied to her, but she claimed to love a part of him. Besides, it was easier to survive with his generous help.

With trepidation, I began my journey to confront Melvin Green and, I hoped, discover the truth. Melvin had promised me that if I came for a visit he would at long last give me what I was waiting for, the information that would make me understand Anita's murder. I had heard all this before, but never had he said it so passionately. I felt that given the fact that he had not had a visitor in several months, he was probably desperate for company and was not really planning on confiding anything. He couldn't.

I had learned that Melvin Green covered his world with a thick blanket of denial. He had always dealt with his problems by denying their existence. This was his coping mechanism. He holds tenaciously to his belief that he has never wronged anyone. Denial is really all he has left. In a sense, if Melvin were to admit the truth, his life would be over.

Our journey took us through five counties before we reached the prison. We traveled through the barrio of Boyle Heights, the once thriving Jewish community where Melvin Green had spent most of his childhood. We passed Los Angeles's Central Jail, where Melvin had lived for over a year while awaiting trial. Some miles past the Los Angeles Civic Center, the freeway changed to Interstate 10, which is known as the Christopher Columbus Transcontinental Highway. I realized that this was the only thoroughfare that Melvin could have traveled to reach the Calipatria State Prison.

Highway 10 leads directly to the desert cities of Palm Springs, Indian Wells, and finally Indio. From Indio, looking ahead, one saw nothing on the horizon but a few scattered date trees, cows, and the turnoff to Route 111. Ironically, the desert cities that Anita once frequented with her girlfriends to escape Mel's wrath might be the last civilization her husband will ever see.

Route 111 is a narrow two-lane highway that begins the ninety-six-mile jaunt from Indio into Calipatria. The scenery is reminiscent of a nuclear wasteland. There are farmlands, but in October, most were barren. Occasionally I would pass a forsaken house standing alone in the once fertile earth.

The desert stretched out before me. Visually, I was so bored that I looked forward to reading the city-destination signs every few minutes because they were literally the only familiar things that I passed. Even the Salton Sea Recreation Area was desolate; there was only one abandoned, decaying motel and a boarded-up chili-dog stand to mark North America's largest inland sea. The empty horizon played games with my eyes, and sometimes mirages created the illusion that if I tried to pass another car I would hit something.

As I drove, I realized that I was very frightened about seeing Melvin. I was going to tell him that I no longer believed there was even a possibility he was innocent. I did not know how he would take my news. If I forced him into admitting to me what had really happened, he would be giving up his chance for freedom, and I would have that guilt to carry for the rest of my life. If I told Mel everything I was certain of, like the coins, as well as the details I could only guess at, like my suspects, there was always the possibility that I would be placing my family in even graver danger.

Alexandra was frightened as well, but for her own reasons. She was terrified of entering a prison. She worried about what she would find there. Though she claimed she wanted to hear everything about the case, she was not ready to listen. Alexandra insisted that she had no prior knowledge of what had happened and that Melvin had never told her any of the details. But as I drove, she turned to me and said, "Melvin did admit to me that Anita deserved to die. He is the only one who can say what happened, and I don't think he ever will. I am not by any means convinced of his innocence. I am scared every day of my life. But I don't know what I can do about it. I can't abandon him. He needs me as much as I need him."

It was the same old story. Alexandra Leeds was trapped. Melvin's money gave her the financial security she lacked and allowed her to live the life of luxury she craved. For Alexandra, Melvin's guilt would be the worst of all possible truths. To live with herself, she would have to leave him. She liked her big house in Encino, her live-in maid, her children's private school, and all the fancy new clothes. So Alexandra had turned her back on many things over the past few months to avoid colliding head on with the truth.

After driving for nearly five hours, we finally saw the prison. It appeared on the horizon like a sinister cousin of the Emerald City, with an ominous shroud hanging over it. It was huge and foreboding, and it actually glowed in the afternoon sunlight. From a distance, it appeared to be radioactive.

A few minutes later, while Alexandra waited in the car, I met an armed escort, went through a metal detector, and signed a waiver that stated I had been informed by prison officials that they failed to recognize hostages in riot situations. I was now as ready as I would ever be to pass through those double electric gates and enter Melvin's world.

I met with Melvin at one of the small round tables in the prison's C-complex visiting room. Calipatria's two C wings housed the prison's most dangerous criminals: the level-four murderers, rapists, and serial killers. These men would be Melvin's family and friends for the rest of his life. They stared at me as I waited for his arrival. I had a sense that their vacant expressions would be part of me forever.

I shuddered. I was reassured by the proximity of two high foreboding metal fences, both topped with barbed wire. One of the fences was electrified, and the current helped make escape from Calipatria nearly impossible. Behind the fences stood fourteen guard towers, each containing a guard armed with a rifle. I noticed that my escort was fully armed. There is no shortage of security at Calipatria.

Within minutes, Melvin literally ran across the visiting room to meet me. He hugged me and thanked me for making the long trip. He promised me that it would be worthwhile. Then he sat down and began the interview with his usual proclamation of innocence.

He started, "I have an appeal pending. Your book is nothing. This is my life." Melvin continued to deny even the simplest of truths. He told me he was never abusive toward Anita; he never threatened her; and he always treated people with love and respect. Then he added, "What else do you want to know? Don't ask me anything about the coins. I will not talk to you about them. Maybe they never existed at all."

Once again, total denial. Even when I asked Melvin a question taken directly from a previous interview, he would often say that he had never said that. In these cases, if I played him a tape of his remarks, obviously in his own voice, he would still insist that the words were not his own. Why had I expected anything different this time?

I decided to stop questioning and just visit with him. I had to admit that he looked wonderful. He was, in his own words, "Two hundred six pounds of solid muscle and hanging dermis." His weight was under control. His nose was no longer swollen and red, and the bags and circles under his eyes had all but disappeared. Though he was one of the oldest men at Calipatria, and the only Jew, prison seemed to agree with Melvin.

"It really is not that bad," he explained. "I am innocent, and my freedom in very important to me. But if I was guilty, this place is better than most. I make the best of it and get on with my life. Sure, there are some weaknesses in the system, but it's not bad here. The system works, and I am trying hard to get rid of the problems here."

I was shocked. "It's not that bad? Aren't you scared?"

"Scared? What for?" Mel asked. "I am the brightest person here, Michele. People leave me alone; they respect me. They call me Mr. Green. I am not like most inmates. I am far beyond them. I can figure out how to survive here. They all want my help and advice. They seek me out to write their letters, work on their appeals. They don't forget. See this glass case? It represents almost fifteen hours of work."

"Someone paid you with that?" I asked.

"Yes," he replied. "I helped a man with his appeal. I help a lot of people. Helping and reaching out is unusual here. People usually respect me for it. When I get uncomfortable, or I feel threatened, I react as I deem appropriate."

"Is that what you did when you felt threatened by Anita?"

"I really don't know. Threatened, how? Money never meant anything to me. I didn't care what she wanted and would have given her whatever the court decided was fair. I wasn't really worried about the IRS because I had already been through it all once before and I knew that I had nothing to hide. It would just take up time that I didn't have. I was already doing her job and mine, while she played with the rabbi. I was exhausted. Anita and I had simply grown apart. We parted, and like in all divorces, some things were said that were pretty adversarial."

"That's all? Some things were said that you didn't mean to say?"

"Yes. Ray Hernandez wanted to put me in prison. He did not care about evidence or whether or not I was guilty. He cared about his job and about solving a high-profile murder."

I stared at Mel as he continued, "I try to look at the bright side of all of this. I am stronger than I have ever been before. I work out, write letters, and I read a book every two days. I have the time for myself that I never took before. I want to set an example to others in here. I want to show these guys what to strive for. These are the miscreants of the world in here. Most of them have committed hundreds, maybe thousands of crimes. These are the people I deal with every day. I do what they would never do. I pick up the mop to help out anytime there is a mess. I am the fastest mopper here. I help with any problem that arises and usually can use my brain to devise a solution. They've never seen anyone like me here."

Melvin said all this proudly, as if he had finally made it to the top. His arrogance was so tragic that I would have laughed if I was not already crying. Mel simply did not seem to recognize that he was at the top of the bottom of society.

Apparently, Melvin still based his life on gaining control

over those around him. The inmates whom he associated with in prison needed the skills he could dispense: his intellect, his knowledge of the law, and his understanding of the system. They even needed the liquor he could concoct with his knowledge of chemistry and a few cinnamon rolls. Melvin's deepest fears of prison could be controlled by his total dominance over those around him. He was the same man that he had always been.

At that moment, I realized that Melvin Green had been hiding from himself for so long. He hid behind a fake diploma; he had hidden for many years behind several hundred pounds of excess weight; he hid in his office day and night; and he was always looking over his shoulder to see if he was going to get caught.

In prison, Melvin could hide forever from the world. He was safe here. I realized that from his perspective, at least on a subconscious level, this was the first vacation he had ever taken, and, ironically, it was a vacation from himself.

I left the prison without the information I so desperately craved. But for the first time, I was certain that I was right on, at least about the coins. And I now knew Melvin Green would never change. But in this maximum-security prison, he had attained the only thing he ever wanted. He was finally the best and the brightest, and he had at last found his sanctuary.

Less than a month later, in November 1992, at a wonderful French restaurant overlooking the police academy, where all the waitresses followed Ray Hernandez around as if he were a god, the detective told me only half jokingly that even if my theory was wrong, he would be my partner anytime. He wanted to know if I would like to team up with him to solve the "Black Dahlia" case, Los Angeles's most notorious unsolved homicide.

"No, Ray," I answered. "You solve the crimes; I'll write the books. Just promise me you'll find an answer and arrest the gunman, whoever he is, soon."

Ray gave me a hug and promised to do just that. But by the end of 1992, an arrest had still not been made. Ray, at his own request, had been transferred downtown to kidnapping. He no longer worked homicide, and the other detectives in North

Hollywood's busy station had their hands full. I understood Michael Coffey's dilemma. He did not have enough detectives to go around. I grew more uncomfortable daily.

At my husband's request, I went to lunch with Kent Cahill and explained the situation I was now facing. I did not want to live my life forever looking over my shoulder. Kent listened patiently. He explained that he was as frustrated as I was. He did not like having me beaten up, and he was worried about my kids. Since the Green verdict, he had carried a gun, but he knew I never would. He worried about my safety and told me to be careful.

Sometime after our lunch, Kent went to his boss, Billy Webb, and told him about my discoveries. Kent explained that there was a good chance I was right and an equally good chance I wasn't. Webb was fascinated. Unbeknownst to me, he called a meeting with Cahill, Coffey, and Coffey's boss, Lt. Ron LaRue, a few days later. The result was that a new detective, Steven Hooks, was assigned to the case.

Hooks and I met almost weekly during January and February of 1993. A bright and aggressive young detective, Hooks willingly listened to my theories. Although I cannot act as an agent of the police, I am working closely with them to help find the answers and missing pieces. At this time, I am hopeful that, with continued investigation, Anita's killer will one day be brought to justice.

Still, I am growing more impatient. I have never liked cliffhangers. Although two years have passed since Anita's tragic death, I still can't sleep at night. I would have liked to have had more conclusive answers by now: an arrest, some closure.

Though personally I have long since overcome my doubts about Melvin Green's guilt, there are times when I continue to harbor uneasiness about the jury's verdict. There are so many missing pieces. I've never been able to prove that Melvin bought anyone a house after Anita's murder like he claimed to have done. He did buy a van for the fellow I'd seen at the jail. But what did that mean? I don't know if I will ever find the whole truth, as long as Melvin has an appeal pending.

Melvin's new appeal was prepared in February 1993. This was about the time that I met the private investigator working on Melvin's behalf, James Sloman. An intelligent and compassionate man, Jim is the one person who shares my interest in Melvin Green. Sloman wonders as I do about all the missing pieces, and he desperately wants to know the entire story. Obviously, with this shared passion, we have become good friends. Though we don't always agree with one another, we have made a vow to share all information and to find all the answers.

Jim Sloman and I have spent the past two months going through boxes of transcripts, notes, documents, and letters. Though I have nineteen boxes of material, Jim's data fills several rooms. He feels as passionately as I do that somewhere the nugget of information exists that will finally help make sense of everything.

Until then, Jim and I continue to visit Melvin Green in prison, a man both of us consider the most perplexing and difficult person we have ever met, yet a man from whom neither of us can escape. There are many nights that we phone one another at all hours just to share another Mel story, a new bit of information, or a theory that hasn't as yet been explored.

In a sense, I find that Jim has become my conscience. He has shown me that no matter how inappropriately a person acts, no matter how blasphemous or lying, he deserves a chance. Perhaps the jurors really hated Melvin too much to be fair. Our laws and systems are set up to protect people like Melvin Green, even if they only protect him from himself. Until we know everything, we can never really be certain of anything.

With Jim's careful training, I will soon become a licensed private investigator. During the past two months, I've gone undercover with him, been out on surveillance, and have even taken a stab at some of his easier cases. My life is quite different from what it was just a year ago when I began this book. I am hopeful that with the skills I've learned, along with the information all of us involved with this case have painstakingly gathered, we'll eventually find the answers that will lead the police to an arrest. If that happens, the police even promise I can have a badge.

Epilogue

Few who knew Anita or Mel Green or Rabbi Jacobs remain untouched by Anita's murder. The number of people who have been affected is astonishing. But two years later, life for most had returned to normal, or as normal as could be expected.

Professionally, Rabbi Steven B. Jacobs continued to shine in the spotlight for a while. He could be seen on television talking about Christmas and Chanukah with a minister and a priest. He made the papers with his response to the Los Angeles riots when he formed a coalition to reach out to the needy.

Rabbi Jacobs continues to push for the building of Shir Chadash, but after raising money in Anita's name, some claim he asked his temple board to consider removing her name from the memorial chapel because not enough money was collected in her honor. With over a million dollars spent on the "new temple," two years after the groundbreaking not one brick has been laid. The rabbi remains the leader of the Shir Chadash congregation, which still holds its services in a Christian church.

Though the rabbi worked diligently to get Shir Chadash built, there were rumors circulating that he was ready to abandon ship. The strain of the past two years had taken its toll, and the rabbi appeared to be close to giving up. As his dream slipped further and further from reality, Rabbi Jacobs had resumes made. He quietly registered with the Reform Movement's rabbinical search committee and began the interview process. At one large congregation, Temple Emmanuel, in San Francisco, Steven Jacobs even flew up with Miriam and stood on the bimah. The congregation hired another rabbi with far less experience.

331

It appears that most of the congregants at Shir Chadash remain completely devoted to Rabbi Jacobs. No longer do they deny that the rabbi and Anita's relationship attributed to Mel's anger and perhaps even indirectly to Anita's death. But they remain unconcerned about this and about what it teaches their children.

Apparently the Central Conference of American Rabbi's Rabbinical Ethics Board is willing to let temple congregants make their own decisions about their leadership. When one member of Shir Chadash formally asked the committee to investigate Jacobs' actions in April 1993, his request was denied. It seems the board discussed the situation, accepted Rabbi Jacobs' explanations for his actions and instead of investigating him, sent him a letter of reprimand.

But the incident forced Rabbi Jacobs into acknowledging his errors to his board. He began one April meeting with a prayer followed by a plea for forgiveness. "Accept me for what I am today and not for what I have done in the past," the Rabbi begged. One board member told me about the strange meeting, "It was haunting. Perhaps a little bit like Jimmy Swaggert. We all felt so sorry for him. What he is going through because of your book is so tragic. Don't you think he feels bad enough about Anita's death? Rabbi Jacobs is a human being and all of us make mistakes. No matter what happens, no matter what he does, he will always be our beloved rabbi. You can't change that."

His career was not the only thing in turmoil; the rabbi's personal life remained a constant struggle. After the trial, Miriam Jacobs said, "I asked him questions, and he got angrier and angrier at me. He told me that he had never loved Anita and that it was just a sexual thing. He said that Anita threw herself at him and that he did not want to make her feel worse by rejecting her. But I kept asking questions, and he did not like that. He could not control my questions anymore. Pretty soon he left me."

Just a year after her marriage, Miriam Jacobs finds herself no longer a *rabbitzin*. She is back at her old job and living in her old condominium. Her year-long marriage had faded to nothing more than a few bitter memories. For now, at least, she remains a Jew. But her new Jewish friends from Shir Chadash have abandoned her, as they blindly continue to follow their leader.

Miriam and Steven Jacobs's divorce was bitter. They continued to live in the same house for many months. Finally, Miriam moved out, on Yom Kippur 1992, while the rabbi was at services. She claimed to remove all the shoe lifts from his shoes the night before. She said, "It was my way of telling him to find another way to elevate himself before the congregation."

The Shir Chadash congregation has also been affected. Of the original thirty-two families that put up their fortunes to personally guarantee the temple's multimillion-dollar loan, a significant number have left the temple, annoyed and frustrated. Nonetheless, the temple's bank has refused to release them from their weighty financial obligations. Though he languishes in prison, Melvin Green's assets still guarantee the temple's loan. Given the recent turn in the California economy, should the temple fold, more than a half dozen families no longer even affiliated with the congregation stand to lose their money and possibly even their homes. Melvin Green's family is one of them.

In December 1992, the Shir Chadash board members were approached by the board members of another floundering Woodland Hill synagogue, Temple Emet. They had a problem. Their temple was facing financial peril, and they were losing congregants at a rapid pace. They needed a new rabbi, one who would be more involved in his congregants' lives and a financial anchor for them. The board members suggested a merger: They had the facilities, Shir Chadash had the leadership and financial stability.

By early 1993, the merger was tentatively approved by both boards. A full congregational vote was set for May 1993. Basically, Rabbi Sharwood was out, and Rabbi Jacobs was in. Shir Chadash agreed to buy out Rabbi Sharwood's five-year contract and make him rabbi emeritus. They would continue carrying their land costs and assume all Emet's expenses as well. Rabbi Jacobs claimed Temple Emet's facility was not ideal and promised that in the near future Shir Chadash would finally build on their land. At that time, Temple Emet's facility would be sold. Meanwhile, the money contributed toward the

Anita Green memorial chapel has been spent on the temple's other weighty financial obligations. But the rabbi was quoted in one paper as saying, "The temple has not yet been built, so nothing has happened to the memorial fund."

Perhaps in anticipation of the negative impact of *No Sanctuary* on their proposed new congregation, the two temples decided to drop their respective names. Their new congregation would be called Kol Tikvah—The Valley Community Temple. The congregation translates *kol tikvah* as "Voice of Hope," but some scholars translate the words as "every hope"—which is what some people thought about the chances of ever being able to build on the land purchased by Shir Chadash in 1988. To many it seemed that Anita's dream had died with her.

Alexandra Leeds, Mel's intended third wife, lived with her daughters for two years in the home Melvin and Anita Green once shared. She remodeled and redecorated the house as soon as she had moved into it.

Alexandra carried Mel's credit cards; in fact, the cards belonged to Anita, but apparently Alexandra had no intention of ever marrying him. Her main concerns are for her children, and she has no problem spending Mel's money to make their lives easier.

Finally, in late January 1993, Alexandra moved out of Melvin's house with a police escort. She left no forwarding address, and the Greens have not been able to reach her. Alexandra took most of the new furnishings Melvin had purchased for their home. "I deserve it all after what I went through believing that man's lies," she said. Alexandra claims that she is now certain Melvin is guilty of the crime he still claims he did not commit. "If he had only been honest with me, I might have stood by his side. But he has never been honest with me about anything. Melvin Green is a very sick man. I tried to help him, but he has only gotten sicker." Alexandra plans on moving home to Ohio when her children's school term ends in June. "I've had enough. I need to move on."

Mel's youngest son by his first wife, Cary, lived alone in the large Encino house after Alexandra and the girls left. Cary, always faithful to his father's wishes, tried valiantly when Alexandra moved out to stop her from taking anything she had not brought into the house. But in the end she prevailed, and he could not save his legacy. Just as Cary predicted she would months earlier, Alexandra took as much as she coult get and their house now stands close to empty. Cary and his pet chimpanzee had taken over Mel and Anita's master bedroom.

Cary Green is the new president of Melvin Green, Incorporated. He runs the company, goes to school, takes care of his father's numerous requests, and is considering law school. But there is something missing in Cary, and the added pressures of school and watching over his father's interests seem to be taking their toll. In December 1992, Cary Green enlisted in the army. He left for basic training in early April 1993. He has finally escaped from the nightmare his life had become.

Michael Green lives with Mel's ailing eighty-six-year-old father, Hy, and Hy's new girlfriend, Dorothy. His father's incarceration is still a mystery to him. He worries because in his letters Melvin seems to be adapting too well to prison. "He sounds just like them now. How will he cope if he ever does get out?" he asked Alexandra one night.

Hy Green recovered from his son's trial. He is too old to worry about Mel. He thanks God every day that June, his beloved wife, did not live to see their only child convicted of murder and that Dorothy only had to meet him once. He went to visit his son in prison in the early fall. They fought during the entire visit. Still Hy Green continues the Green family tradition of total denial. He swears his son is an innocent man who was wrongly convicted. He is so convinced of this that in March 1993, Hy mortgaged his home to help pay for Melvin's appeal and hopefully for a new trial. "He'll be home in no time," Hy explained to me.

Mel's staff remains faithful to their paychecks. But even one of his secretaries says, "His armor is beginning to tarnish." One of the conditions of their employment is that they write Melvin at least once a week.

Anita's only child, Scott Arnow, is getting by. He is finishing his schooling and working hard at his job as a youth probation officer. But there is a void in his life that will never be filled.

Scott is still unable to think about Melvin Green without bitterness. "I guess what shocked me the most was the murder and then all the deception. The deception and the lies. . . . Mel was a fraud and we never knew it. I was really surprised about the diplomas. I kept thinking that at least seventy percent of our life was a fake. Life with Melvin was total fraud."

Phyllis Baltin continues to live a life filled with drama. In February, her boyfriend, Lance, collected a portion of the city council's fifteen-thousand-dollar reward for information leading to the capture and conviction of Anita Green's murderer. He is currently waiting for the temple to make good on their offer to match the city's payment.

Phyllis has recovered, but she will never be the same. "Before this happened, I looked at people differently. I was more fun loving and trusting; now I always wonder." Tears began to pour from Phyllis's eyes as she continued. "I learned many things from Anita's death. You have to live each day as if it was your last. You have to cherish the good moments and look past the bad. Anita taught me that. She always lived her life that way."

Phyllis reflected on Anita's generous legacy and added, "She left me many gifts. She left me you, someone who would listen to all of my problems as attentively as she had." Then she added softly, the tears pouring down her cheeks, "Anita left me the most magnificent woman I have ever known, her mother. Think about it. Riva is the bravest person I have ever met. She never really understood Anita, and I know that Anita never knew the woman that I have come to know. Nevertheless, Riva always loved her more than life itself, and her love was unconditional."

The lawmen who worked diligently to put Melvin Green behind bars—Ray Hernandez, Mike Coffey, David Arnold, Sonny Medina, and Jorge Armenta—all continue as Los Angeles Police Department detectives, and they are among our city's finest.

Mike Coffey continues as the homicide supervisor at North Hollywood's busy police station. Murders are up, and he is overworked and exhausted. I caught up with Mike one day, and over the phone he told me how bad things had gotten in a city that averages over ten murders a day. He is beginning to feel like he can no longer be the little Dutch boy sticking his finger in the dike to hold back the flood of mayhem.

Still, Michael took the time to listen to me and promised

that he would try to make sure that Anita's shooter whoever he is would one day be arrested.

Detective Steven Hooks works steadily on doing just that. A compassionate and caring man, he appears to worry about my safety almost as much as I do.

Ray Hernandez feels that the courts' latest interpretations of criminals' rights have made it nearly impossible for him to effectively arrest and interrogate homicide suspects. He is now working downtown, where he investigates kidnappings. But Ray will never forget his hunt for Anita Green's murderer. He was obsessed by it for months, and it came close to destroying him.

"This case definitely ranks among the top murder cases I have ever worked on. I was very, very gratified when we got Melvin because I was obsessed by this case. I couldn't sleep because, damn it, I knew Melvin paid somebody to kill his wife. I knew what a devil and monster he was just by talking to him. I knew how he treated her, and that is why I just kept after him. Thank God the arrogant son of a bitch will never again walk the streets."

The lawyers would never forget Melvin Green either, especially his defense team. Arthur Alexander, fed up with life in Los Angeles, is now practicing law in Tucson, Arizona. In his free time, he is trying to become a Jewish cowboy. The Melvin Green verdict still perplexes him.

"Forgetting Mel Green for a minute, as a lawyer I am offended that somebody could be convicted based on the character of this evidence. There is nothing wrong with circumstantial evidence, but this was of the shoddiest kind. This was ten-year-old stuff. This was statements taken out of context, all put together in a jigsaw puzzle. That's what still offends me."

Then he added, "The letters really hurt us. You read those letters and, I mean, they are horrible. You know, this guy is the guy who, when you are stopped at the red light and you look over, is in the next car dictating into his tape recorder. There are only two people that I can think of who think that everything they say is so important that it must be recorded for posterity, and both of them have been hung by it. One is Melvin Green, and the other is Richard Nixon. Then you think about the personalities of those two people, and you see how similar they are. I feel bad for the man, though. I went to see him before he was transferred to prison just to tell him that I hope things work out for him."

Though he planned on retiring before the Green case, the esteemed Gerry Chaleff is once again back in court, working on the highly publicized Stuart and Neil Woodman case, dubbed by the press the "Yom Kippur murders." I met him in his office on one of his rare days off. "Well, what do you want to know?" he asked.

I asked him one more time, for the record, what he thought about Melvin's guilt or innocence. He leaned back in his chair and rubbed his beard. There was a slight twinkle in his eyes as he answered. "I can't tell you what I thought or what I knew, or why I did what I did. I'm sorry. But if it makes you feel any better, I will say that Mel never once told me that he did it. You know more about certain things than we ever did. It's all very interesting. This case was all about control. Melvin could have cared less about the money. He could not stand that she had left him, that anyone could have left him."

Then Gerry Chaleff added, "Kent Cahill sent Melvin Green to prison. He did an excellent job on a very difficult case. I think that because you have this unknown, this ambiguity, because nobody knows how it really happened. I was just rereading his closing argument; it was brilliant. We had answers for everything, except the hairdresser. I couldn't argue her away."

In another conversation Gerry explained, "I could never have put Melvin on the tand because he denies everything. If something is white, he'll say it is black. The jury would never have believed anything he said."

Prosecutor Kent Cahill remains one of the Los Angeles' finest young prosecutors. After the Green verdict, many said he walked on water. But more likely, Kent Cahill was to be found flying his new Grumman Tiger over the skies of California, as he savored his victory.

Kent once told me that pilots have a saying: "'If you don't think you are the best pilot in the sky, then you shouldn't be there.' The same can be said of trial attorneys. It takes a certain type of arrogance to do the job."

Over two years after Anita's murder and a year after his

work sent Melvin Green away for life, Kent waits patiently to be given a case in which he believes as strongly. Ironically, Kent Cahill has been transferred to downtown Los Angeles and he's as mierable as ever about the long commute. But in the criminal courts building where he tried *People* v. *Green*, Cahill remains somewhat of a legend. Often in the halls people whisper, "That's the guy that won the Green case."

Melvin Green sits in prison and waits. He waits for a prison job and for his appeal to be granted. He writes letters, volunteers in the prison law library, and obsesses about his latest loss, Alexandra. He wants to be out of prison in time to participate in the 1996 Senior Olympics.

Melvin's appeals team consists of his knowledgeable lawyers, Robert Gerstein and Aaron Shelfon, and his compassionate private investigator, James Sloman. James in particular takes the time to spend one day a week at the Calipatria prison patiently interviewing Melvin Green, his most interesting client to date.

In late February 1993, we spent several days together at the prison interviewing and visiting with Melvin. It was the same old story. Melvin had grown even more obsessive since the recent departure of his fiancée, Alexandra Leeds. He simply could not believe that she would want to leave him. Melvin showed us the dozens of letters he had written about her. He spent hours dictating into the tape recorder James had brought into the interview room.

As I watched Melvin frantically pour his tormented thoughts into the machine, I began to cry. At that moment, I was certain that money had nothing to do with Anita's murder. This was all about loyalty and betrayal. Melvin Green simply does not allow people to walk away from his life, especially those with whom he's been intimate.

When we finally left the prison, James looked at me and smiled. "We'll probably be coming here together for ten years, and everything will be exactly the same. He'll keep insisting that he didn't do it, and I will still be searching for the missing facts. And you, Michele...maybe by then, with a little luck, you'll have a great sequel. Just be careful," he added, with a concerned smile.

Though the legal wheels move slowly, Melvin Green's appeals lawyer, Robert Gerstein, appealed Melvin's conviction in April 1993 on a number of grounds. His most convincing argument, and the one that Melvin pins his hopes on, is that the letters he wrote his attorney in the months before Anita's murder were confidential; that is, they should never have been let into the trial in the first place.

It is doubtful that, given the quality of evidence presented at Melvin Green's murder trial, a jury would have convicted him without the letters. They were a tremendous obstacle his defense team was never able to overcome. If the California Supreme Court rules that they were indeed privileged, the reversal will give Melvin the new trial he hopes for.

At our last visit I asked Melvin what would happen if he was granted a new trial. "There is not a bit of evidence that says I killed Anita. It was all a crap shoot, a card game. That's all. I gues I'd hope to be dealt a winning hand." Melvin laughed, then went on to tell me that his greatest dream was to prove them all wrong. "I will make them all understand. There has to be reasonable doubt. I mean it is obvious that I didn't pull the trigger."

In his lengthy appellate brief, Gerstein argues another issue eloquently. He says there was simply too little evidence to convict Melvin of anything, let alone murder with special circumstances. Though an appeal on insufficient evidence is very hard to win, in this case there was nothing ever found directly linking Melvin to Anita's murder. For these reasons, there could never be a jury verdict of guilty beyond a reasonable doubt. If the courts reverse the jury's verdict on this ground, *People* v. *Green* would be dismissed, and Melvin would be a free man.

Several months earlier, on Anita's birthday in January 1993, Riva and I stood at her graveside and cried together as we remembered Anita on the day she would have turned forty-five. It was true that Riva had never understood her eldest daughter, and my book was not likely to bring about the understanding for which she so fervently prayed. Riva had always wondered about her daughter's choices, but in her heart she knew that Anita was special.

"She was very, very good, and she was very loyal to Mel. She would never, never have hurt him. I will never understand why Anita was killed."

Then she said, "Anita loved her father so. She always wanted his approval, and he would have done anything for her." Riva looked at her beloved Joseph's grave next to Anita's. "I think about my husband every day. I am so glad he was not around to see what happened, because it would have really killed him."

Then Riva turned back to her daughter's grave and said, "See what your beloved rabbi did to his wife? Do you think things would have been any different for you? I hope you are watching all of this, Anita, and I hope you finally understand what I was trying to tell you. I love you, my sweetheart."

We left the graves and walked toward our cars. Despite the surroundings, Riva's spirits seemed to be up and her mood was particularly optimistic. She told me that sometimes she thought about moving back east to be closer to her surviving daughter, Linda, and to her three grandchildren. She had not made the decision to leave because once again she was finally enjoying her life here. I looked up at her eyes, and I knew that she was telling the truth.

It all began for me in this cemetery, just two years before. I had never been to a funeral as tragic as Anita's. I found that I simply could not fathom what had happened, and I was so overwrought with sadness that, at the time, I could barely stand. I knew, somehow, that Anita's death would change my life, but I had no idea that the changes would be so drastic.

Lately I find myself wondering if it has all been worthwhile. I am filled with a deep sadness as I wrestle with this question that seems to have overtaken my life. I have made more enemies than I can count by writing this book, and as Judge Trammel once told me, I will probably never again feel completely safe.

But who of us is ever really completely safe? Is life not supposed to be a constant struggle? Certainly Judaism requires a willingness to pursue the right path even when everyone around you is threatening you. Working on this book and seeing what happened to Anita have taught me this lesson.

If I guarded the community's secrets and kept silent, then I too would become one of Anita's killers. I believe with all my heart that it was the silence, as well as the shooter's bullet, that killed my friend.